Brookings Occasional Papers

The Future of European Security: An Interim Assessment

CATHERINE McARDLE KELLEHER

THE BROOKINGS INSTITUTION
Washington, D.C.

Brookings Occasional Papers

THE BROOKINGS INSTITUTION is a private nonprofit organization devoted to research, education, and publication on important issues of domestic and foreign policy. Its principal purpose is to bring knowledge to bear on the major policy problems facing the American people.

On occasion Brookings authors produce research papers that warrant immediate circulation as contributions to the public debate on current issues of national importance. Because of the circumstances of their production, these Occasional Papers are not subjected to all of the formal review procedures established for the Institution's research publications, and they may be revised at a later date. As in all Brookings publications, the judgments, conclusions, and recommendations presented in the papers are solely those of the authors and should not be attributed to the trustees, officers, or other staff members of the Institution.

Acknowledgments

A monograph of any significant size necessarily involves help from a long list of contributors. Rachel Epstein and Ian Campbell assisted in the research, preparation, and presentation of the manuscript. Laura Paros, David Bird, Rainer Baumann, Tanja Schümer, and Michael Kelleher contributed to specific portions of the manuscript. Caroline Lalire edited the manuscript, and Lisa Bevell helped to ready it for production. The evolution of arguments in this monograph benefited from the comments of a number of readers—Elizabeth Pond, Kori Schake, Steve Flanagan, Gale Mattox, Angela Stent, Janne Nolan, Harry Dolton, Susan Woodward, John Engels, and Kirk Wolcott. Responsibility for the arguments and factual content of this monograph is the author's alone.

Funding for this occasional paper was provided in part by the John D. and Catherine T. MacArthur Foundation and the Carnegie Corporation of New York. Brookings gratefully acknowledges their support.

Abbreviations and Acronyms

ARRC	Allied Command Europe rapid reaction corps
ATTU	Atlantic to the Urals
AWACS	Airborne warning and control systems
CBMs	Confidence-building measures
CE	Central Europe
CEE	Central and eastern Europe
CEI	Central European Initiative
CFE	Conventional Forces in Europe
CFSP	Common foreign and security policy
CIS	Commonwealth of Independent States
CJTF	Combined/Joint Task Forces
CNN	Cable News Network
COCOM	Coordinating Committee for Multilateral Export Controls
CPC	Conflict Prevention Center
CRS	Congressional Research Service
CSBM	Confidence- and security-building measures
CSCE	Conference on Security and Cooperation in Europe
DDR	Deutsche Demokratische Republik
DPQ	Defense planning questionnaire
EBRD	European Bank for Reconstruction and Development
EC	European Community
ECSC	European Coal and Steel Community
ECU	European currency unit
EDC	European Defense Community
EFTA	European Free Trade Association
EMU	European Monetary Union
ERM	European exchange rate mechanism
ESDI	European security and defense identity
EU	European Union
EURATOM	European Atomic Energy Community
FSC	Forum for Security Cooperation
FSU	Former Soviet Union

G-7	Group of Seven industrialized nations
GATT	General Agreement on Tariffs and Trade
IEPG	Independent European Program Group
IISS	International Institute for Strategic Studies
INF	Intermediate-Range Nuclear Forces
ITAR-TASS	Post-Soviet news agency (Russia)
KOBRA	Kontrolle bei der Ausfuhr (German export control system)
MBFR	Mutual and balanced force reduction talks
MNCs	Major NATO commands
MSCs	Major subordinate commands (NATO)
NAC	North Atlantic Council
NACC	North Atlantic Cooperation Council
NAFTA	North American Free Trade Agreement
NATO	North Atlantic Treaty Organization
NIS	Newly independent states
NNA	Neutral and nonaligned states
NORTHAG	Northern Army Group (NATO)
NSC	National Security Council
ODIHR	Office of Democratic Institutions and Human Rights
OECD	Organization for Economic Cooperation and Development
OEEC	Organization for European Economic Cooperation (later became the OECD)
PFP	Partnership for Peace
PHARE	Pologne-Hongrie: actions pour la réconversion économique
PRIF	Peace Research Institute, Frankfurt
RFE-RL	Radio Free Europe-Radio Liberty
RRF	Rapid reaction force
SACEUR	Supreme allied commander, Europe
SAMs	Sanctions assistance missions
SHAPE	Supreme Headquarters, Allied Powers, Europe
SIPRI	Stockholm International Peace Research Institute
SPD	Social Democratic Party (of Germany)
TACIS	Technical assistance to the Commonwealth of Independent States and Georgia
USIA	United States Information Agency
UN	United Nations
UNECE	United Nations Economic Commission for Europe
UNIDIR	United Nations Institute for Disarmament Research
UNPROFOR	United Nations Protection Force
WEU	Western European Union
WTO	Warsaw Treaty Organization
YPA	Yugoslav People's Army

Contents

1. The United States and European Security:
Overview and Introduction   1

2. The Organizational Framework of European Security   22

3. The Politics of European Security: Organizational
Transformation and the Competition over
the Security Agenda, 1989-94   45

4. Outreach to the East, 1989-94   78

5. Operational Choices: The Management of Conflict
and Peacemaking Outside Europe   106

6. What Is to Be Done?   136

Appendix A: Selected European Security
Chronology, 1948-94   160

Appendix B: Partnership for Peace *Invitation*   174

Appendix C: The North Atlantic Treaty,
Washington, D.C., April 4, 1949   179

Selected Bibliography   183

Notes   187

Index   210

Europe 1995

1

The United States and European Security: Overview and Introduction

In the five years since the fall of the Berlin wall, one of the most challenging conceptual tasks has been to redefine the nature and requirements of European security. Viewed superficially from the perspective of western Europe, Europe is now more secure than at any other time in the past two centuries. The threat of an expansionist Soviet empire is gone; so too is the ideological competition with the communist system. Germany has united peacefully and democratically; it is firmly bound by its own choice into an integrated European economic system and into a transatlantic security community. Prosperity at unprecedented levels has created a continentwide preference for stability, democracy, a set of thoroughgoing constraints on the use of force, and an aversion to war. Instability and conflict on Europe's periphery are regrettable but ultimately excludable from the European security context.

It is the argument of this monograph that, however appealing, such a view misstates both the present reality and the future horizon of European security. Europe and the United States now stand at a critical junction of policy choice. The challenge is twofold: to preserve and deepen what has been achieved in western Europe and to extend the European zone of peace and stability as far east as possible. To meet these challenges will require at least as much ingenuity and commitment as did the building of the Western security arrangements that began in the late 1940s and early 1950s with the Marshall Plan, the North Atlantic Treaty Organization (NATO), and the European Community. It will demand an equivalent understanding of the benefits of security cooperation over unilateral national action and of the fundamental interrelationship of economic prosperity, political stability, and military security. It will require equal levels of European and American interdependence and significant amounts of American leadership, at least in the medium term. And though in cold war terms, there is no urgent military threat to be faced, the costs of ignoring or postponing action on these challenges will be enormous.

Why is that so? Post–cold war Europe faces a range of both new and familiar challenges to its security. Although the cold war nightmare of massive conventional invasion of Europe is long over, the most obvious challenges are still those that arise from changes in the east, in particular the political and military revolutions in central and eastern Europe (CEE) and the former Soviet Union.[1] There is a small but still measurable possibility that Russia will revert to its authoritarian and expansionist ways and will use its still significant nuclear weapons to gain political and military advantage in the "near abroad," over its former Warsaw Pact allies, or even over western Europe. Far more plausible in the next several decades are the threats that may arise from Russian political stalemate and military disintegration: continuing turbulence, political uncertainty, and a military vacuum to Europe's east that is a continuing source of instability for all Europeans but especially for the newly democratizing states of central and eastern Europe.

Risks in central Europe itself also arise from the dangers of isolation, of political and economic failure, and of increasing ethnic tensions. Many fear a resurgence of the aggressive nationalism and the political polarization experienced in the 1930s. Such a result would be most likely if the present reforming regimes that enjoy uncertain political support are denied the eventual option of integration into the Western economic and security frameworks. To be buffer states between western Europe and Russia is unacceptable over the long term. To be shut out of an equitable share in the prosperity and the stability that the Euro-Atlantic community has achieved for itself is to betray the bases of democratic reform, and perhaps to hasten a return to the social, political, and economic chaos so characteristic of central Europe in the interwar years.

Western Europe faces a different set of challenges, arising more out of complacency and policy drift. There is a need to renew understanding of how much present security derives from the great cooperative achievements of the past four decades and of how much it is in mutual interests to protect and deepen those security "investments." Most important is the transformation of the long-standing continental rivalries, especially that between France and Germany, into a framework of mutual commitments to cooperative security and to maintaining a European zone of peace. A central goal was and is to embed a reviving, increasingly powerful Germany in a network of mutual security structures and guarantees, supported by a common commitment to transparency and multilateral action through NATO and economic integration through the European Community. Very important, too, is the role of the United States in creating a transatlantic security community, bound not only through its force commitments within NATO and by the habits of day-to-day cooperation but also by a common vision for a peaceful international order.

To meet all these challenges, the search must now be for ways to adapt the existing European security architecture and to strike a new political and institutional balance in light of the critical changes since 1989. To be taken into account are the new role and vulnerability of an uncertain Russia, the evolution of a more powerful united Germany, and a far wider, more ambitious European union that stretches to the Russian border. To be tested as well is the willingness of the United States to take a central role, again to help shape cooperative institutions and craft processes for multilateral consultation and joint action. Security cooperation that is extended Europewide will, at a minimum, maintain and expand military capabilities to deter and contain direct military threats. More important, it will also lessen or forestall their occurrence by creating a new framework of mutual security guarantees and of commitments to multilateral action to preserve peace and nourish democratic order.

Security in Europe: The Cooperative Framework

Four decades of division and cold war stalemate in Europe have left a promising foundation on which to strengthen and expand the framework of cooperative security. (For a chronology of European security since 1948, see appendix A.) In no other region has there been more progress toward mutual regulation of military capabilities and operations, toward mutual reassurance and the avoidance of tension and uncertainty. In the West, most of the progress has come through the evolution of NATO from a traditional interstate organization into a unique system of standing military forces and an integrated command in peacetime to ensure continuous political reassurance as well as joint defense in crisis. By the end of the 1960s the core elements of the framework were standard NATO practices: mutual agreement on the size and distribution of offensive force, transparency in operations and in doctrine across the allied states, commitments not to change intra-alliance borders by force, and commitments to combined border defense in war, to name only the most important.[2]

In the East, progress was more limited. The central and eastern European states remained within the Soviet sphere and the framework of the Soviet-dominated Warsaw Pact. But by the 1980s they had gained new access, a new political voice, and new channels for mutual consultation, with one another but especially with the West. This was true whether they engaged in a growing international dialogue on mutual security and the creation of simple confidence-building measures (CBM)—as within the loose, pan-European Conference on Security and Cooperation in Europe (CSCE)—or in more formal negotiations about specific arms control measures in the interest of mutual threat reduction—as in the Conventional Forces in Europe (CFE) talks.

The fall of the Berlin Wall in 1989 and the political change that swept through the East led to a rash of reassessments of the future value of this foundation. Some people, in the first wave of euphoria, argued that the cold war legacy could be disassembled, that Europe, now whole and free, could grow together organically.[3] As difficulties and uncertainty mounted, others argued that the prospects for regional cooperation and stability were too limited to permit the eastward spread of a Western-style European security community.[4] Commitments to mutual defense and to security cooperation, they felt, could not be created in the context of a painful transition to democracy in central Europe or of the political tumult that followed the disestablishment of the Soviet Union. Russia itself was an uncertain and, for at least the foreseeable future, probably an inappropriate partner. There would be time and opportunity later, once the civic revolution was firmly rooted and stability regained. Cynics even argued that though there was serious risk of negative outcomes—such as rapid renationalization of defense doctrine and operations or fragmentation of existing structures—these would be short-term effects that could be reversed or corrected once the central Europeans were offered the carrot of economic integration.

A quite different scenario is offered here, one that builds on many of the aspirations and initiatives put forth at the groundbreaking NATO summit of January 1994. The changed character of the security challenges in post–cold war Europe now make it possible, and in all significant ways urgent, to extend and deepen the western European cooperative system to a continentwide regime. One key to any future European security architecture will be to build on the minimal pan-European processes that existed before the Wall's fall—to extend and enrich the process of mutual agreement and reassurance achieved through the interaction of an open CSCE dialogue and the specific weapons limitations and regional balances guaranteed by the CFE treaty. The ultimate goal of this process will be to move toward a system of expanding regional stability and reciprocal reassurance, which will in turn foster an environment for greater cooperation and for more continuous exchanges about doctrine, force structure, and future military planning.

New forms of cooperation also flow from the 1994 summit initiatives. Of the greatest importance in the short run will be the NATO Partnership for Peace (PFP), a cumulative set of agreements on security cooperation between the alliance and those CSCE states that are appropriate. As discussed in more detail in chapter 4, the immediate aim is to foster more regular cooperation on peacekeeping and emergency humanitarian assistance, as under UN-NATO aegis in Bosnia. Such an effort should complement parallel political advances within the CFE-CSCE process to expand joint cooperative efforts from the Atlantic to the Urals. But the PFP is also designed to pave the way for the eventual expansion of NATO's core, with those democratizing states that prove themselves able and willing to take up all the responsibilities expected of NATO members bound by NATO's article 5 pledge of mutual defense.

Perhaps the critical categories of cooperation to be built, however, are those that emerge from NATO practice as it has evolved since the 1950s. Defense guarantees about borders and territorial integrity now seem far less urgent; at least as important is to establish regular communication and constant cooperation, as well as a pattern of openness and "no surprises." The basic mode to be sought with the new PFP partners is the habit of policy coordination and cooperation and a widening of the NATO commitment to multilateral action that has become the norm for relations among the allies. The scope will certainly be regional, and probably global; in the new environment there is no longer great validity to the out-of-area concept.

At a more fundamental level is the need to develop shared political values and mutual standards for state behavior, including the use of military force. NATO in its present incarnation appears to be an alliance of relatively homogeneous polities, all with similar views on the nature of civil order, on political accountability and the processes of political change, and on the rights of majorities and minorities. It has not always been so; indeed, for much of NATO's existence, it was only generally true. The experience of NATO's more than four decades suggests that cooperation at the required levels is possible among a wide range of political systems at different levels of political and economic development. There was, for example, effective cooperation with a Federal Republic in the process of democratic creation and with an uncertain, democratizing Spain. Conversely, although formal membership remained intact, NATO's organizational culture led to continuing but seriously circumscribed interaction with a Turkey, Greece, or Portugal under a military junta.

To permit future cooperation, the irreducible minimum is for the partner state to have at least the potential for mutual agreement on principles of democratic control and of equitable civic order, including political guarantees for minorities. Again, what now seems normal among the Western partners in those domains is the result of long years of dialogue, policy convergence, and, in critical areas, increasing functional integration across borders. A learning process has occurred, not only within the sphere of NATO's security policy but perhaps even more dramatically within the European Community, designed from the outset to create European political stability through mutual involvement.

Unquestionably, within the PFP circle as within NATO itself, national differences remain; national interests and concerns are still to be recognized and defended. But if reassurance and transparency are the minimum goals of the expanding NATO-PFP process, cooperation, coordination, and eventually mutually acceptable policy should follow. This assumes that electorates and elites across Europe come to see mutual policies and jointly set standards for behavior not as infringements of sovereignty or as last-ditch measures but as policies of first resort and choices that, on balance, serve to enhance national interests.

Active military cooperation is the arena of greatest short-term concern— and as the United States has recognized in several of its 1994 summit initiatives, the arena of greatest political opportunity. Much cooperative practice that already exists can be easily extended and intensified. There are, for example, the formal confidence- and security-building measures (CSBMs) adopted in the past under the CSCE, which focused on the announcement and monitoring of exercises and data exchanges. There are also the specialized on-site monitoring systems created under the late cold war treaty to limit U.S. and Soviet intermediate nuclear forces and carried forward under the CFE treaty. In the recent past, CFE inspections of weapons destruction events have been largely done by joint military teams and through the pooling of national inspection quotas.

Most of these measures still have symbolic value, although they were all initially designed for an era of limited information and minimal transparency.

Of importance now is the complete acceptance of transparency as a guiding principle, as the instrument through which international accountability is expressed and measured. Crucial, too, is the growing store of common operational experiences—in humanitarian missions in Rwanda, Bosnia, and Somalia in the CSCE monitoring missions in Nagorno-Kharabakh and Tajikistan, and in multilateral observation of the protection of minority citizen rights in the Baltics. Not all the relevant states have been involved—not all the members of NATO, nor all those that have joined PFP, and certainly not all of those in the looser intergovernmental North Atlantic Cooperation Council (NACC), established in 1991.

Countries have also learned a range of different lessons from these experiences, not all of them positive. Bosnia is a case in point. Nevertheless, in both the operations in and the planning for Bosnia, operational differences have at least been sorted out. There has been a mutual learning about chains of command and instruments of communication, about the differences in national military style of operation, and more than a little practice in the mutual frustrations and benefits gained through day-to-day coordination and contingency planning.

More important opportunities lie in planning together for the future. Transatlantic military establishments, East and West, are searching for new concepts and attempting to define new missions with which to ensure a continuing sense of purpose and to preserve present resources. The opening of eastern and central Europe has already led to selected military-to-military exchanges and limited seminars on doctrine and training. Most have been bilateral, but new opportunities exist for multilateral cooperation, as in the first PFP exercises in the fall of 1994 and the multination effort to build and train the "Baltic Brigade."[5]

But the full measure of doctrinal change, of the force restructuring and downsizing that the post–cold war period will require, is yet to come. Especially in Europe it will be crucial to provide for a more systematic organization of discussion and change, of mutual adjustment on the widest possible regional basis, rather than to rely on solely national considerations or convenient or comfortable bilateral excursions. It is necessary to protect and indeed expand the CFE regime, not simply as an arms control regime but as one of the chief pillars of a regional security system that takes transparency and reassurance for all as the critical goals. CFE inspections and the related activities under CSCE and the pending Open Skies treaty arrangements provide hard evidence about "no surprises," about the seriousness of jointly measuring capabilities as well as intentions, and about the usefulness of intrusive cooperation to create mutual reassurance and control. These regimes must be made even more robust, with sufficient flexibility to allow problem solving and to meet new challenges, and with sufficient rigor to guarantee standards of mutually acceptable behavior.[6]

A host of major new needs should also be addressed cooperatively, to gain not only cost savings but also new levels of trust and transparency. The requirement to build a new, open continentwide system for military air traffic control is one; the possibility of automated continuous data exchange under the CSCE-CFE regimes about forces, deployments, planning, and budgets is another. And as discussed later, there are many more: from cooperative acquisition or coordination of weapons planning for new security missions (perhaps as peacekeeping to be undertaken jointly) to the real-time sharing of intelligence and the design of cumulative joint exercises and field maneuvers.

The Role of the United States in Future European Security

A second key argument here is that the United States can and should take a central role in both the widening and the deepening of future European security arrangements. Part of the reason lies in the simple continuity of American national interest in the post–cold war environment. In the five decades since the end of World War II, the security and stability of Europe have been a constant goal of American foreign policy. Successive administrations have endorsed the change from the disinterested bystander–occasional balancer role Washington played in the 1920s and 1930s to that of full participant (and even benevolent hegemon) in shaping Europe's security. For that reason the remarkable Marshall Plan for European economic reconstruction and integration was launched; for that reason the United States accepted its first "entangling alliance," the North Atlantic Treaty Organization, and its first continuous peacetime deployments and security guarantees outside the continental United States.

From Washington's perspective, Europe's postwar security presented three critical challenges: to deter Soviet domination or attack, to repress any revival of Nazi aggression or German militarism while building a stronger European framework for Germany, and to allow a security framework that fostered the political and economic reconstruction of Europe. At stake was an overriding American national interest: the need of the United States for cooperative democratic allies committed to a similar vision of an open international order with free trade and access for all. Increasingly as the postwar era lengthened, Europe was not the only place to find such partners. For reasons of history, cultural affinity, and economics, however, it was the first place to look.

It is the argument of this monograph that American interest in a stable and secure Europe and its need for cooperative allies and partners are as great now as at any time in the postwar period. The task of countering a Soviet bloc is gone; the scope of transatlantic military planning and the balance of political and military concerns in the Euro-Atlantic alliance may well be adjusted to a lower level of continuous American military presence. But the role of American commitment remains a central factor, as does American leadership in preserving past achievements in western Europe and in extending the security dialogue to central and eastern Europe, including Russia. And the instruments to forge new cooperation, to enlarge the European zone of peace, are those honed and practiced within the NATO system of cooperative security over the past four decades.

In intensity and in scope, the task of restructuring Europe's security framework equals that undertaken and successfully implemented by the United States in the creation phase, from 1945 to 1955. In conceptual terms, it represents a unique opportunity to renew and reshape the ideals of multilateralism and of core economic security that were central to Washington's planning for postwar Europe during World War II and that inform the American approach to post–cold war international relations. In political terms, it requires a reconsideration of America's critical European relationships and the crucial functions, international and domestic, that are now seamlessly subsumed under NATO's security cooperation and commitment. These are questions, indeed, that go far beyond even a broadened definition of Europe and are at the heart of the looming debate about a transformed American foreign policy.

In taking up this task, the United States confronts a radically changed political context from that of the immediate postwar period. Both the economic and the political environment are considerably more complex: more sophisticated capabilities and more access to information through advanced technology, yet more accountability for political elites, which have less ability to keep domestic politics from shaping (or indeed dominating) foreign policy decisions. The United States remains the only military superpower and the inescapable leader if it chooses, yet it is less able and willing, politically and economically, to act alone. Its choice of partners is thus critical: so too is the consideration of the broad processes and specific projects that will be creative and long-lasting responses to the complex challenges ahead.

Europe's Security: The Necessary Partners

In the search for future security in Europe, the United States faces a new array of partners as capable and as strong willed as those in the cold war. The three most important sets of partners are the European Union as an organization, France and Germany as national states, and Russia.

The Emerging Power: The European Union

A primary change since the cold war is the emergence of a formal political western Europe, the European Union (EU), formally the successor to the long-standing European Community. The EU was created under the Maastricht Treaty of December 1991. The core of the Maastricht design is a fundamental Franco-German consensus on the accelerated, comprehensive integration of Europe beyond the level of a successful customs union. The proximate stimulus came from the joint initiatives of President François Mitterrand and Chancellor Helmut Kohl that began in the mid-1980s and were developed in part to offset what was perceived as a growing American unilateralism and inexorable path toward disengagement from Europe. After German unification, Franco-German agreement intensified, with both states seeing the EU as embodying Germany's unequivocal commitment to multilateral action and to integration in all areas.

The EU action agenda is a long one, cutting across simmering national differences and complicated already by the planned addition of four new states (Austria, Sweden, Finland, and Norway) in 1995. Directed by the European Council, or what might be described as a cartel of governments, the EU focuses primarily on effective financial and monetary integration in the shortest possible time. Common policymaking initiatives lag somewhat. Yet seen as integral to this process is the development of a common European foreign and security policy, including the eventual evolution and institutional expression of a European security and defense identity (ESDI). Acting as an interim organization is the transformed Western European Union (WEU), which after long debate serves both as the EU's security instrument and as the European pillar within NATO. Ultimately, the EU itself is to absorb the WEU and transform the key security functions through a common defense policy.

Some of this reorganization now seems to be set aside for development in the long-distant future; Europe's security integration outside NATO has advanced little since 1991. The obvious reason has been the continuing European failure to agree on how to treat the conflict in the former Yugoslavia or to take action there. This failure has further deepened what has been termed Europe's post-Maastricht blues. First came the weariness and the letdown that occupied much of the year following Maastricht. Now there is anxiety about maintaining momentum and building agreement toward the next critical milestone, the EU's planned intergovernmental conference of the spring of 1996 to set Europe's future direction. In addition, the longest European economic recession in postwar history has had devastating consequences: much higher unemployment, voter disillusionment, youth disaffection, and the disturbing rise of right-wing reaction and violence.

Perhaps the key political barrier to progress toward union, however, has been the self-absorption of Germany and France, neither of which has many spare political resources to maintain the political campaign. The Germans have been preoccupied with the mechanics and burdens—economic, political, and psychic—of unification. The French have become enmeshed in political and generational cleavages—the split between Mitterrand and both his political allies and his political successors. Yet both in rhetoric and in what limited action has been taken, the German and French leaders remain committed to at least the promise of ESDI. There are the beginnings of the Eurocorps, with French and German units now joined by the Belgians, Luxembourgeois, and Spanish. There is talk of common arms production and the push toward European arms export controls. There is the development of a common–issue catalogue, to be highlighted during 1994–95, the year of German, then French, presidency of the EU. And in 1994 there were clearly related French and German proposals that the EU in 1996 at least decide to allow core states to push ahead toward closer economic, political, and security integration.

The reaction of the United States was initially active opposition within a cloud of positive rhetoric. Particularly during the first three years of the Bush administration (1988–90), every European initiative toward greater unity and autonomy in security affairs seemed couched in the language of confrontation, not continued transatlantic cooperation. Not surprisingly perhaps, these initiatives met hostility and direct riposte—as in Bush's famous 1991 words, "if your ultimate aim is to provide for your own defense, the time to tell us is today."[7] A separate European organization would weaken the NATO keystone and, therefore, the transatlantic "community of fate," which had been so carefully constructed and defended against opponents and domestic critics. At the very least, it would result in the de facto extension of NATO's article 5 guarantee, without prior American agreement; at the most, it might destroy the integrated command structure that was the operational heart of NATO.[8] By 1992, however, the Bush administration pronounced itself satisfied with European responsiveness and the concept of a united European effort within the primary NATO framework.

The Clinton administration has been enthusiastic about European defense cooperation from the first. Bill Clinton has emerged as the first president since Dwight D. Eisenhower to be genuinely accepting of European integration as a complement to, rather than as a constraint on, American foreign policy. This stance may have been made easier by the lack of conspicuous European progress and the dramatic failures in mutual action in the former Yugoslavia, ultimately leaving the burden of coordination and planning to NATO. But the three presidential trips to Europe in 1993 and 1994 all emphasized Clinton's support for mutual security efforts as being integral to the goal of European union.[9] The furthest reaching measures were the initiatives at the January 1994 summit, especially the American initiative for the Combined/Joint Task Forces that would allow the combined European allies in the WEU to use NATO assets and forces at times when NATO (or the United States) cannot or will not act.[10]

The Crucial Partners: Germany and France

A cooperative security strategy for Europe, however, must do more than deal with the nascent EU potential or the day-to-day coordination with a fledgling WEU force. The primary challenge will be to engage and secure commitments at both the national and the multilateral level from Germany and France to share in such a strategy. Each country possesses critical assets but puts new constraints on or poses fundamental difficulties for the preservation and the extension of the European zone of peace.

The German case is by far the more important, but also the more straightforward. For much of the past five years, Germany has been fully absorbed in the process of unification, in the mobilization of its economic and political resources to incorporate the former German Democratic Republic (DDR). What energies remained were spent attempting to adjust to the status of an enlarged Germany and to allay the resulting fears and concerns of others.

Foreign and defense policy, never major discussion topics in postwar Germany, usually receded into the background, the general presumption being that the previous consensus on multilateral action through NATO and the EU still held.[11] Perhaps the one exception brought unforetold and unwelcome international opprobrium: the unswervable German campaign in 1991 to obtain early European recognition of the independence of Croatia and Slovenia, which resulted in the irreversible breakup of the Yugoslav federation.

By 1994 there were a number of indicators that Germany would be increasingly attentive to its international role and its role in European security. Some simply reflect the passage of time: by the end of 1994 Germany had experienced the second national election after unification, the final withdrawal both of Russian troops from the former DDR and of the symbolic Berlin garrisons of all the wartime allies, and the end of the first economic restructuring program. Others reflect the burden of increasing international demands: the calls of the United States for Germany to exercise the responsibilities of full strategic partnership; the clear hopes of Poland, Hungary, and the Czech and Slovak republics that Germany will be their advocate for admission to the EU, NATO, or both.

But the most striking changes have occurred in the domestic debate. Germany, and particularly former foreign minister Hans- Dietrich Genscher, were long the most articulate proponents of security through cooperation and engagement, especially vis-à-vis the East.[12] But this always stopped short of the direct involvement of German forces, even for humanitarian purposes. The use of German forces for purposes other than article 5 defense was the subject of intense public debate, sometimes verging on ritualistic, about the interpretation of a constitutional prohibition. Germany also had a historical legacy that made it wary of any military involvement in areas of previous Nazi occupation. And the future of NATO itself was the subject of partisan discussion. In the euphoria immediately after the Wall, there were indeed voices, predominantly (but not only) on the left, looking forward to NATO's replacement by the more détente-oriented, cooperative CSCE or by a new, more engaged, autonomous all-European security organization.[13]

The Kohl government now has had a court interpretation and a full Bundestag debate describing the grounds on which German military forces may be used for purposes other than border defense. It has a limited, but beginning, record of direct support for multilateral missions—in Cambodia, in Somalia, in AWACS (airborne warning and control systems) duty over the former Yugoslavia, and in indirect support of UN-NATO operations in Bosnia.

More important, there is no substantial domestic opposition to the general concept of such future ventures, even though decisions will still be on a cautious, case-by-case basis. No party except the reformed communists of the Party of Democratic Socialism opposes a primary role for NATO or the maintenance of a somewhat pared down, more professional armed forces. And there is even marked enthusiasm domestically as well as internationally for greater German global responsibilities, especially if expressed as a permanent German seat on a new, reformed UN Security Council. That would ensure a German voice in decisions on the use of force, give new expression to the German belief in multilateralism and cooperation toward security, and be more consistent with German economic power and increased political responsibility.

The task for the United States will be to encourage and support the German transition to a more public role and more assertive European leadership on security issues. What must be done is to achieve a new transparency in and reassurance about German security decisionmaking. Germany remains of critical concern to many, in part because of its history of military expansionism but also because of its predominance, politically, economically, and militarily. Although never directly acknowledged, the United States is still seen by many states as the counterweight to a strong Germany, the guarantor of a continuing European balance. This view is particularly widespread in a still fragile eastern and central Europe, as relevant in a skeptical Balkans as perhaps in a proud Moscow or uncertain Kiev. The U.S. channel also still provides some reassurance to some Germans, both those interested in a fair share at the "top table" and those still anxious to avoid a gathering of their once and future enemies. And the German military, concerned about crafting and defending its future, still sees intrinsic value in mutual exchange and planning.[14]

France presents a different and far more mixed challenge in its claims as the first protector of the interests of an integrated Europe and in its potential as a "blocking" power, especially in NATO. Since the late 1980s France has gradually abandoned some of the trappings of its previous public opposition to NATO and its adamant refusal to participate in integrated NATO activities. Considerable debate and mutual irritation still continue, however; the legacy of decades of mutual suspicion dies hard. There is a clear and primary commitment across the political spectrum to the creation of a functioning European defense organization and an unquestioned expression of a European security identity vis-à-vis the United States in all aspects of security.

Moreover, French leaders of every political stripe and generation have also reiterated France's unwillingness to rejoin the NATO integrated command structure under any formal guise. To be sure, the imperative of President Mitterrand's personal opposition to NATO military integration diminishes as his time in office wanes. But there is a fundamental French policy consensus that still seems to condemn every interaction between France and much of the rest of NATO to the maximum of negotiation and debate, despite what in the end is often a generally favorable outcome.

France is showing a new sense of engagement and has made progress in both the scope and the level of its military cooperation and involvement in alliance political-military debate. By any measure, it has now surpassed the benchmark of cooperation of the 1960s; short of directly assigning troops or taking a permanent seat in NATO's Defense Planning Committee, it may be close to the greatest alliance role it has ever assumed. Albeit outside the formal alliance military structures, there is new shared military experience—from the formal joint operations in the Gulf War to the coordination of planning for Bosnia, now and after a peace accord.[15] And several interview discussions suggest that for some Americans France is the equal of, or even has now replaced, Britain as the partner the United States can most count on "to be there on the day."[16]

The task for the United States is therefore to maximize French involvement or, at the very least, to ensure its consent to the formation of transatlantic "coalitions of the willing" in the event of serious threats to international peace and security. It must do so, however, without simultaneously sacrificing or downgrading crucial benefits to be gained from the formal integrated alliance structure. French diffidence may change with foreseeable political changes, or it may not; in any case the pace of change will almost certainly continue to be gradual. Formal military integration of French forces must matter less; actual contributions and mutually preferred outcomes must be made to matter more. This means greater stress on improving communication and coordination in all channels, bilateral as well as multilateral, military as well as diplomatic, indirect as well as direct. It also means American willingness to share leadership. Washington must abandon future efforts to play the "German card" in negotiations with the French (if only because it will be unsuccessful) and focus on what unites, rather than on what divides, the two countries.[17]

Most important, serious efforts must be made to foster joint planning for cooperation and convergence in the future. Of all the western European countries, France has been the most engaged in thinking strategically—about global order and security, about peacekeeping and humanitarian intervention, and about its future commitments and force structure. It has had an ongoing elite debate about the necessity for international protection for noncombatants and refugees as well as about the use of military force to create political stability. It has had perhaps the most exposure of any NATO country to the problems of intervention in civil conflict, of re-creating order in "failed states," and in peacekeeping between rival factions in former colonies. Whatever the final outcome, the French attempt to create a safe zone in Rwanda was a unique and commendable contribution to the few alternatives available to the international community. A public debate on France's nuclear investment has also started, mirroring the private discussion of the past several years about the costs and the alternatives now available to France in terms of testing, alert status, and continued technical development.[18] The outcome will be of critical importance for the general nonproliferation regime and particularly for the continuing commitments to nonproliferation in Europe.

The Essential Partner: Russia

The last critical partner for the United States and its allies will be a cooperative Russia. Over the five years since the effective collapse of communism and the Soviet empire, Russia has occupied an ambiguous place in Western strategy. In NATO's first strategy review in 1991, the Soviet Union and its uncertain political future was still the source of threat and instability. Russia, the primary successor state, has since progressed to the status of uneasy but essential partner. This is true formally in Russia's long-discussed application to join NATO's Partnership for Peace, a controversial development both in Russia and in the West.[19] But it is at least as important in other spheres: for example, Russia's critical and somewhat unexpected participation in the Contact Group (the Western Four and Russia, or the "quad plus one"), which has designed a settlement plan for Bosnia and pressed Serbs, Croats, and Muslims alike to accept it, was the most dramatic instance of Russian-Western political cooperation in late 1994. Of perhaps greater importance for long-term stability are Russia's agreement of economic association with the EU and its de facto accession to the Group of Seven (G-7).[20]

As discussed in more detail in later chapters, institutions and memberships do not in themselves guarantee either dialogue or commitment to uphold standards of behavior. Although now at a lower level, Russia's economic turbulence continues; political authority and the patterns of political decisionmaking still seem uncertain, unaccountable, and ineffective, at least at the center. Most observers believe this pattern may well continue for a decade or more.

Increasingly, some Russian elites—old and new, on the right and the left—call on the symbols of Russian power and military potential.[21] They view the West with suspicion and reproach, asserting the imperative for Russia to find its own way both on its own territory and in the "near abroad." According to them, Western promises have produced little in the way of concrete help or continuing respect for Russian interests. Russian efforts to pursue long-standing foreign policy interests—as in Iraq—are scorned because they do not accord with Western policies or national postures. Western offers of security partnership will be similarly hollow or, worse yet, further reduce Russia's potential for independent action or its standing as a military superpower.

Others, including many in the present Yeltsin government and in the centrist factions in the parliament, stress Russia's inevitable return to greatness and the necessary role it plays in the European balance, especially against a stronger, united Germany. They see the necessity for Russia not to choose between Asia and Europe, its Janus-like stance paralleling that of the United States in the Atlantic and the Pacific. They see Russia and other interested former Soviet territories working together in the transformed Commonwealth of Independent States (CIS) and assuming responsibility for security and stability within the former Soviet space and at its periphery. The CIS under Russian leadership would then parallel NATO working in Europe under U.S. leadership on similar problems; their coordination would be achieved within the CSCE or a CSCE-like umbrella organization of equal participants.

Those Russian elites who do favor a positive response to Western invitations to cooperate in a broad European security framework do so for a range of motives. Some see such an attitude as the best opportunity to preserve Russian leverage over security arrangements in central Europe and the Baltic—a direct, unmistakable channel to ensure that Russian interests and preferences are still given due respect. Some see it as the entry price for global cooperation on issues ranging from economic support to strategic arms control. Perhaps the most interesting groups are those, a few in the higher military leadership, that see strategic dialogue, some greater transparency, and some mutual planning and training as defense against their domestic critics and insurance within the Western framework against fragmentation or micromanagement.

Few view the prospect of direct membership in NATO as either a likely or an appropriate outcome. Many give priority to the superpower special relationship with the United States and to the looser dialogues Russia already enjoys with Germany, France, and Britain. Interestingly enough, their reasons parallel those of Western critics. Russia is simply too large and too important to be accommodated within the NATO framework, however transformed and recalibrated to provide for Russia. ("How is NATO to digest a [Russian] elephant?")[22] A looser association—in the PFP, in the North Atlantic Cooperation Council, in a limited G-7 extension—will be best until Russia has completed fundamental economic reform and a transition to democratic accountability. The critical cooperative connection will be sustained at numerous levels, not least in Russia's role as an essential partner within the Security Council of the United Nations.

It is in the fundamental interest of the United States to nourish and extend Russia's cooperative involvement in safeguarding Europe's security. The possibility of a reversion to an expansionist Russia seems slight at present; so too does any attempt to restore Soviet-style influence over the central Europeans or the Baltic republics. But clearly to reduce the range of conceivable threats—political or economic pressure as well as military action—to a Poland or a Hungary involves Russian cooperation as a first priority. Russia must see what is being done and be reassured of peaceful intent and of adequate notice of important changes. Alternatively, an engaged Russia may be less vulnerable to the risks of military and political fragmentation. With assured information flows and access on demand to events as they happen, Russians will have less grounds for paranoia or a sense of victimization or isolation.

The tasks involved are complex and substantial. Russia's participation in the PFP will be an optimistic sign as is the process by which NATO recognized Russia's special weight but not its preference for exclusive rights or control within the PFP. One conceptual parallel is the treatment of a recovering West Germany within the NATO of the 1950s and the early 1960s. Germany's initial status had more to do with mutually accepted constraints on German forces and behavior than with the guarantee of autonomy or preference in crucial areas. The status was imposed but shared; sacrifices were made (albeit unequal ones) by all the states participating to the common enterprise.

In the end it is, of course, Russia's choice to participate or not, to seek broader opportunities for cooperation and interaction. The sense of imposed inferiority and Western delight in Russian weakness is already strong in some Russian circles; Western initiatives seem only to confirm these feelings. But the United States must take the lead in ensuring that the door to cooperation is always open, that there is both time and incentive to develop the forms of interaction that will support the farthest possible extension eastward of the European zone of peace.

The Domestic Framework

The last constituencies the United States must include in this cooperative security framework are the American public and especially the U.S. Congress. The ahistorical nature of American political debate makes every international commitment appear renegotiable and subject to reconsideration. Before the Wall fell, for example, continuity in NATO arrangements was often held rhetorical hostage to greater burden-sharing efforts by European states. After the collapse of the Soviet Union, some in Congress saw no further need for a continuing American role or presence. Europe was now capable and willing to provide for its own security, and, as was dramatically demonstrated in the Bush policy toward the crisis in the former Yugoslavia, should be left to do so.

The challenge faced by the Clinton administration is probably less difficult with regard to the American public in general.[23] Most Americans continue to see western Europe as within their sphere of concern and as worthy of direct defense. Eastern and central Europe is somewhat more remote but increasingly included in the definition of the Europe with which the United States should ally itself. The enthusiasm of émigré groups for the newly democratizing states, the flow of visitors and information, and the level of engagement among selected business and social groups all suggest a latent mobilization base for greater cooperation and involvement. The principal barrier is cost, particularly any substantial amounts that would subtract from the resources available for long-postponed domestic agendas.

Americans have somewhat different attitudes toward U.S. cooperation with Russia. Most no longer consider Russia a threat; individuals and groups show widespread support for the positive benefits of the "second Russian revolution." Every step toward defusing military confrontation has met with majority approval. Military exchanges, Russia's entry into NATO's Partnership for

Peace, and Russia's involvement in the Bosnian settlement along with traditional arms control agreements have all generated positive images of Russia and of Russian-American interchange, taken increasingly as normal. Many Americans are indeed cautiously optimistic about Russia's gradual evolution toward economic reform and democratic control and accountability.

But for large segments of the electorate, and its congressional interpreters, direct security cooperation with Russia, in Europe as elsewhere, must be approached with caution.[24] In part, this approach turns on cost; how, for example, can it be justified to pay for Russian defense conversion or homes for displaced Russian officers when funds for similar projects in the United States are unavailable? In part, too, it reflects congressional skepticism about possible diversion and waste in the present economic chaos.[25] To some degree it also reflects a sense of distance, perhaps even the belief that the most fundamental problems of importance to Americans—expansionist communist ideology and a globally competitive Soviet Union—have been resolved. As a result, American support for programs aiding Russian reform has been less enthusiastic on both the individual and national levels than support for similar programs in central Europe, with levels for Russia often dipping far below those expressed in Germany, Russia's most consistent Western supporter. And even those efforts most directly related to immediate American and European security interests and policy concerns have attracted little continuing attention—to mention only the central issues of demilitarization, denuclearization and dismantlement, CFE weapons reductions, and chemical weapons destruction.

Past experience suggests that these attitudes may change with time and, more directly, can be shaped through presidential and especially congressional leadership. What is required is a compelling explanation, in terms of American interests in Europe and throughout the world, of the need to engage Russia in security dialogue and cooperation. Without that, the majority belief that Russia poses no threat will seem an acceptable basis for a policy of benign neglect. There will be little basis on which to provide the intellectual and material resources needed to offset the most probable threats: the risks arising out of Russian political and military fragmentation or of Russian self-isolation or withdrawal inward in the face of crisis. And it will be too easy for Congress to continue the narrow politics of the usual, driven by short-term economic interests and demands, and by the confusion of the existence of military forces and authorization of a large military budget with the creation of security.

Conclusion

The task of extending the cooperative security regime in Europe presents significant challenges to post–cold war American foreign policy. The costs in the short term seem high, the specific benefits perhaps only appreciated in the long term or through the absence of conflict or tension. The task requires an explicit statement of vision, an exercise that is hard for both presidents and practitioners and one that runs counter to the hallowed Anglo-Saxon tradition of "muddling through."

What is remarkable, however, is how much has already been accomplished in the five years of rapid political and economic change since the Wall fell. As described in greater detail in the rest of the monograph, organizational frameworks have been transformed and have been turned to a host of new cooperative functions. Processes begun in the waning days of the cold war have been adapted to the requirements of the new security context, not always with maximum effectiveness but with cumulating results. The main challenge so far, the continuing civil conflicts in the former Yugoslavia, has been bobbled and often mishandled—but by all. An end to the violence has not yet been secured; both political and military outcomes appear uncertain. Yet lessons have been learned, and new forms of cooperation in peacekeeping and conflict prevention have been tested and expanded to involve a range of European and non-European actors.

2

The Organizational Framework of European Security

Institutions and their post–cold war responsibilities have been the central focus of debates about European security since days after the fall of the Berlin Wall. The goal, first set in U.S. secretary of state James Baker's Berlin speech in December 1989, was to establish a new security architecture, one that preserved what had been achieved in the West but encouraged adaptation to the new political and military context.[1] Baker's primary concern was America's relationship with an evolving European Community, and the need to ensure both NATO's continuing preeminence and the rejection of a "Fortress Europe" strategy by the Community. But Baker and his successors increasingly emphasized the new security needs in the East and the need for new institutional arrangements to secure a Europe increasingly whole and free.

The Question Catalog

Throughout most of the Bush years, the principal, often stormy search was for a balanced European-American framework that allowed for a transformed NATO, for a newly ambitious Western European Union, and for an equitable division of labor and leadership between them. But there was also no escaping the issue of security institutions in and for the states in what was now to be defined as central and eastern Europe, and in particular the role of Russia. Direct pressure came from transforming events such as the threatening Moscow coup attempts in 1991 and the executive-parliamentary standoff in 1993. Most emphatic too were the escalating demands of the non-Russian central and eastern European states for both guarantees and a secured seat at the major organizational tables. In addition, the intertwined future of the pan-European Conference on Security and Cooperation in Europe needed to be defined.

From the vantage point of late 1994, many of the basic directions of institutional change seem clear, and the period of debate and rapid change at a close. NATO has emerged as the primary framework for European security and seemingly will be so as long as the United States wishes it and remains engaged. The role of Russia has still not been addressed directly. But NATO has created two new mechanisms for expanding dialogue and cooperation with Russia and the other CEE states: first the intergovernmental North Atlantic Cooperation Council in 1991 and then, in 1994, the Partnership for Peace initiative, a set of bilateral agreements on cooperation between NATO and most of the NACC states. (See appendix B for the text of the PFP.)

The other interlocking security organizations are still in transition but are now fairly well sorted out. The European Union (EU) and its transitional security arm, the Western European Union (WEU), have a set of goals and potential capabilities for the future realization of a common foreign and security policy. More important in the present are the clarified relationships between the European Union and NATO, which are no longer directly competitive or contradictory. The CSCE has gained more permanent structures and a set of narrower, more focused missions, but it has only qualified support and is hampered as much by its cumbersome size as by its traditional intergovernmental decisionmaking procedures. A host of other organizations are working on new or specific aspects of European security: to highlight only two, the UN effort with NATO in Bosnia and in peace monitoring in Georgia, and the international Council of Europe on the protection of citizenship and political rights of ethnic minorities in the central European and Baltic states.

But the transformations achieved over the last five years should not obscure the many institutional issues about European security and stability that must still be addressed. The fundamental challenge is still how simultaneously to widen and deepen the European cooperative regime. The most important issue is still how to ensure European security with and through Russian engagement or, at the least, without drawing new lines of confrontation against Russia. Of great concern is the scope of and timing for an expansion of NATO membership to appropriate or "willing" CEE states, an issue at most postponed by the PFP concept. Daily reminders of the significance of Russia's role come from the Bosnian conflict, where any outcome other than continuing civil war depends on the closest possible cooperation of the West and Russia.

The choices are not easy; the tasks involved are at least as difficult as constructing the North Atlantic Treaty Organization itself and securing the peaceful rearmament of the Federal Republic of Germany. Any significant extension eastward means a return to first principles, the reflection in institutional form of new, expanded agreements on the core elements of cooperation. Most basic is to define the borders and indicators of Europe. Which states of the CEE claimants, for example, must be included in the primary security institutions to ensure the best prospects for the security and stability of all? What are the costs and risks of excluding some states or allowing them to exclude themselves? What security guarantees are desirable, necessary, or realistic for any new members? Are there acceptable workable substitutes for these or for formal institutional membership itself either during a transition period or in the longer term?

In western Europe the questions are less dramatic but equally complex, politically and militarily. NATO still faces major transformation challenges: the need to adapt organizationally and procedurally to new missions and new threats; to smaller, less well funded military forces; and to new decision-making requirements. Also at issue are the evolving political consequences of a European political union in the making, of a stronger, more independent German voice, and of the new "northern" members of the EU.

For all states in the former East and West, there is also the overriding need to convince domestic publics of the continuing importance of institutionalized cooperation, indeed of cooperation itself. Popular sentiment in almost every state supports drastic reductions in military forces and budgets and longs for overdue attention to domestic needs. Most leaders still see multilateral action and cooperative guarantees as the preferred outcome in crisis. Now, though, they are more focused on selective engagements and on crisis prevention and management than on the institutional and operational implications of new missions. The horrors of Bosnia and the challenges of Somalia and Rwanda have shaken this viewpoint but have not decisively altered it.

Moreover, how Europe came to develop the foundation for a cooperative security regime seems in retrospect to have been a straightforward and perhaps inevitable process.[2] Traditional analysis links the process of building confidence and limiting military capabilities in Europe to the impetus provided by the cold war. In the West, fear of Soviet attack and the need for fundamental political cohesion allowed for continuous progress under U.S. leadership toward cooperative control over all aspects of military security, from standing forces to common efforts to achieve arms control. As the cold war competition changed or ebbed, episodic progress was also made toward East-West détente, toward cooperative actions and mechanisms to allow for lowered tension.

However broadly accurate, these conclusions probably obscure the complexity of the evolution of cooperative security concepts. Indeed, they understate many of the lessons that will be critical to guiding present efforts to transform the European security system. The key distinction is between the cooperation achieved in Atlantic Europe and the convergence achieved under a pan-Europe approach, especially in the 1980s. But it is also important to assess the relative value of formal structures and informal procedures to the process of security regime building. One needs to understand the complexity of the organizational efforts involved, the changing mix of bilateral and multilateral elements as catalytic factors in cooperation.

Evolution in the West:
The European-American Security Relationship, 1947–89

Traditionally, analyses of the European-American security relationship are essentially histories of the NATO alliance.[3] Such works recounted NATO's positive attributes: its uniqueness as a standing military alliance with broad-ranging formal and informal guarantees of mutual help and continuing deterrence, its level of alert and integrated command, and its impressive mobilization potential of conventional and nuclear capability against the forces of the Soviet Union and its Warsaw Pact allies. More dramatic notes were provided by the recurring NATO crises—over nuclear weapons doctrines and deployments, over power sharing and burden shedding, over the role of the United States as benign hegemon, and over the dilemma of French membership but nonparticipation.

Committed Atlanticists on both sides of the ocean often contrasted the successful NATO pattern to what was until 1989 a somewhat inconclusive postwar search for a European defense identity. The start was an ambitious attempt to establish a supranational European Defense Community (EDC) in the early 1950s, a highly integrated framework that was designed to contain a rearming Germany and that was ultimately rejected by France and, more indirectly, by Britain.[4] NATO then oversaw Germany's military rehabilitation, with guidance of only its economic potential left to the emerging European institutions. Even to some European enthusiasts, the central theme of the 1970s and 1980s seemed the inability of Europe to overcome its cold war

Figure 2-1. European Community Chronology, 1951–94

1951 *April:* European Coal and Steel Community is created.

1957 *March:* Treaties of Rome are signed, creating European Economic Community and European Atomic Energy Community. The two are later merged into European Community (EC).

1985 *June:* EC white paper calls for completion of the internal market by January 1, 1993 (the Europe 1992 program).

1987 *June:* Single European Act enters into force.

1989 *April:* Delors Report is presented, calling for establishment of Economic and Monetary Union in three stages by 1999. EC launches PHARE (Pologne-Hongrie: actions pour la réconversion économique).

1990 *February:* United States and EC announce regular meetings between foreign ministers and EC and U.S. presidents.

1991 *June:* EC negotiates cease-fire between Slovenia and Yugoslavia and later begins peace conference for Serbo-Croatian conflict.

---

dependence on the United States for security and therefore the dominance of NATO and U.S. preferences over any European organizational efforts.

This approach, however, poses NATO and the European Community as false alternatives rather than as interdependent institutions within a common concept and thus obscures critical interactions in the postwar search for European security. From the outset, both Americans and Europeans defined security in terms of both military and economic requirements. The direct threats, especially in the first postwar decade, were seen as Soviet expansionism and the uncontrolled growth of the German military. But the fundamental fears were of a return to the dangers of the 1930s: the lack of economic security eroding political allegiance to democratic values and the lack of military security, given a looming totalitarian threat and weak national militaries. The EC and NATO thus presented intertwined answers to the same question: how to preserve peace in Europe against internal and external threat.[5] Clearly differentiated functionally at first, each grew to have impacts on both economic and military cooperation in Europe and across the Atlantic.

October: Anglo-Italian "Declaration on European Security and Defense" is presented. Franco-German proposal follows.

December: Maastricht Treaty, establishing European Union, is signed. EC concludes association agreements with Visegrad states. Others follow.

1992 *January:* EC recognizes Slovenia and Croatia.

June: Lisbon summit declaration specifies goals of common foreign and security policy.

1993 *June:* EC eases terms of association agreements and agrees to consider eventual full membership for central and eastern European states.

October: Maastricht Treaty enters into force after German court at Karlsruhe approves text.

1994 *June:* EU signs Partnership and Cooperation agreement with Russia.

The European Community

From the first days of the Europe of the Six and the European Coal and Steel Community, the EC was the primary vehicle for achieving transparency in political and economic policies, as well as the integration of national economies deemed essential for true security. (See figure 2-1 for a chronology of the EC.) The central premise was that solid ground for peace in Europe would exist if Franco-German competition could be harnessed and their relationship thus stabilized and if the German-European balance became a task for all, with positive economic incentives for those who participated in common actions and limits. Competition would give way to free trade and specialization; beggar-thy-neighbor policies, such as those that had bedeviled the 1920s and 1930s, would be replaced by cooperative patterns of comparative advantage and the evolution of a single European trading area. Transparency and cross-border access would be the watchwords of governmental cooperation at all levels and the best security guarantees against the politics of fear and the risk of surprise.

The pace of Community development was slow, and the expectations of the postwar functionalist leaders about cooperative cross-border solutions were often disappointed. Progress was sometimes reversible. The dashing of the great hopes attending the EDC and the stillborn European Political Community in 1954 led to a relaunching of a broadened European Community, but one with a traditional international decisionmaking structure. It was the intergovernmental EC Council of Ministers, not the more integrated European Commission, that had the key responsibilities and decisionmaking authority. The practical limits of integration were the set of activities and functions in which European states could not achieve national outcomes, in which their national interests dictated joint efforts that blurred border distinctions or required the giving up of sovereignty. Moreover, although the potential for expansion of membership seemed clear, especially in the cold war context, actual entry was sometimes obscured by Community disagreement and occasionally, as in Britain's first application, lockout.

But the effort to build an integrated Europe continued, and slowly but surely it fulfilled the dreams of Jean Monnet and the original functionalists. From time to time there were attempts to surge forward politically, toward the definition of the basis for a common European foreign policy and eventually for security policy as well. In the 1970s and 1980s there were several efforts to make a breakthrough; most remained at the rhetorical level. Others tried to become more operational—such as the tantalizing Genscher-Colombo initiative, an ambitious plan to merge and deepen European political and defense cooperation in 1981—but these attracted little broad political support. An occasionally recurring French theme was to revitalize the WEU as the core of an independent European defense identity buttressed by autonomous planning capacity and capabilities. A second, more successful set of efforts stressed Franco-German defense cooperation, often with an explicit challenge to the Anglo-Saxon allies.

More important, however, for the building of a broader, deeply rooted European security regime were the consequences of the growth and increasing competencies of the Community bureaucracy and the evolution, somewhat fitful, of the Commission itself. These created new ways of doing business across borders, new patterns of governmental and bureaucratic interaction, new sources of mutual reassurance, and new perceptions of the inevitability of a European "zone of peace." By the mid-1980s, with the design of a single European economic space, there might still be debate about final goals and forms, but the process of building Europe seemed irreversible.

A critical new stimulus came with the Franco-German initiatives of the mid-1980s to accelerate the pace of European union.[6] Franco-German rapprochement was always the Community's political core. But however well maintained by both sides, the relationship was often buffeted by suspicions in Washington, the impact of personalities in Paris and Bonn, and the critical differences over security agendas after France's withdrawal from NATO in 1966. But by the mid-1980s the focus had shifted substantially, reflecting both the waning of cold war hostilities and the growing German disenchantment with Washington's European priorities. The personal commitment of President François Mitterrand and Chancellor Helmut Kohl galvanized the push toward Europe 1992, the final steps in the creation of the common European economic space. But their vision also included dramatic progress in critical new areas toward the securing of a deepened EU: the creation of a European monetary union and the intensification of political cooperation, including progress toward a common foreign and security policy (CFSP). A common defense policy would come to be an intrinsic part of the EU only at the very end of a long process, but it, too, would eventually be Europeanized.

One of the more innovative Kohl-Mitterrand proposals led to the design in 1988 of a joint Franco-German brigade, explicitly described as a precursor to the eventual establishment of an independent European defense identity. Not all the Community partners were equally pleased, and it was apparent from the outset that the French and German approaches differed considerably. The position of the French rested on their traditional opposition to the NATO integrated military organization and their continuing sponsorship of a European alternative, preferably through the still underused WEU. Although wishing to retain an American commitment to European security, the French sought to eliminate continued European dependence on a United States that would inevitably withdraw from Europe according to its own timetable and needs. Kohl's Germany had more complex goals. Bonn was far more interested in balancing its European and transatlantic relationships, in legitimizing its European identity but also maintaining a U.S. presence and involvement. But both countries were committed to an accelerated European union and placed increasing significance on a clear differentiation of European and transatlantic institutions.

Figure 2-2. Nato Chronology, 1949–94

1949 *April 4:* North Atlantic Treaty is signed in Washington by Belgium, Canada, Denmark, France, Iceland, Italy, Luxembourg, Netherlands, Norway, Portugal, United Kingdom, and United States.

1952 *February 18:* Greece and Turkey join NATO.

1955 *May 5:* Federal Republic of Germany becomes member of NATO.

May 14: USSR founds Warsaw Treaty Organization (WTO) with Albania, Bulgaria, Czechoslovakia, East Germany, Hungary, Poland, and Romania.

1966 *March 10:* France formally withdraws from NATO's integrated military structure; SHAPE and NATO headquarters leave Paris for Mons and Brussels.

1967 *April 6–7:* Initial meeting of the Nuclear Planning Group (NPG).

1982 *May 30:* Spain joins NATO.

1987 *February 17:* Vienna talks open between NATO and WTO countries on mandate for negotiations on reducing conventional forces in Europe from Atlantic to Urals (later known as CFE talks).

1990 *July 6:* NATO Summit publishes "London Declaration" on transformed North Atlantic Alliance; outlines plans to develop cooperation with all countries of central and eastern Europe across a wide spectrum of political and military activity, including regular diplomatic liaison.

The Transatlantic Community

NATO's evolution was more strictly related to controlling postwar threats. It drew explicitly on the lessons of World War II: to counter the Soviet threat and to manage Germany in military terms required a continuing transatlantic framework and the direct involvement of the United States in European security arrangements. The North Atlantic Treaty, or Atlantic Charter, of 1949 contained the first step toward collective defense, the guarantee under article 5 of cooperative defense of all NATO territory if attacked. (See appendix C for the complete text.) The evolution from a traditional security alliance composed of a series of bilateral treaties to a collective security pact guaranteeing the defense of all by all continued with the creation in the early 1950s of standing military forces and a permanent allied command structure headed by a supreme commander of allied forces (SACEUR). Decisions were

1991 *March 31:* Formal dissolution of military structures of WTO.

November 8: NATO Rome Summit unveils new Strategic Concept.

December 20: First meeting of the North Atlantic Cooperation Council (NACC) of sixteen NATO allies and nine central and eastern European states; Soviet Union ends.

1992 *June 4:* NATO foreign ministers announce readiness to accept on case-by-case basis CSCE taskings for peacekeeping missions.

December 17: Foreign ministers broaden peacekeeping cooperation and agree to accept UN peacekeeping mandates, including in former Yugoslavia.

1993 *April 12:* NATO begins combat patrols to enforce UN no-fly zone over Bosnia.

1994 *January 10–11:* Brussels Summit launches Partnership for Peace (PFP) open to all willing NACC-CSCE states and endorses concept of Combined Joint Task Forces (CJTF) to support development of European defense identity (ESDI).

February 28: NATO fires first shots in combat, downing four Serbian planes.

September: First NATO-PFP exercise held in Poland.

to be made collectively by the intergovernmental North Atlantic Council (NAC), which soon began to meet in fairly continuous session. (For a chronology of NATO, see figure 2-2.)

From an American perspective, NATO's emergence was the indirect and unforeseen consequence of European, and especially British, efforts to entangle the United States in a long-term economic and military alliance. American aid to a recovering Europe—whether in military assistance or in the broader Marshall Plan for economic recovery—was made conditional on Europe's ability to demonstrate cross-border cooperation and the clear will to defend itself. The goal seemed to have been met after the signing of the Brussels pact for cooperative defense in 1948 and the planning of the EDC, under the broad umbrella of the traditional North Atlantic Treaty of 1949. The United States itself was eager to cut its defense budget and, after full demobilization, to return to "normal." Well into the 1950s politicians and military leaders alike described a continuing American military presence in Europe as "temporary" or until "Europe (or Germany) is on its feet again."

Increasing military confrontation with the Soviet Union and the outbreak of the Korean War transformed both the alliance and the American role. By the mid 1950s NATO emerged as a fully implemented alliance, with not only commitments to common territorial defense (article 5) and comprehensive political consultation (article 4),[7] but also a unique integrated military command charged with force management and planning in peacetime. The United States provided the bulk of the initial resources and forces and successfully lobbied for expansion to Greece, Turkey, Germany, and eventually Spain, beyond the original Atlantic Charter signatories of 1949.

Over its first two decades, moreover, NATO added the functions of a cooperative security organization. In no other region of the world was there more progress toward mutual regulation and coordination of military capabilities and operations, toward mutual reassurance and the avoidance of uncertainty. Military establishments were bound in a consciously designed, thickening web of equipment and structural constraints, mutually devised and with mutual oversight and transparency. The SACEUR (supreme allied commander, Europe), always an American, and the integrated command structure at SHAPE (Supreme Headquarters, Allied Powers, Europe) had wide and intrusive powers and increasing authority, reflecting American interests and influence.

Politically, by the mid-1960s NATO had also become in effect the permanent diplomatic conference for the region, led and presided over by the United States. The critical elements were not just the formal political representation or even the standing military forces and supporting cooperative structures for planning, training, and operations. Involved, too, were hosts of formal and informal networks, primarily bilateral but also multilateral channels for consultation and coordination on a wide-ranging security agenda.

NATO's list of potential members from the first was far less clearcut than the EC's. Viewed with hindsight, NATO's admissions to membership mixed targets of opportunity (Norway), issues of geostrategic necessity (Iceland, Greece, and Turkey), and particular political imperatives (democratizing Spain). NATO was set to reach as far as possible across the European "free world," with the tightest integration and largest number of standing peacetime forces in its central front, the zone considered of maximum danger. The northern and southern flanks saw looser forms of military organization and more traditional interstate cooperation. And military integration on the seas was still looser, often seeming merely an extension of the Anglo-American mutual assistance efforts of World War II.

NATO in both its military and political activities evolved specific and sometimes unique ways of doing business, all with wide-ranging implications for the intensity and the general success of interstate security cooperation. The general mode was one of U.S. leadership accompanied by formal interstate bargaining and, most often, compromises struck on the trading among the major allied partners of issue-specific benefits and risks. But the level and the extent of cooperation seemed to increase yearly, having important implications for the mutual direction and joint limits of policy even within bilateral channels. Patterns of managed burden sharing developed, never as many as the United States insisted on but probably more than most national parliaments would have arrived at independently. Given the day-to-day facts of a permanent integrated command structure and the resulting necessity of mutual transparency, there was de facto mutual oversight over all offensive forces in the European theater. And there was the impact of common experience among the military, trends that changed patterns of decisionmaking at home as well as within the multilateral command and planning functions.

NATO developed many critical initiatives on economic security as well. These were not the formal efforts toward coordination and the elimination of economic competition foreseen in article 2 of the North Atlantic Treaty; those duties were left first to the Organization for European Economic Cooperation (the OEEC, which later became the larger Organization for Economic Cooperationand Development, OECD) and then to the evolving Community. Rather it was the effect of defense cooperation on national economies: the specific calculation of burden-sharing formulas, the relatively full disclosure of the economics of national weapons development and acquisition, and the issues of mutual stakes in continuing research and development. By the 1970s and 1980s NATO sharing indeed entailed comprehensive engagement: joint agreement to an infrastructure paid for and maintained in common, an annual survey of budget plans and commitments, and far-reaching consultations at every level about military research, force structure changes, and plans for new weapons systems.

Unquestionably, complementary approaches to security did not eliminate points of competition and mutual irritation in the NATO-EC relationship. The usual flash point was the role of France, particularly after France, under the leadership of Charles de Gaulle, left NATO's integrated military command in 1966. France consistently argued the case for a united Europe, assuming responsibility for its own security and not being dependent for its destiny and ultimately for its survival on the United States. From the Gaullist perspective, the common NATO military structures were simply instruments of U.S. control over the choices of European states. The United States neither could nor would meet its commitments to Europe's defense with all available means, nuclear or conventional. Therefore, all that should survive of NATO was a traditional treaty between a uniting Europe and the United States and whatever special arrangements were needed to fulfill American pledges as a postwar victor to ensure the protection and good behavior of Germany.

Equally significant irritations arose at other levels of allied political interaction. The United States never hesitated to link the value of its military support to demands for European economic agreement or to promote the purchase of American military goods and services as an economic offset within NATO. The European arms industry and ultimately the European governments within NATO's Independent European Program Group chafed at the "buy American" emphasis in decisions on arms and strategy. The NATO bureaucracy was jealous of its foreign policy prerogatives and until well into the 1980s reacted vigilantly to any EC initiative that dealt directly with issues in the NATO area. The EC and its bureaucracy often found means of political and economic payback, if not in kind, then in intensity.

But despite all the rhetoric and the Franco-American shrillness, at a fundamental level there was recognition of the basic division of labor within the West. NATO and the EC were seen as two instruments serving the same ends, with broadly accepted trade-offs of advantage and disadvantage and no disagreement about the geographic and political scope of the respective efforts. Competition and nationalization were moderated, if not entirely checked, in the interest of broader and deeper cooperation. The specifics of policy were sometimes controversial and a source of interorganizational irritation; the general framework and policy outcomes in both economic and military security were quite the opposite.

In some ways the most telling success of the broadly complementary approach of the EC and NATO came in a common approach to a key question: how to balance military strength and economic potential in a Europe twice savaged by German expansionism. The special wisdom of postwar European international politics was that security was most easily achieved by making

Germany a partner in this balancing process and by enmeshing all states co-operatively in Germany's containment. Germany was always a formal equal in NATO and in the EC, whatever its special obligations were or however it implemented the military constraints required. Avoiding an isolated Germany, vulnerable (as after World War I) to demagogic legends, meant developing mutual security structures in which Germany would both give and receive hostages against the future in the form of mutually binding guarantees.

The treatment of Germany thus became the core demonstration of how to extend cooperative security guarantees to an erstwhile enemy turned ally. For example, although Germany accepted stationed forces on its territory to bolster its own security and to help alleviate the fears of other states, its own forces interacted and coordinated with foreign forces on the basis of parity. Its military arsenal in all but the area of nuclear capability represented an equal (and sometimes greater) share in the collective security apparatus; its strategy and doctrine were open to the influence of others and also decided in common. Guarding against German "singular-ization"—allowing for the principles of self-limitation and regulation to gain acceptance—became more and more important for all of Germany's allies as a political foundation for broad areas of European cooperation.

By mid 1989 the basic framework of Western security cooperation was an accepted part of the political landscape—with obvious political and economic benefits for every member state, even with spillover benefits for the security of the neutral states outside both NATO and the EC. Proponents of ever closer European union did cite the distance still to go toward a new European Defense Community or toward developing Europe's own effective collective security measures. American presidents and pundits railed about persistent shortfalls in economic as opposed to military cooperation, about the difficulties in burden sharing in an age of increasing East-West thaw, about the unwillingness of Europeans to concert out-of-area initiatives, political or military. The U.S. Congress regularly threatened limits on American deployments and a schedule for force withdrawals if burden sharing was not satisfactory. And during the 1980s European opposition parties and those on the Left focused noisily on the outdatedness of NATO and the need to develop a common security system that would encompass a freer, more open eastern Europe as well.

But the basic course seemed set; the critical building blocks were in place, and cooperation toward mutual security, economic and military, the well-practiced and established norm.

Cooperative Security across Europe: 1975–89

Progress toward a cooperative security regime embracing eastern as well as western Europe has been far more uneven and unpredictable then the evolution of western Europe alone. The critical element was always the military stalemate in Europe, the unwillingness, if not the inability, of East and West to change the political division of the Continent. The eastern European crises in the 1950s, especially the danger-laden confrontations in the second Berlin crisis of 1958–62, demonstrated how high the stakes were for Moscow and for Washington and how high the risks were for the European states. Particularly as set forth in Germany's Ostpolitik, any move toward greater security required states to acknowledge the division and then to use transparency and reassurance to overcome the consequences of division.

The first concrete steps toward a pan-European regime emerged in the context of the East-West détente in the early 1970s, stimulated both by the Nixon-Brezhnev arms control agreements and by the succession of eastern European political agreements that were the essential elements of German Ostpolitik. Of central interest were two somewhat contradictory policy initiatives: the linked decisions to begin the thirty-five–member Conference on Security and Cooperation in Europe and to initiate the mutual and balanced force reduction (MBFR) talks between the twenty-three states of the NATO and Warsaw Treaty Organization alliances. The CSCE was the more innovative and broader of the two initiatives. Pushed first by the Soviet Union, the CSCE was then taken up by western Europeans and especially by German foreign minister Hans-Dietrich Genscher in the first flush of détente in the early 1970s. The western Europeans saw the CSCE as an attempt to address the nonmilitary aspects of security in Europe, to open a security dialogue with the East, and to reduce uncertainty about national intentions and military operations. (For the evolution of European security negotiations, see figure 2-3.)

The United States, on the other hand, dismissed the CSCE either as a holdover from the earlier utopian dream of collective security or as a Soviet or French attempt to craft a pan-European alternative to NATO. It constantly tried to delay the start of talks and showed little interest in participation and even less expectation of a useful outcome from any such "talk shop."

Washington finally agreed to participate in the conventional forces in Europe talks only if there were to be simultaneous efforts toward an MBFR agreement. Fostered largely by the United States, the MBFR was the first of

Figure 2-3. Evolution of European Security Negotiations, 1973–92

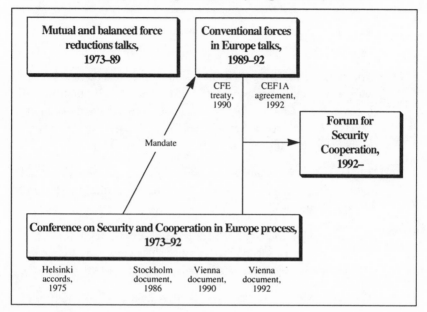

several efforts to use formal arms control negotiations to limit Soviet conventional capabilities and to lessen the risks arising out of the massive military concentrations in Europe. At the same time the initiative was an effort to outflank domestic critics of growing military budgets in the United States and throughout western Europe. The MBFR was to achieve a binding multilateral scheme aimed at producing reduction in forces and budgets in the East in return for equal reductions in the West.

To Washington and many in Europe the arms control path seemed the more legitimate, if not necessarily the more promising, approach to achieving military stability in Europe.[8] After an initial flurry, any hopes for substantial progress were abandoned. Beyond years of formal negotiation sessions, the MBFR process itself produced few tangible results, although it did open interesting channels for East-West European back-channel interactions. Progress toward reductions and a lowering of threat came only after the Gorbachev revolution. The specific breakthroughs toward agreement for arms reductions came in the late 1980s, with the Intermediate-Range Nuclear Forces (INF) treaty for asymmetric reductions in Soviet and American nuclear systems leading the way to new approaches to U.S.-Soviet agreements.[9]

Figure 2-4. CSCE Chronology, 1975–94

1975 *August:* Heads of state and government of Europe (except Albania), along with Canada and United States, sign Helsinki Final Act.

1990 *November:* CSCE adopts Vienna document on expanded confidence and security-building measures (CSBMs). Paris CSCE summit meeting establishes Charter of Paris for a new Europe, which reaffirms the values of Conference on Security and Cooperation in Europe and prescribes new structures and institutions for CSCE process.

1992 *July:* CSCE claims status of a regional organization for political and cultural cooperation according to United Nations criteria at Helsinki Review Conference.

December: CSCE Council of Foreign Ministers creates new meeting group known as the Vienna Group, which will meet weekly and recommend action on violent conflicts to Committee of Senior Officials. (CSO).

1993 *February:* Meeting of CSO in Prague. A joint CSCE-EU Office of Sanctions coordinator is established to support CSCE teams based in nations bordering Serbia and Montenegro.

The MBFR's successor, the CFE agreement limiting conventional weapons levels from the Atlantic-to-the-Urals (ATTU) area,[10] was the capstone of this changed environment. Both the INF and CFE accords still assumed competing alliances and adversarial interests. But both also involved new levels of cooperation, including bold steps toward transparency and verification. For example, it became routine to hold regular and short-notice intrusive inspections on national territories and to seek multilateral approaches to a wide range of issues, from the character of weapons deployment to agreed methods for weapon dismantlement and destruction.

As the political climate changed dramatically in the 1980s, the MBFR stalled and the CSCE gained new hope. The CSCE in its initial phases had built only a fragile consensus resting on very different national goals. For the Soviet Union, the CSCE was the political legitimation of the status quo; for the United States, the CSCE was primarily a vehicle for stabilizing East-West military relationships (MBFR). For the western Europeans, the con-

---

March: CSCE meeting on Nagorno-Karabakh in Rome approves document setting forth draft mandate for advance group of observers. Fact-finding mission authorized for Slovakia and Czech Republic.

May: Creation of ODIHR's (Office of Democratic Institutions and Human Rights) Office of Free Elections in Warsaw.

September: First Human Dimension Implementation meeting in Warsaw.

October: Election monitoring in Azerbaijan by observers from CSCE states, coordinated by ODIHR.

November: CSCE decides to send a four-person mission to Latvia to reduce tensions between the government and the Russian speakers located there.

December: 600 observers are sent to Russian Federation to monitor elections.

1994 *February:* Parliamentary elections are held in Moldova. Elections are monitored by representatives of ODIHR, the Parliamentary Assembly, and CSCE mission to Moldova.

---

sistent hope was for a return to the détente agenda of the early 1970s, the humanitarian but also political imperatives to overcome the division of Europe and especially the division of Germany. (For a chronology of the CSCE, see figure 2-4.)

During the 1980s efforts in the CSCE became more focused on changing European military concepts and operational practices as the instruments with which to offset the worst consequences of the stalemated military confrontation in the center of Europe. Highest on the agenda was mutual regulation of those military activities that raised perceptions of the risk of surprise attack, heightened uncertainty about intentions, or seemed to lead to automatic crisis escalation.

From the outset, CSCE negotiations reflected the inherent tension between attempts to stabilize the existing confrontational nature of the East-West relationship and a commitment to change the status quo. The Helsinki documents of 1975 were statements of principles and declarations of intent. They did not amount to a binding international treaty or even formal agreements among like-minded states. Still, they reflected some requisites of cooperative security: the promise to use force only for defensive ends, the commitment not to try to alter borders by force, the use of transparency to eliminate uncertainty and risk, and the legitimacy of an international interest in the way other states treat their own citizens and minorities.

Progress over the course of the CSCE's first decade was still slow; it focused largely on increasing communication flows about nonmilitary aspects of security (human rights, transparency) and ensuring the autonomous participation (and thus the independent voice) of the eastern European states. The first truly cooperative steps were the relatively limited confidence-building measures agreed to in Helsinki: the agreement to provide prior notification of military movements involving more than 25,000 personnel and the voluntary exchange of observers at military exercises.[11]

After a rocky start, these measures were observed by all parties almost without exception and thus served as a body of experience and a precedent for more far-reaching agreements achieved at the review conferences in Stockholm (1986) and Vienna (1990).[12] The agreement to increasingly intrusive confidence and security-building measures, meant, for example, more stringent restrictions on military exercises and the need for information about national alert procedures; open exchange of data on forces, weapons, and deployments; new rights allowing for challenge inspections; and increased exchanges among high-ranking professional military and civilian officials.[13] The CSCE was also the formal convener of the CFE negotiation, allowing the neutral and nonaligned European states for the first time to have a right of oversight and occasional influence over East-West military arrangements.

Ultimately, the CSCE's critical contributions came less in moves toward disarmament than in the legitimation of a comprehensive political framework for ongoing security cooperation among all European states. Many of the concepts of mutual security and defensive restructuring discussed were unworkable; many of the sessions revealed only the degree of division and the influence of superpower competition among participants. The United States softened its objections to the CSCE in general only at points of particular partisan utility vis-à-vis the Soviet Union. And Soviets from the outset saw the CSCE as only one of the channels through which to exploit the attractions of détente.

But even a weakly organized CSCE created channels and habits of discussion, giving credibility to regular contacts among states on security questions. In the domestic politics of many European states, most particularly in eastern Europe, the CSCE locked in patterns of popular expectation about compliance and, at least at the rhetorical level, set goals and standards to which governments could be held accountable at home and abroad.

Perhaps most important was the fact that the CSCE was a guaranteed international forum for the non-Soviet members of the Warsaw Pact to reinstate their political credentials, at least rhetorically, as Europeans.[14] Largely because of French objections to bloc-to-bloc talks, the CSCE accorded full and equal formal rights to each state, rights that the central Europeans to different national degrees soon learned to use. As the political changes sparked by Solidarity in Poland during the early 1980s reverberated throughout the central European states, the CSCE provided opportunities for back-channel diplomacy and the exchange of information with the West, and occasionally with one another.

In the late 1980s national differences with Soviet preferences became more open, making the CSCE "window" less necessary and less important for the reformers of Poland and Hungary. But the CSCE still constituted another option, another channel, and further evidence of irreversible dialogue and European-ness.

Institutional Lessons Learned

It is far too easy now to dismiss all this institutional development as of limited significance for post–cold war security challenges. But the developments in Europe, East and West, over the past five years suggest that these organizational developments cast long shadows for the future organization of cooperative security in Europe. The pace of change, the critical nature of the security tasks faced have left little room for new organizations; policymakers and publics alike have mined the experience of the past four decades for the critical institutional lessons to be learned for the future.

My analysis here suggests four lessons. The first is the role of architectural redundancy: the compatible, if not always convergent, evolution of different organizations, some with overlapping responsibilities for security tasks, all moving along the same general path. Both NATO and the EC were required to bring Germany back into a peaceful cooperative western European regime. Secondary but vital roles were also played by the Council of Europe in social and cultural affairs, the OECD, the WEU, the European caucus within NATO, and many more. Security was the product of a number of interlocking organizations, without hard and fast borders, all available to be used according to political need and circumstance.

Moreover, clear changes in organizational structure and power occurred in response to both the international and the domestic context of the participating states. Few organizations died; most adapted to changing priorities and capabilities. An ambitious European Defense Community or European Political Community failed to develop in the 1950s, but a looser WEU and a narrowly focused Independent European Program Group went on, both as special caucuses within NATO. The significance of a European Free Trade Association, a European Atomic Energy Community, or a Council of Europe waxed and waned with changing political conditions and changing participation, but all did so within an increasingly "normal" multilateral framework.

Not all, of course, were of equal importance to member states or equally useful for the advancement of national interests. NATO remained the dominant organization, reflecting the power and the preferences of the American leadership. But the other institutions provided alternate channels for consensus building or problem solving or rallying points to counter American agendas. No single institution was deemed sufficient to meet all requirements; there was no single architectural choice.

The second lesson is the necessity of multiple levels of relationships, which were always key to security and the establishment of mutual political reassurance. Traditional alliance theory posited that the existence of a common compelling threat—the Soviet Union—would provide a sufficient basis for international cohesion. But, as Karl Deutsch argued quite early, what was really at stake was the building of a security community rooted as much in shared values, intentions, and attitudes among like-minded states as in effective fighting capabilities positioned against a common enemy.[15]

Success in every multilateral forum turned on key bilateral relationships that undergirded the formal organizational structures. In Europe, for example, the core was Franco-German rapprochement, the convergence of both national policies and popular perceptions. But there were other critical bilateral ties as well: Anglo-French, Anglo-German, and most particularly American ties to Britain, Germany, and France.[16] Although obscured by the more positive experience of later years, European relations involved disputes and irritation, issues of competition and hierarchy, and conflict over who was to be defined as part of "us." All these interactions ultimately resulted in what became increasingly irreversible national decisions to embed bilateral relations within a broader multilateral framework, decisions that sought to provide offsetting forces, to allow for greater scope and benefit, and even to promote greater mutual harmony.

In NATO the support and cohesion generated by bilateral relationship was at least as central. For both the United States and its allies there was constant switching between multilateral and bilateral channels—to clarify, to intensify policy pressure, to achieve side payments or broker deals blocked in the other channels. For the allies the advantage of a multilateral alliance was to benefit from the greater transparency and from chances for influence over American decisionmaking. But with few exceptions, the principal focus was on the relationship with Washington. More advantages flowed to the United States, with NATO providing the chance through one institution to exert and track regional influence and to deflect or moderate the particularist demands even of the most important allied states in the region.

The third lesson is the indispensability of a commitment to transparency as a process.[17] The transparency measures in the CSCE are the most obvious examples of how important the cumulative impact of information exchange and guaranteed access was to the development of a sense, however limited, of East-West reassurance. The critical element was never the specific data gained, for instance, from exercise observation. Rather it was the continuing pattern of compliance, of responses to legitimate queries, of the development of mutual expectations of convergent behavior. The more intrusive inspection measures of the CFE built directly on this record of compliance and with similar results. The critical gains were only in part the results observed; at least as important were the cooperative efforts involved in arranging and implementing the inspection regime itself.

Transparency in the western European and transatlantic realm, without question, was more far-reaching. In NATO, for example, there was de facto mutual regulation of all offensive forces in the European theater. An integrated command posited continuous operational consultation about interallied forces, regular intrusive inspections and evaluations, and joint assessments of present and future technologies and capabilities.[18] Every other year saw the formal process of a defense planning questionnaire, with responses given by each state about plans for forces and for alert status and reserve capabilities. Even more important were the negotiations that the NATO international military staff and the major NATO commands held with each state before the formal reply and the iterative process of adjustment, trade-offs over time, and political as well as economic burden sharing in light of domestic conditions.

In the EC, broader functional integration entailed requirements for openness and regular unrestricted access to information about national policies and plans that went even further. Increasingly, the free flow of goods and individuals across European borders implicitly allowed for continuous communication about national economic arrangements and planning, including regular reporting to allow cooperative regulation of national sectors. It demanded the development of common standards and the common assessment of penalties for multiple forms of activities and continuing reaffirmation of the costs and the risks to national interests of any breakdown in cooperation among Community states.

The fourth lesson is the development of broad popular support for multilateral solutions as being at least equal in legitimacy and effectiveness as national decisions. In the military area in the immediate postwar period, this conviction stemmed in part from disillusionment with national capabilities or a pragmatic judgment that cooperation in NATO was the price of security derived from an American guarantee. But the habit of cooperation and the expectation of multilateral effort grew on both the public and the elite level throughout the successive years.

Renationalization of security was never an acceptable alternative in political or military terms. The heyday of détente in the 1970s did not change this basic conviction of the 1950s and the 1960s. For all of the American threats in the 1970s and the 1980s to leave Europe, the emphasis was always on more equitable burden sharing, not a return to the unrealistic alternative of 1930s-style isolationism. In European states, if only because of the continuing German question, the scope for national security efforts seemed even narrower. Even when there were widespread calls in the 1970s and 1980s for the elimination of NATO, or its transformation into an independent European security organization more attuned to a lessening threat, the alternative security framework being promoted was multinational. It always contained a high degree of cross-border cooperation or functional integration that was seen to provide more benefits than risks and that would encourage trust and continuing cooperation on a more or less equitable basis.

3

The Politics of European Security: Organizational Transformation and the Competition over the Security Agenda, 1989–94

To understand the evolution of Europe's security regime, it is essential to probe the remarkable changes in political context over the past five years. Even with hindsight, it is hard to encompass the magnitude of change and policy challenges involved or to comprehend the organizational and intellectual burden it posed for the central-state actors and political leaders. By every measure, the pace and scope of change, especially during 1990–92, were revolutionary. They were all the more awe-inspiring given the long-frozen divisions of the cold war era. The unification of Germany in less than a year, the transformation of the central and eastern European states toward populist, if not democratic, principles and market economies would each alone have been revolutionary. Unquestionably, however, the watershed mark was the collapse of the Soviet Union, both as imperial system and as the fountainhead of the global communist system. The lodestars of cold war security in essence vanished, seemingly taking with them much of the logic of European security efforts for more than four decades.

Sorting out the details of these enormous shifts will require far more analytic distance than five years allows. So too will delineating the interaction of the many causal factors in producing specific outcomes in Europe or throughout the world. All that can be attempted here is to assess three central issues in the politics of post–cold war security in Europe: the organizational transformation and competition over the new security agenda; the efforts to bring Russia and the other CEE states into a new security dialogue; and the new efforts at peace management operations in Europe and outside of it, first in the Gulf and then in the former Yugoslavia.

Given the revolutionary shifts from 1989 to 1994, what is remarkable is how much of the organizational structure of the old order was preserved and adapted to the requirements of the new. Few new organizations emerged;

those that did were usually of an intermediate, facilitating character—transitional steps toward expanding or changing an older structure. Adaptation was in fits and starts, almost always partial and evolutionary. The changes that did occur built on concepts and agreements that were in prospect before the Wall fell, as the move toward a totally open internal market through the Europe 1992 program and toward political union demonstrate. The image presented to publics anxious to reap the benefits of revolutionary change and the budgetary dividends of present peace was of a broad continuity of purpose and effort.

Why has this been so? In part, it almost certainly demonstrated the tyranny of the pace of change. In security arrangements even more than in other areas, there was simply no time to build a consensus about new practices or procedures, about new distributions of organizational power and resources. What was at hand and operating was the preferred mechanism.

The broad pattern of organizational continuity also reflected a basic conservative tendency in the face of uncertainty and confusion to retain the familiar. That was particularly demonstrated in the preferences and the habits of the states that saw themselves as "winners," the major status quo states of the West. They, and especially the United States, were anxious to preserve tested instruments and were unwilling to sacrifice the continuation of past advantage prematurely. Even the principal debates about change followed familiar lines. The grounds for many of the most important transatlantic and European disagreements still derived from the Franco-American axis. In Washington, the preference for a NATO-first formula remained strong, perhaps even stronger than before. In Paris and much of the time in Bonn, the chances seemed at hand to move toward the long-discussed European union, including for the first time significant integration in both foreign policy and security policy.

Moreover, those states that emerged most transformed by the changes—a united Germany and an uncertain Russian Federation—had little to gain (and much to lose) in attempting at such an early phase to force organizational adaptation to their own design. Realistically, too, they were self-absorbed in the management of their domestic politics and changes. Only the European Community, stimulated by the earlier economic boom and spirited Franco-German initiatives, tried to accelerate its organizational evolution. Its emphasis in the Maastricht Treaty was on establishing new competences and ensuring a dynamic of expanding powers. Yet its design almost immediately faltered in the face of popular skepticism and was proved largely inadequate in meeting the challenges arising from the conflicts that consumed the former Yugoslavia.

But the appearance of overriding continuity should not obscure the magnitude of the fundamental changes that have taken place. Most important are the new contacts at all levels between central and western Europe and in all organizational realms—political, military, economic, social, in both the private and public sectors. Russia and its transatlantic interlocutors are in constant negotiation—in the G-7, in the Contact Group searching for settlement in the former Yugoslavia,[1] and in new cooperation channels set up under both the EC and NATO. The agendas have changed radically, away from formal arms control agreements and the mitigation of the consequences of military stalemate to a search for compatible military structures and cooperative ventures in peacekeeping, crisis containment, and joint security outreach.

The challenge for the United States and its allies and partners is still twofold: to preserve the core of the cooperative security success that has been the hallmark of the transatlantic-European area for the past four decades and to spread the zone of peace as far eastward as possible. It is a process still in transition, for which all the risks and the consequences are not clear. But many of the lines of future evolution now seem set, and the issues, if not all of the answers, seem clear.

How to organize cooperatively for security was the obvious first question in the post–cold war adaptation of the European security regime. Organizational continuity was not what many observers predicted in the weeks and months that followed the fall of the Berlin Wall. The mood of central as well as western Europe was one of "Europhoria,"[2] the overturning of all the old forms of division and confrontation and the growing together again of all that had been unnaturally separated in the East-West struggle. Peace seemed at hand; the Soviet Union might still pose a threat but soon only from behind its own borders. Emerging democracy would do much to fill the security vacuum in central Europe; democracies did not wage war with one another, and democratic publics would press for the peaceful resolution of dispute. The risks to security that would be left would be mitigated by the urgent building of economic security in central Europe, fueled by Western economic and political aid and the construction of a new European security framework.

For many in central Europe and on the left in western Europe, the obvious candidate for this organizational role was a transformed and newly empowered Conference on Security and Cooperation in Europe.[3] It alone encompassed all the states of the new Europe whole and free. The CSCE principles, enunciated at Helsinki and Stockholm, set out the standards by which the new and reborn states would be judged, particularly the commitment not to change borders by force and the guarantees of human and civil rights. All states to be considered European would have to adhere to those standards, as demonstrated by the celebration of the Charter of Paris codifying and extending the CSCE principles in October 1990.[4] Moreover, a CSCE with new organizations and new operational capabilities for conflict resolution and peacekeeping would represent a clean break with the old machinery of the cold war (such as NATO) and reflect the new political balance in Europe.

What is clear at the beginning of 1995 is how little Europe's recent experience has matched this set of expectations. The CSCE's prospects for transformation seem far more limited now. So, too, seem the prospects for a strictly European approach to security, realized either under a traditional pan-European framework or, in the near future, under a tightly integrated European political union with far-ranging security policy coordination. What seems most probable in the decade ahead is a transformation and rebalancing of the transatlantic framework, with a revised and refocused NATO. There is a new set of initiatives to the East, especially the Partnership for Peace, launched in 1994. There is far more scope accorded to a European pillar within the alliance, a role to be filled at least for the interim by a transformed Western European Union. And the question of expanding NATO membership to some states in central Europe, and even to an interested Russia, is now an issue of time, not possibility.

This chapter focuses on the evolution of the three leading candidates for the management of European security in the post–cold war world. It looks especially hard at the often negative relationship between NATO and the WEU, with an eye to determining what degree of cooperation between the two is likely in the future as well as what the institutional hierarchy is likely to look like in the years to come. It is useful first, however, to review why the CSCE, to many an obvious choice for a transformed security agenda, failed to emerge as a major organizational component in the European security regime.

The Rise and Fall of the CSCE, 1989–94

CSCE developments in 1990 and 1991 seemed relatively encouraging to its principal supporters, with perhaps German foreign minister Hans-Dietrich

Figure 3-1. CSCE Membership as of October 1994

Albania	Greece	Romania
Armenia	Hungary	Russia
Austria	Iceland	San Marino
Azerbaijan	Ireland	Slovakia
Belarus	Italy	Slovenia
Belgium	Kazakhstan	Spain
Bosnia-Herzegovina	Kyrgyzstan	Sweden
Bulgaria	Latvia	Switzerland
Canada	Liechtenstein	Tajikistan
Croatia	Lithuania	Turkey
Cyprus	Luxembourg	Turkmenistan
Czech Republic	Malta	Ukraine
Denmark	Moldova	United Kingdom
Estonia	Monaco	United States
Finland	Netherlands	Uzbekistan
France	Norway	Vatican City
Georgia	Poland	Yugoslavia
Germany	Portugal	*(suspended)*

Genscher and Czechoslovak president Vaclav Havel being the most outspoken. Successive declarations by NATO and European Community meetings recognized the centrality of the CSCE principles for future security and expressed the need to strengthen the CSCE for new cooperative tasks.[5] Institutionalization proceeded, albeit somewhat slowly; the CSCE for the first time acquired permanent organizations and a secretary general. Vienna once again was the central site of the increasingly continuous discussions and oversight functions of the CSCE. There were new conflict-monitoring missions and extensive attempts to define and design operational guidelines for future peacekeeping functions. (See figure 3-1 for a list of CSCE members.)

Yet by the CSCE Helsinki summit in July 1992, optimism about the CSCE potential as a comprehensive framework for new security arrangements had largely vanished. Some of this change reflected increasing disenchantment among those states that had always been skeptical, particularly the United States and Britain. The CSCE still meant in their eyes a return to the politically discredited images of a collective security system like the League of Nations. Moreover, the end of the cold war seemed to intensify the tendency of small states to claim a due share in political control, the so-called Malta syndrome that had so infuriated Washington and London during the 1980s. To the cynics, too, the CSCE had been a forum sufficient only to bring pressure against the Soviet Union on issues of human rights violations and other "un-European" practices. With the demise of the Soviet Union, even that function no longer existed.

The CSCE's fall as a possible alternative framework was perhaps made more obvious by two French proposals to replace it as the pan-European forum. The first was President François Mitterrand's essentially still-born proposal advanced in Prague in the spring of 1990 for the establishment of a European Confederation, a new continentwide organization for Europeans only.[6] The second, three years later, was the plan Prime Minister Edouard Balladur proposed for a more focused security organization, this time including North Americans.[7]

Adopted as a European Union initiative at the EC Copenhagen summit, the new organization is to be concerned with the most pressing problems of security cooperation: minority rights and stabilizing borders. The Balladur plan, also known as the Pact on Stability in Europe, builds on and replaces Mitterrand's confederation idea. There are, however, important deviations. Balladur maintained that, as a means of ensuring a strong EC as well as pan-European stability and security, the eastern European nations needed to work out their respective conflicts before entry into the EC. A follow-up meeting on May 28, 1994, led to an agreement by nine eastern European nations to attempt to mediate their internal and territorial disputes with the aid of the EU. The agreement reached was part of Balladur's efforts to establish principles of "good neighborliness" among eastern European nations.[8]

The critical blow to the CSCE, however, was the growing wariness of the Helmot Kohl government and of the CEE leaders, including Havel himself. These leaders were increasingly disillusioned about the willingness of the West to treat them as equal partners and feared being consigned permanently to a pan-European limbo. Moreover, their sense of broad security was shaken by the CSCE's weakness and inaction in the face of two clear crises. The first was the attempted Moscow coup in August 1991, and the dramatic implications it might have had for central European security. The second was the inadequacy of CSCE principles and procedures in staving off the clear run-up to conflict in the former Yugoslavia, with fighting that finally began in Slovenia and Croatia in the summer of 1991.

Although the CSCE has since enhanced its visibility in Yugoslavia and the former Soviet Union (FSU), its effectiveness as a peacekeeping organization has remained constrained. Between September 1992 and June 1993, around Kosovo, Sandjak, and Vojvodina, the CSCE limited itself to fact-finding missions to monitor human rights abuses, the democratic process, and the media. A similar monitoring and communications mission is still going on in Macedonia, involving eight CSCE officials. Additionally, the CSCE, in conjunction with the EU, has established sanctions assistance missions (SAMs) in countries neighboring the rump Yugoslavia, including Albania, Bulgaria, Croatia, Hungary, Macedonia, Romania, and Ukraine. The 146 officials in these SAMs are supposed to provide assistance and ensure that these countries are in fact complying with the UN sanctions against Serbia-Montenegro and the arms embargo against all republics of the former Yugoslavia.

The CSCE also has missions in both Latvia and Estonia on the issue of the rights of Russian minorities, and it has been active in monitoring conflict in other parts of the FSU. In Moldova, for example, delegates are trying to implement a plan by which the Trans-Dniester region would have some autonomy but would be incorporated in Moldova.[9] The CSCE is trying to assist in negotiating a settlement in Tajikistan and again is monitoring the human rights situation there.[10] In addition, the CSCE has a mission in Georgia monitoring two conflicts: one involving separatist Abkhazian forces in the west, the other, South-Ossetian forces in the south. But because these CSCE missions are being conducted in conjunction with 3,000 Russian Commonwealth of Independent States troops, delegates have had to coordinate (some argue, subordinate) their activities with those military forces, thus limiting their effectiveness.[11]

In only one instance, the conflict in Ngorno-Karabakh, has the CSCE considered deploying a peacekeeping force of its own. The CSCE is planning to send approximately 2,500 lightly armed forces into the region to enforce the fragile cease-fire of the spring of 1994.[12] The plan has been complicated by Russia, however, which would like to send in its own peacekeeping force, and by the conflicting preconditions set by the factions themselves.

This may appear to be a lengthy list of peacekeeping involvement by the CSCE, but the missions are small (numbering between fewer than 12 and 2,500 personnel in all cases), and their impact thus far has been minimal. Although the CSCE exercises have certainly contributed to a growing body of knowledge about the source and character of post–cold war conflicts, the CSCE has failed to mitigate the brutalities of war or to promote conflict resolution.

The assessment, even among diehard enthusiasts, is that, as a traditional international organization of fifty-three members, the CSCE cannot and will not become the organizational framework of first resort. At Helsinki in July 1992 the CSCE did claim the status of a regional organization according to United Nations criteria, but as an organization for political and cultural cooperation rather than for self-defense.[13] Clearly it could at most play a contributing role to European and global security, given that its prevailing political consensus is still at the limited level of the cold war. This level of political interest and of political will has been adequate to sustain reassurance through confidence building among stalemated adversaries but not sufficient even to begin the process of political and organizational transformation. Even with its new institutions and its new "less than unanimous" decisionmaking rules,[14] the CSCE's structure is simply too vague and thus too cumbersome to allow rapid response or timely action; the time and resources to build a consensus for crisis management would in most instances not be available.

Most important of all in the short run, the CSCE no longer has a major power champion equal to Genscher's Germany. For everything but consultation toward preventive diplomacy (and maybe not even then, given the potentially disruptive role of the "Maltas"), the CSCE is the last choice of venue for all the major European players, including the European Community. Even Russia and the other CEE states remained lukewarm toward the CSCE until discussion of NATO expansion turned serious in 1993.[15] The CSCE, while performing some valuable monitoring missions and serving as a venue for arms control and preventive diplomacy issues, is a forum waiting to be used, a dialogue awaiting serious discussion partners.

The CSCE's quasi-moribund condition is hardly due to a lack of mechanisms, institutionalization, or organization. On the contrary, there has been rapid progress in the last two years in devising new forums for consultation, fact finding, and monitoring. The CSCE's main obstacle to greater influence in the Atlantic-to-the-Urals area is the reluctance of members, especially the most powerful states, to empower the CSCE by using the tools established since the fall of the Berlin Wall.

This does not mean, however, that post–cold war Europe cannot benefit from a more active, powerful, and engaged CSCE. Given its broad membership, it is unlikely to show competence in peacekeeping (although there are moves being made in that direction). But the CSCE is making a substantial contribution as a forum of preventive diplomacy, early warning, and human rights monitoring, all of which are much needed in the European sphere. The

CSCE's broad membership has given it unprecedented credibility in providing a forum in which rich and poor countries, from East or West, can exchange views on an equal footing. This broad membership lends the CSCE an air of openness and perhaps impartiality that no other European security organization can claim.

Simultaneously, broad membership is also the CSCE's greatest weakness; the organization is somewhat ahead of its time. Interests among its members are not yet congruent enough to warrant unified action in the wide range of crises that are now emerging. Moreover, many of the original principles outlined in the Helsinki Final Act of 1975, held sacred by the dissidents of the 1989 revolutions, have been rendered obsolete by the war in the Balkans and ethnic conflicts throughout the FSU.

Still, the CSCE now functions as a repository of ready institutions such as the Forum for Security Cooperation (FSC), the Permanent Committee, and the Conflict Prevention Center (all located in Vienna); the Office for Democratic Institutions and Human Rights in Warsaw; and the Economic Forum in Prague. Maintaining this potential is a sound policy for all its members. The FSC, in particular, has emerged as an increasingly important arena for furthering CSCE goals. Since its mandate was laid down in the "Program for Immediate Action" of the 1992 Helsinki document, the FSC has focused on strengthening the most effective institutions in the CSCE's purview. Using a two-track approach to separate issue areas, the FSC has facilitated discussion and cooperation on arms control, disarmament, CSBMs, and nonproliferation on the one hand, and force planning, defense industry conversion cooperation, establishment of a "code of conduct" in security measures, and preliminary nonproliferation issues on the other.

Progress on these sorts of issues, divisive and halting though it may occasionally be, illustrates the strengths and indeed the indispensability of the CSCE. Should current conflicts worsen or should common interests converge further, the CSCE may come to play a leading role in conflict resolution. In the interim it is advantageous to have at least one organization working to keep the channels of communication open between warring parties. Moreover, the CSCE's future role could eventually be expanded to carry out other security-related tasks, such as ensuring the safe return of war refugees to their homes and villages or overseeing traditional peacekeeping functions like the interposition of external forces between former adversaries that have reached an initial political settlement. Bosnia and Nagorno-Karabakh are two obvious candidate locations. Expanding the CSCE's role sooner rather than later,

however, will certainly entail providing resources, including perhaps fire-
power, to which the organization does not yet have access.

The Transatlantic-European Competition, 1990–94

Unquestionably the greatest transformations and the liveliest organization
competition turned on the adaptation of NATO and the European Community to the new post–cold war security requirements.

The stakes were the highest; the expectations about deciding now for the
long-term future, very intense. In the flurry of change, much was forgotten
on both sides of the Atlantic about the earlier complementarity of NATO and
the EC and the essential interconnection between economic and military security. Atlanticists and Europeanists alike offered many good reasons moti-
vating the competition: the need to find a new or renewed framework in
which to embed a stronger Germany on the one hand, and to deal with the
power vacuum left in central and eastern Europe while simultaneously rebalancing European and American security roles on the other.

The Western European Union: Competitor or Pillar?

Although the WEU had its genesis in 1948 with the Brussels Treaty, it did
not become an active player on the security scene until the mid-1980s. In
1984, after disagreements with the United States over new nuclear deployments in Europe, the strategic defense initiative and détente with the Soviet
Union, France (supported by Germany) began vigorously promoting an autonomous, unified European defense voice supported by combined military
forces independent of the United States. This initiative led to the 1991 Rome
Declaration, which outlined plans for reforming and empowering the WEU.
Technically, besides promulgating a new agenda, the Rome declaration re-
activated the union by reinstating regular meetings (twice a year) of the WEU
council. More important, the declaration provided impetus to action that pre-
cipitated the accession of Portugal and Spain in 1987 and the minesweeping
initiative in the Gulf during the Iran-Iraq war in 1988, the WEU's first coordinated military undertaking.[16] The organization's military competence
was tested again during the coalition war against Iraq in 1990 when the WEU
sent naval vessels to enforce the trade embargo against Iraq as well as mine
hunters to clear the area.

At each juncture, however, efforts to fuse European defense capabilities
have been thwarted. Not only has the WEU faced resistance because of the

possibly negative impact of WEU development on NATO's responsibilities and mandate. It has also been a divisive issue among the European powers themselves. The run-up to Maastricht, the Maastricht compromise, and immediate post-Maastricht developments have highlighted the challenges to the WEU's institutional development both from NATO and from within Europe itself.

In 1989 the Community was already deeply engaged in the process of widening and deepening, with its moves toward Europe 1992 and the creation of a common European space that would reach over the boundaries of the Community to include the remaining states, largely neutral, of the European Free Trade Association (EFTA). The main impetus had been the initiatives of France and Germany, beginning in 1985, to press for greater economic integration, including a monetary union, and for the widening of EC competences to new "natural" areas, including security and (ultimately) defense policy. The limits of European political cooperation in foreign policy seemed to have been reached, a view clearly shared by the European Commission anxious, under the leadership of Jacques Delors, to expand its scope of responsibility. What was needed was a new push, especially in view of the growing détente with a reforming central Europe and a Gorbachev in Russia open to dialogue and change.

Dramatic political change in Poland, Hungary, and then Germany accelerated this push for change. By far the greatest impetus was German unification and the new converging reasons it gave both Bonn and Paris to push even harder toward European political union. After a few ill-fated Mitterrand efforts to resurrect an anti-German, or at least an antiunification, coalition with the Soviet Union and Poland, France sought reassurance of control over Germany through the deepening of Community integration. A key element would be progress toward development of a common European foreign and security policy, led essentially by France and Germany. One particularly ambitious program, begun in 1988 and given more urgency by unification, was the formation of a joint Franco-German brigade (later renamed the Eurocorps). The brigade began largely as a showpiece, with full operability set only as a very long term goal. But unification drove the French (and to some extent the Germans) to make more substantive progress toward a functional brigade in an effort to tie Germany—and especially the German military—more solidly into a European framework. Efforts like the Franco-German brigade emphasized a familiar theme of French diplomacy: tying Germany within a unified Europe, given greater urgency because of new fears about Germany's future orientation and new convictions that the United States would no longer be needed (or perhaps willing) to right Europe's security balance.

From the first talk of German unity in January 1990, the Kohl government gave high priority to linking unification directly to progress toward European union. The German goal was broader than that of France: an immediate push both to widen and deepen the Community, although on slightly different time scales. Widening was essential to providing positive reassurance to Germany's neighbors to the East about the intentions and the policies of a united Germany. Deepening would occur perhaps earlier, to secure what had already been achieved by Germany's politics of reassurance vis-à-vis western Europe.

Last but hardly least was the renewed calculus of the European Commission under Jacques Delors, which was seeking to maximize its role as well as its vision of Europe and of supranational policymaking. The Commission had long smarted under the Community's self-denying ordinance that left security matters strictly to NATO and to the "hard" sectors of intergovernmental decision. A common foreign and security policy and an eventual European defense and security identity meant a new international standing for the Community and a higher international political profile for a Europe speaking globally with one voice. Political union meant not only new economic power but also the ability to wield it. What was required was a common strategy and an institutional basis for the melding of external economic and diplomatic influence, particularly in terms of additions to European security—East and West—at a time of revolutionary change.

Negotiations toward the Maastricht Treaty on European Union progressed steadily throughout 1990 and 1991, with considerable debate within the responsible European intergovernmental conference and in elite circles about what control the new EU could or should claim over security policy, particularly at NATO's expense. By the fall of 1991 it became clear that what could be sought was only an agreement on future competence, not a blueprint for immediate action.

The primary debate over the WEU within Europe revolved around a conflict between Atlanticist members, led by Britain and (somewhat surprisingly) Italy, and Europeanists, led by France and an occasionally more ambivalent Germany. The Atlanticist vision of the WEU—set out in the Anglo-Italian "Declaration on European Security and Defense" of October 4, 1991—essentially subordinated the organization to a NATO-dominated framework. It sought to establish the WEU "through an evolutionary process involving successive phases" as "the defense component of the [European] Union and as the means to strengthen the European pillar of the alliance." The proposal sought a very limited mandate for the WEU that would not conflict with, but only "reinforce," the alliance.

NATO was, in the Atlanticist view, the necessary organizational framework so long as the United States was willing to remain committed and involved; any change must come first within that framework. An eventual European defense organization might oversee capabilities for missions outside the scope of the North Atlantic Treaty, the so-called out-of-area missions; NATO would remain primarily responsible for defense in Europe. In the longer term Atlanticist states were also generally against any further transfer of national sovereignty to the European Commission, especially in areas as sensitive as foreign policy, let alone in security arrangements or plans for operational defense.

The Europeanist response was vastly different. In a joint "Letter to Mr. Ruud Lubbers on European Security,"[17] François Mitterrand and Helmut Kohl set out a much more ambitious plan for the WEU. They envisioned a much broader mandate for the organization, incorporating (among other things) "increased cooperation on arms with a view to establishing a European Arms agency" and the "formation of military units under the authority of WEU." They saw the WEU as a component of a developing CFSP, and set the WEU up as a coequal partner to NATO by calling for "closer military cooperation in compliment to the Alliance" and by allowing for the WEU to coordinate common European security positions before discussion in NATO. Finally, the letter incorporated the Eurocorps initiative, announced in 1991 as an expansion of the Franco-German brigade of 1988 to participation by other interested European states, as the backbone of an eventual common European army. The end result would be a Europe that would take responsibility for the security and, therefore, the defense of its constituent elements whatever NATO's situation and wherever threats might arise.[18]

The reaction of the Bush administration to the Europeanist initiatives was swift and harsh, with a full campaign of aggressive diplomacy and backchannel pressure. Washington on several occasions shrilly warned the Europeans about precipitous, unconsidered action or organizational expansion that put NATO's achievements and guarantees at risk. There could be no European autonomous decisions that would commit an unconsulted United States to preserve security outside the existing NATO area or NATO membership. Nor would a free-standing WEU, perhaps extended to states like the

EFTA neutrals or others, be permitted to entangle the United States in guarantees or missions to which it had not consented.[19]

Perhaps the most telling evidence of American anxieties about a European undermining of NATO came at the November 1991 Rome NATO summit, staged to highlight NATO's new post–cold war strategy and force structure. President Bush directly challenged the allies: "If your ultimate aim is to provide for your own defense, then the time to tell us is today." He then went on to argue forcefully that the United States did not see "how there can be a substitute for the Alliance as the provider of our [U.S.] defense and Europe's security." [20]

The announcement of the Franco-German Eurocorps initiative in October 1991, and its inclusion into the overall Franco-German proposal, was a particularly unpleasant surprise. The design of a joint Franco-German military unit, freestanding and eventually to be supplemented by force contributions from other European states, proved especially galling to the NATO stalwarts not only in Washington but also elsewhere.[21] Political and military figures alike protested the creation of a Eurocorps outside NATO, especially one involving German troops already pledged to NATO. They demanded operational coordination with and linkages to the NATO integrated command.

The Maastricht Treaty of December 1991 marked the striking of a relatively fragile security bargain among the Europeanists and the Atlanticists: in the short term recognizing NATO's primacy but clearly defining the path for future independent Europeanist evolution.[22] The WEU would look forward to the "eventual framing of a common defense policy, which might in time lead to a common defense," as part of the broader CFSP. Decisions on CFSP in general and the eventual defense identity in particular would require unanimous agreement on questions of principles, with qualified majority voting only on issues of implementation. Moreover, the WEU would be simultaneously both "an integral part" of the staged evolution of the EU and a means toward a strengthened European pillar of NATO.

In a separate declaration, the nine WEU members tried to give a more substantive profile to their efforts to establish a "genuine" European defense identity and to assume "greater responsibility" for European defense.[23] The WEU would strengthen its linkages to both the EC and NATO through a move to Brussels and the development of an operational role through joint planning in a Brussels-based planning organization and logistical and other support cooperation "complementary to the alliance." States that were members of the EC or NATO but not members of the WEU could participate in

Figure 3-2. Membership in the Western European Union

WEU activities as members or associates as they chose. (See figure 3-2 for
a map of WEU membership.)

Agreement at Maastricht, however, soon appeared to be the high point, at
least in the short term, of Community agreement on security policy. Tensions
arose again over the next steps in establishing the Eurocorps. WEU ministers, meeting at La Rochelle in June 1992, issued a communiqué outlining
the basic tasks for the Eurocorps. These were delineated to include (1) joint
allied defense under either the Brussels or NATO treaties; (2) "maintaining
or re-establishing peace"; and (3) "humanitarian missions." Thus the La
Rochelle communiqué declared that the corps would be compatible with
NATO but also identified its functions to be such as to allow Europe "to have

its own means for military action at its disposal."[24] Once again Atlanticists raised the question of the relation of the Eurocorps to the NATO command structure; answers from Paris and Bonn were often contradictory, and irritation again arose on both sides of the Atlantic.

The June 1992 EC foreign ministers meeting at Lisbon made some headway toward broader agreement, specifying CFSP goals and outlining security issues for joint European action.[25] But the consensus was possible only at relatively high levels of abstraction. Quite apart from American irritation or opposition, the fundamental debate of Atlanticists and Europeanists continued. There was no real European agreement on either the substance or the procedures for initiating a broad-reaching decisionmaking process on security. And though renationalization of defense, particularly a German renationalization, was a dreaded alternative for all but a small proportion of the French political class, there was still another option, the transformation of NATO.

Moreover, the prospects for CFSP as a whole sank in the general gloom over the limited support for Maastricht, shown by the Danish rejection and the tepid political approval elsewhere. The treaty was ratified more than a year behind schedule, in the midst of a major economic recession and at a time of collective political burnout. The EU's failures to contain the conflict in the former Yugoslavia, or to agree even on the preferred policy outcome, soon overtook all theoretical discussions of joint action. Managing the Yugoslav crisis was a task that Europe set for itself in the initial aftermath of Maastricht; it was a test that it, even with the help of institutions (notably the UN and NATO), would continue to fail well into the mid-1990s.

The Western European Union: Current Developments

The WEU has so far fallen short of providing for Europe's defense, but the underlying framework already exists, and it continues to evolve sporadically. The WEU Ministerial Council's Petersberg Declarations of June 1992 build on Maastricht, more clearly defining the WEU's role as both a European defense organization and a pillar of the Atlantic alliance. In Petersberg the signatories agreed to "support, on a case-by-case basis and in accordance with [their] own procedures, the effective implementation of conflict prevention and crisis-management measures, including peacekeeping activities of the CSCE or the United Nations Security Council."[26] According to the declaration, the WEU may become engaged in peacekeeping, search and rescue missions, humanitarian aid, and military combat.

Shortly after the Maastricht summit, the WEU was confronted with escalating violence in the former Yugoslavia. Following an extraordinary Ministerial Council meeting in Helsinki in July 1992, the WEU took action against
Serbia in conjunction with UN resolutions 713 and 757 by providing air and
naval equipment to strengthen enforcement of the economic embargo against
Serbia.[27] In addition, the WEU provided special technical assistance to Hungary, Bulgaria, and Romania to bolster patrolling efforts and sent its own
monitoring vessels to the Danube to inhibit illegal trade with embargoed
ports.

WEU monitoring missions were strengthened and expanded again with
"Operation Sharp Guard," which began monitoring UN sanctions in the Adriatic on June 15, 1993, as a combined WEU-NATO effort. By August 11,
1994, Operation Sharp Guard had challenged 25,300 merchant vessels
headed for Serbia and Montenegro, and of those, 2,480 were inspected. Between this and other patrolling missions that came before it, more than
37,000 vessels were challenged, and more than 4,700 were sent to port or inspected.[28] The WEU is also developing a plan to deploy a police force for
peacekeeping in the Bosnian town of Mostar. If such a force is established,
it will be a large step forward for strengthening the legitimacy of the WEU.

Institutionally, the WEU has also enjoyed some moderate success. The
Maastricht Final Act and the Petersberg Declarations provided for substantial expansion of the WEU planning cell and secretariat—taking care not to
explicitly challenge NATO. Also, the WEU's administrative organs have
been moved from London and Paris to Brussels, which has increased efficiency and proximity to other European institutions as well as to NATO. Finally, the WEU has developed a "two-hatting" formula to "share" ministers
with NATO, increasing the level of experience in the WEU while providing
a cooperative link to NATO. Though the WEU still lacks an integrated command structure, these steps should make it more capable of coordinating action within its mandate.

The organization has also made strides in other areas. The WEU signed
association agreements with the central European and Baltic states and began in June 1994 to meet formally with these states in the Ministerial Council. Also, in 1993 the WEU established the Centre for the Interpretation of
Satellite Data in Torrejon, Spain,[29] marking a great step toward reducing
WEU reliance on NATO strategic assets. As for the Eurocorps, its development remains somewhat stunted, primarily because of opposition within Europe, particularly from small states that fear Franco-German hegemony in

Figure 3-3. Chronology of the Western European Union, 1948–93

1948 Brussels Treaty Organization, WEU's forerunner, is created.

1954 Paris agreements change the name of Brussels Treaty Organization to Western European Union and define its purpose as creating unity and progressive integration in Europe. Germany and Italy accede to the organization.

1984 WEU is revived in response to widening divisions within NATO (especially over strategic defense initiative). French government calls for a harmonization of views on defense, security, and military issues.

1987 Operation Cleansweep, a WEU-organized minesweeping operation, is initiated by Netherlands in an attempt to secure free navigation during the Iran-Iraq war.

1990 WEU coordinates European participation in naval embargo against Iraq in Gulf War.

1991 WEU headquarters move from London to Brussels, closer to NATO.

April: WEU organizes Operation Safe Haven, the European Community airlift of humanitarian relief to Kurdish refugees.

---

the EU if those two states dominate a European army. Some strides, however, have been made. Belgium and Spain have joined the Eurocorps (though not without significant problems). In addition, France and Germany announced in October 1993 that they were discussing the creation of a joint armaments agency, initially focused on procurement for Eurocorps but with obvious implications for further future integration Europewide.[30] Yet even with these successes, language and command and control problems, as well as declining defense resources, have kept the corps from being much more than a showpiece, a sort of "parade army" for Europe to march down the Champs-Elysées, at least for now.

The assessment of the WEU to date, then, must be mixed. (For a chronology of the WEU, see figure 3-3.) Clearly, the organization has made important institutional strides toward effectiveness and autonomy. The WEU has had some (admittedly quite limited) success operationally—in the Gulf twice and in the Adriatic. Yet it is equally clear that the value of the organization

December: "Declaration on the Role of the Western European Union and its Relations with the European Union and with the Atlantic Alliance" annexed to Maastricht Treaty.

1992 *June:* Petersberg declaration issued, allowing WEU forces to serve as peacekeeping forces under CSCE or UN auspices. Allows for three types of relations with WEU: full membership, observer status, and associate membership.

July: Operation Sharp Vigilance, involving the monitoring of sanctions against Yugoslavia in Adriatic, is established under Italian coordination.

1993 WEU establishes Centre for Interpretation of Satellite Data in Torrejon, Spain.

May: Concept of forces answerable to the WEU (FAWEU) is introduced.

June: Operation Sharp Guard, a joint WEU/NATO mission aimed at strengthening the existing naval embargoes against Serbia and Montenegro, begins under Italian coordination.

---

lies in its potential, not in its present achievements or basically nonexistent capabilities. Without political consensus in Europe, security cooperation independent of NATO and of American leadership will remain only an option for the distant future, largely dependent on American choices.

NATO: Transatlantic Transformations

NATO's first reaction to European initiatives for change reflected the slower, frustrating pace of NATO's own decisionmaking toward what seemed to many to be an uncertain future. NATO's only initial success came in the critical role that the organization played in facilitating German unification in 1990. Its London summit in July 1990 recognized the Soviet Union as no longer an enemy but as a partner in the building of security in Europe. To cushion the consequences of continued German membership in NATO, the organization decided that the Soviet Union and its former Warsaw Pact partner states were to be given access to NATO and to be helped to maintain diplomatic and eventually military liaison at the Brussels headquarters. The NATO allies also agreed to Soviet demands for the special status of eastern German territory during the period of Soviet force withdrawal; no foreign forces or nuclear weapons to be introduced before the end of 1994.[31]

NATO meeting followed NATO meeting, with what was clearly a European and transatlantic agenda crowded with a number of distracting events and several contradictory initiatives on the division of security responsibilities. It was not just the challenge of nascent European separation and a reinvigorated WEU that concerned NATO and the Bush administration. With the progressive dismantlement of the Soviet forward military presence and then of the overall Soviet military threat itself, NATO found itself unable to reach a clear new definition of functions and structures. Most of NATO's proposed changes did not go to the heart of the post–cold war alliance dilemma; that is, how to define a new overarching purpose that would garner public support and that went beyond preparing for defense against uncertainty. For many in the United States and Europe, particularly in eastern Europe, NATO's principal function was to frame U.S. involvement in Europe, as well as to demonstrate the continuing commitment of the United States to the evolution of a cooperative security system. Decisions about force commitments, basing, or even specific command arrangements were seen as less important than the fundamental missions.

For others, notably in France before the change in government in 1993, the basic structure of NATO remained that of the cold war era and was not susceptible to change, especially given the dominant role of the United States. NATO's continuation had therefore to be limited to a transitional period, sufficient to allow Europe to absorb the initial impact of German unification and the revolutions in the East and to allow the United States to phase gradually into inevitable withdrawal.

Moreover, the initial efforts to revise NATO strategy were less than satisfactory. The alliance's new Strategic Concept, presented at the Rome summit in November 1991, was unwieldy, the product of what was unquestionably an ambitious undertaking in a turbulent political context. On crucial points there had often been only general agreement, and clarity was often sacrificed to the continuing imperatives for last-minute compromises. Further, the strategy posited uncertainty and a turbulent Soviet Union as the critical threats to be faced, just a month before the collapse of the Soviet Union itself.

As defined again at Rome, NATO's core functions were four: to act as one (but only one) foundation for stability in Europe, to be the forum for transatlantic political consultation, to constitute the primary mechanism to deter and defend against attacks on its members, and to preserve the strategic balance in Europe.[32] Its new missions were to include collective action in peace and crisis as well as in war, particularly preventive diplomacy and crisis management. NATO and the United States explicitly recognized that these were shared responsibilities and agreed to work in conjunction with European and other multilateral organizations to provide for the "necessary mutual transparency and complementarilty between the European security and defense identity and the NATO alliance."

An ambitious NATO force restructuring program also got under way, sparked by the new political environment and by domestic budget-cutting imperatives in the already shrinking defense industrial sector. The 1991 Rome summit saw agreement on both the need for a new Allied Command Europe rapid reaction corps (ARRC) for crisis intervention and the need for far lower levels of standing forces, organized on a multinational basis and equipped with lighter, more defensive armament. Plans also foresaw lower levels of readiness for main defense forces, while maintaining the advantages of planning and standardization under an integrated command structure. American units would not necessarily be included in the ARRC, although American support assets and individual specialty teams would most likely be mobilized for particular missions. But the transformed forces were still described as operating only within NATO's traditional geostrategic context, under the SACEUR and with planning and coordination being done principally through SHAPE. The ARRC's formal mission was still intervention within the NATO area, and the most binding force assignments gave greatest significance to what increasingly seemed the least likely contingency, an article 5 defense of NATO territory and borders against direct attack.

As the conflict in Yugoslavia progressed in 1992 and early 1993, most NATO allies agreed that this was no longer a probable or sufficient NATO mission. Moreover, the notions of in-area versus out of area no longer necessarily corresponded to NATO's interests in maintaining peace and stability in Europe or in the potentially turbulent surrounding regions to the south or east. The main threats to European security stemmed largely from domestic turmoil, ethnic conflict, and secessionist movements, all originating outside the formal NATO area but with immediate cross-border consequences. Either there would need to be a reinterpretation of the area over which article 5 guarantees of common defense would operate, or a greater number of alliance actions would depend on invigorating or reinterpreting article 4, under which alliance members are to consult and act politically on an ad hoc basis in the event of a crisis.

Peacekeeping on a selected basis seemed an obvious new mission, one that might involve some willing allies (such as Britain, France, and the United States in the Gulf War) or almost all members. NATO indicated in 1992 that it would not anticipate launching many such initiatives on its own authority or in its own area. But it was now prepared to accept peacekeeping tasking both from the CSCE and then from the United Nations.[33] Participation would be the responsibility of individual members; NATO would use assets on the basis of general agreement and the involvement of the willing.

By mid-1993 the horrors in Bosnia provided clear reason to think through what might be required to undertake selective military operations under the article 4 agreement. At the heart of NATO's planning efforts was not peace enforcement or intervention in the ongoing civil war; both of these missions far exceeded the political consensus within NATO then or since. Rather, it was the implementation of what was hoped would be a near-term political settlement in which NATO would act as agent and would gain the cooperation of some nonmember states such as Russia and Ukraine. What was needed at a minimum was to further develop the compatibility of forces, monitor political and geographic areas of tension, and consult on areas of shared military and strategic concern. More questionable for most members were suggestions to allow NATO to provide longer-term guarantees for stability, in essence commitments just short of security guarantees.[34]

By early 1994 the outlines of NATO's broad transformation seemed considerably more ambitious and more durable than had been projected even by NATO enthusiasts in 1991. Many of the specific details about efforts to reach out to the East and to affect peace management are discussed in the following two chapters, but even a brief overview underscores the magnitude and the significance of the organizational changes.

First, in an internal house cleaning and streamlining project, NATO's command structure was substantially changed. The number of major NATO commands was reduced from three to two: European and Atlantic, with Allied Command Channel being absorbed into the former. This reduction was accompanied by the creation of major subordinate commands within Allied Command Europe, responsible for the southern, central, and northwest regions.[35] Also, NATO was deeply involved in a UN peacekeeping mandate, providing a wide range of operational military support to the UN Protection Force humanitarian mission in Bosnia.

But perhaps even more dramatic in terms of past debates was the evidence

of expanding cooperation between France and its alliance partners. Many of
the day-to-day surface irritations remained; any issue that raised new prerogatives for the United States or for NATO's integrated command also en-
countered stiff French criticism and noninvolvement.[36] But 1992 and 1993
saw many advances, almost all related to increasing French concern about
the widening war in the former Yugoslavia and the lack of an effective European response. There was now French involvement in NATO advance planning for Bosnia, a clarification of the interim WEU-NATO relationship in
planning and structure, and a French return—for the first time since 1966—
to participation in NATO's Military Committee for discussions on Bosnia
and peacekeeping.

Current Developments in NATO: The PFP and CJTF

After considerable debate in Washington and throughout the alliance, the
January 1994 Brussels summit decided on two critical new organizational
adaptations. The first, discussed more fully in chapter 4, was the Partnership
for Peace, which included a new basis and new structures for cooperation
with the central and eastern European states toward joint peacekeeping tasks.
The second was to initiate planning for a series of Combined/Joint Task
Forces (CJTF) that would allow both NATO and the WEU access in a crisis
to NATO forces, support resources, and infrastructure assets. The goals were
to keep NATO relevant in the changing environment while meeting European concerns about greater autonomy; the critical premise was that, though
there would need to be general agreement, only some allies would be able
and willing to take specific actions outside the NATO area. They would then
operate together with other member states or perhaps even attract contributions from PFP states and others. American forces in particular would not
and perhaps should not be counted on in every proposed action outside the
NATO area. (See figure 3-4 for a map of NATO members and PFP signatories.)

The seeds of the Combined/Joint Task Forces were planted at the Rome
summit in 1991, where the new "strategic concept" stressed the importance
of highly mobile and rapidly deployable forces in the post–cold war strategic environment.[37] The ARRC provided for this capability within the NATO
area but with a fixed force and organizational structure. What was needed
was a similar instrument with far greater flexibility to allow the Europeans
to form coalitions of the willing under a jointly designated operational commander and act together outside NATO. Two conditions seemed basic: the

Figure 3-4. European NATO Members and Partnership for Peace (PFP) Signatories, October 1994

a. The other members are the United States and Canada.
b. PFP signatories not shown: Armenia, Azerbaijan, Georgia, Kazakhstan, Kyrgyzstan, Slovenia, Turkmenistan, and Uzbekistan.

United States would probably not be included, and the rest of NATO was essentially not opposed. Moreover, provision for the eventual use of the CJTF would be one more political hedge, one more critical answer to the questions increasingly heard in alliance capitals of why NATO and why a NATO force structure were still needed in a post-cold war environment.

The CJTF program is still being negotiated, but the basic directions are now clear. The CJTF is an organizational scheme designed to allow separable but not separate forces for purposes other than the defense of the NATO area. In one stroke the CJTF attempts to preserve NATO's ability to defend its own territory, expand NATO's ability to act out of area, redistribute some alliance costs away from the United States to the Europeans, and give the WEU easy access to NATO forces and equipment for its own missions in which the United States has no vital interest. While contributing to the European security and defense identity, the CJTF planners are also hoping to eliminate competition between the WEU and NATO and to avoid costly duplication of equipment, technology, and training now and in the future.

The proposed division of labor under the CJTF is complex, but if successful, advocates argue, it could resolve several problems at once. Ideally, the CJTF will satisfy Atlanticists because technically and in budget terms the WEU's military might and European defense overall will virtually overlap with that of NATO. NATO's preservation and congressional approval of this new approach to burden sharing will ensure the United States's continued engagement, with American troops on the Continent numbering about 100,000. For those in favor of a more autonomous European defense, however, the CJTF may allow the Europeans the choice to act decisively with military force without the United States (or at least without U.S. involvement beyond support activities). Not only may such an arrangement increase the likelihood of consensus and action on issues viewed as European, but military operations without the United States may carry a lighter political load, both outside NATO and within, especially but not only in France.

Operationally, the CJTF would allow the WEU to take troops and equipment from NATO if the WEU countries wanted to intervene in a crisis in which NATO rejected military options. In addition to establishing an equitable division of labor between the WEU and NATO, the CJTF could conceivably allow NATO and non-NATO forces to coordinate on an ad hoc basis for peacekeeping, humanitarian, or search and rescue missions. This could be done under the political conditions agreed to in 1992, not just on NATO's or the WEU's behalf but for UN or CSCE missions as well. Through expanded joint military training exercises, compatible communication networks, and integrated military structures, the CJTF will potentially bring a greater degree of flexibility to European defense and security arrangements than would be possible under NATO alone. The obvious codependence of NATO and the WEU, moreover, will both strengthen and demonstrate the interlocking character of these organizations. At a minimum, it will prevent another round of fruitless debate, led by Washington, Paris, or any other capital, about one organization undermining the other or succeeding at the other's expense.

It is also hoped that as the PFP evolves and military exchanges develop stronger ties between the long-time members and CEE states that the new members will also be able to take part in selected peacekeeping missions. Together, the PFP and the CJTF are essentially article 4–type functions. Both are structured to bring new states into the cooperative security process, even to conduct joint operations and missions as agreed upon on a case-by-case basis. Neither offers or requires NATO membership in the short term and thus avoids the political debate and the operational complexities that would have to be faced in extending article 5 of the North Atlantic Treaty to potential members.

But there are also potential disadvantages to the CJTF, whatever form it may ultimately take. Although it appears to allow greater military flexibility for both NATO and the WEU, the CJTF in fact demands a greater degree of consensus among a larger number of countries than does any previous arrangement. Although the United States originally formulated the CJTF concept, the Europeans are the ones who must pursue it most vigorously for the plan to come to fruition. Now that Europhoria has passed and Europeans, notably the French, have so far failed to vigorously pursue ESDI, the American political leadership appears somewhat less concerned about NATO's overall flexibility. In essence, a successful implementation of the CJTF would mean participants' willingness to agree to disagree, or at least to draw different consequences about action in a crisis. With limited resources and competing agendas, there is still potential for organizational competition, diverging interests, and gridlock.

Most significant, beyond a basic NATO Council vote, the political structure that would allow the dispatch and the continuing control of NATO forces and equipment is still undefined, and debate and confusion abound over the specific circumstances under which the WEU could call on NATO, and specifically SACEUR, assets. By March 1994 the WEU leadership had already drawn up a list of contingencies and potential scenarios in which it would wish to be able to call upon NATO forces. NATO is seen by some to be lagging behind in the process, in part, some reports allege, because of NATO's organizational inertia or reluctance, partially among planners (again, especially France), to see the process move forward.[38]

A further complication has been a revisiting of past Franco-American difficulties about political control and command authority. Because France withdrew from NATO's integrated military command in 1966 but preserved its position on the North Atlantic Council, NATO's political arm, it has demanded at almost every point of specific implementation that the CJTF answer only to the NAC to maximize its impact on the CJTF debate. The proposed location of the CJTF planning unit at SHAPE, for example, raised contention, as did the question of regional responsibilities. Considerable delay and some carefully crafted special arrangements were then required to accommodate France's request, while trying also to accommodate the preferences of other allies.[39] The irritation recurs every time the issue of the role of NATO's SACEUR and of the integrated command is mentioned.

Several other areas are still unresolved, despite the increasingly overlapping membership of NATO and the WEU. First, if NATO forces were allocated to a WEU mission, NATO might then be unable to meet other central military requirements. Article 5 cases would seem to call for the immediate return of forces to NATO command. But if NATO agrees to act on the basis of an article 4 consultation, is the order of priority, and therefore NATO command authority, foreordained, or will it be determined politically on a case-by-case basis? How many forces will be enough to satisfy the probable range of contingencies, and how do these levels square with the force- and budget-cutting decisions in train in every NATO capital? Second, the division of labor between WEU military capability and the Rapid Reaction Corps under NATO has not been fully mapped out. Third, there is no broad consensus on respective spheres of WEU-NATO interest beyond NATO's current borders. Although there may well be no general basis for European-American agreement on a division of labor, consultative and cooperative mechanisms on the political level need to be available and reliable. Both NATO and the WEU must therefore in theory adapt their operations, training, and political orientations to the same wide range of out-of-area contingencies.

Finally, the specifics of how the CJTF and PFP interlock require further delineation and smoothing. The WEU has tried to extend its influence eastward by offering associate membership to six central European states[40] in addition to the Baltics; the PFP now includes a good proportion of the CSCE participants. Clearly, it is necessary to avoid counterproductive competition between the initiatives and the expensive duplication of political and military burdens and functions.

The congressional perspective on the CJTF is also yet to be explored in detail. It is already difficult after Somalia for the United States to participate in peacekeeping missions, given congressional concerns about potential policy drift, fiscal restraints, and the political justification needed to allow American lives to be put at risk. Despite the burden-sharing advantages, it may become equally difficult to justify defense spending for the assets most crucial to the CJTF initiative—such as lift, reconnaissance, intelligence, and communication—if these appear to be useful primarily for missions at European discretion.

Additionally, it may prove difficult to get Congress to approve the provision of unique U.S. assets to a CJTF contingent led by the WEU in a situation in which no clear U.S. interests are at stake, a fair possibility when dealing with out-of-NATO conflicts. Many Americans see the CJTF strictly as a NATO asset to be made available for operations outside NATO territory. As such, they feel it would be inappropriate to emphasize its application as a vehicle for European-led operations that do not include U.S. forces. According to this view, any contingency—be it led by NATO or the WEU—would require political support from the United States before any involvement.

At a fundamental level, then, the CJTF may at least in the short run exacerbate intra-alliance political vulnerabilities. When finally completed, the program itself may be a military-operational solution for what is fundamentally a political problem. The debate within the alliance, and within each capital, is over what should be the guiding set of principles that determine in which contingencies the alliance and its members will fight and with which partners. The CJTF can address the how; preparation in advance will make it possible to translate a political decision into cooperative action. But it is really the why, and the political divisions that promote action or inaction, that will be critical. To what benefit will it be to spend countless hours on compatible equipment, training, and the logistics of a CJTF if the lack of political consensus means that we will never use it?

In some respects, the CJTF concept is being tested by events. Two ongoing operations in the former Yugoslavia already reflect functions that parallel those foreseen for a CJTF, but both are now under the auspices of NATO. Operation Sharp Guard is the WEU-NATO mission that monitors the Adriatic, and Operation Deny Flight used NATO AWACS to monitor airspace over Bosnia-Herzogovina and NATO air units to enforce exclusion zones. In both instances, there has been general agreement among the allies, and NATO resources, including a deployed headquarters unit, have been used in support of UN decisions. But while there has been general NAC approval, it has not been necessary for every member of NATO to be involved; in effect then, establishing the first use of a CJTF. Moreover, in the event that a political solution is reached in Bosnia and a peace plan adopted, the resulting implementation/peacekeeping force will essentially use a CJTF-type command and control structure (that is, perhaps a non-NATO operational commander with both NATO and non-NATO units assigned to him and supported by NATO communications and intelligence assets). This would prove an important indicator of the further viability of the CJTF concept and flexibility of its proposed structure.

NATO and WEU: Potential for Partnership?

Prospects for cooperation between NATO and the WEU (with the CSCE playing a largely separate role) have become better since the revolutions of 1989 thrust European security institutions into disarray. Early on, however, the balance of power between institutions was well illuminated. The sharp reaction of the Bush administration to the Franco-German proposal in 1991 made it clear that the United States would not tolerate any institutional development of an EC-only security structure if such development were to come at NATO's expense.

Yet since then cooperation has increased to some degree. The United States began to realize, at least by 1992, that with the successful conclusion of the Maastricht negotiations Europe would be in a better long-term position to demand a greater say in security decisionmaking. The realization was softened somewhat by the knowledge that a louder voice for Europe should mandate a larger European financial contribution to burden sharing.

By the spring of 1993 much of the rancor had left the European-American debate over security organizations. Elections had brought in a conservative French government more interested in transatlantic cooperation than in confrontation, especially given the pragmatic challenges of Bosnia.[41] The election of Bill Clinton similarly brought to power the first American president since Eisenhower who seemed more than rhetorically interested in a united Europe and the contribution it could make to joint economic and security efforts. Agreement on the Eurocorps relationship with NATO had smoothed the way: in an operational emergency the force would be available as a unit to NATO or the WEU; in peacetime it would remain under national (read, for Germany, NATO) command. Use for peacekeeping or humanitarian missions outside NATO would require only the agreement of contributing states, but with NATO clearly having first call.[42]

WEU-NATO relations have improved substantially with the Clinton administration's European policy. On his four trips to Europe since being elected, President Clinton has unequivocally stated his support for a stronger

European defense organization. The NATO summit held in Brussels in January 1994 confirmed this support with the U.S. proposal to create the Combined/Joint Task Forces. With NATO moving quickly to expand its influence and operations eastward with the Partnership for Peace, however, and with the WEU making parallel moves, it is not yet clear how the new institutional arrangements will be adjusted to alleviate potential competitive pressures.[43] In all probability, the United States and its European allies will have to come to a new political consensus about the appropriate division of labor between transatlantic and European security organizations. But there now seems much less chance of a return to the rancor and suspicion of the 1990–92 period.

The Way Forward

After five years, the end result is a rather untidy set of organizational solutions and initiatives, with overlapping functions, responsibilities, and membership. By most measures, NATO has emerged as the institutional winner. NATO is unquestionably the security forum of first resort, the framework where ongoing operational military cooperation still undergirds the sweeping political military pronouncements about shared interests and burdens. And it is to NATO that the allies and the new CEE partners turn in crisis.

NATO still has a challenging agenda to confront. The transatlantic transformation is not yet complete; it may still falter if the allies are faced with the long-threatened missions associated with enforcement of a Bosnia peace accord or the escalation of fighting there beyond present boundaries. Clearly, the principal protagonists in Paris and Washington are not totally satisfied with this resolution, and debate and dispute continue about the details of any new initiative, albeit on a lower level of intensity. It is also not certain what concrete meaning NATO's institutional transformation will have in an era of shrinking defense budgets and domestic opposition in Europe and the United States to maintaining present defense commitments, let alone the assumption of new missions or responsibilities.

But if the comparison is in terms of relative share of decisionmaking on security issues, the Europeanists have also won some areas of at least potential advantage. NATO command prerogatives have been maintained, but there is now shared responsibility with, and promised responsiveness to, the WEU outside Europe. For the first time the United States also accepts, and not just in principle, a unified European voice in defense. Its development will mean what Washington has long feared: European decisionmaking out-

side NATO for policies over which the United States may have had little prior
influence through bilateral channels or through its NATO leadership position. But it is hard at present to see just how or when such an occasion in the
European-American dialogue will arise.

As with many of the most far-reaching aspects of the Maastricht blueprint, what Europe wants, or in the medium term what Europe will be, is uncertain. The cockiness of 1990–91 over European unity has passed; simple
economic recovery will probably not be sufficient to revive it, even in
France. And the hard slog to implement the economic provisions of Maastricht seems to some a task more than sufficient for the foreseeable future.
Many observers argue now that the further institutional evolution of a Community security role beyond the efforts of the WEU will be slow and probably hostage to domestic politics in France, Germany, and Britain. And the
trick, in the eyes of a number of domestic publics, will be how to retain the
benefits of the U.S. involvement against an uncertain future.[44] (See figure
3-5 for the membership in the interlocking security organizations.)

Some Americans, particularly in the Atlanticist camp, seem to believe that
a serious European effort to organize security on a European basis will now
be a matter of decades, not years.

But this is once again an American overestimation of the durability and
the utility of the status quo. The structure of the common foreign and security policy may not yet be clear, but consultation within the Community continues to grow in strength and frequency. The search for a common policy in
the Yugoslav crisis has been wrenching, but broad agreement exists on this
and other major issues, particularly among Britain, France, and Germany.
Popular expectations about overall European cooperation may have fallen
from their post-Wall highs, but they are still very strong. Moreover, NATO's
transformation and the American debate on the future U.S. role within it are
still far from complete.

Some argue, indeed, that the United States will soon find itself challenged
more often by a single European policy, once Germany emerges as an active,
increasingly independent international player and at least a core group of European states will be increasingly able to act as a political unit. Mid-1994
found another round of Franco-German initiatives that set forth a new path
to integration, to be pushed during the year in which Germany, then France,
will hold the EU presidency, and after in the 1996 EU Intergovernmental
Conference. The central concept is a variable-speed Europe of concentric
circles: in the first circle, the forging ahead of the willing five: France, Ger-

Figure 3-5. Security in Europe: Membership of North American and Eurasian Countries in NATO, the EU, the WEU, and the CSCE

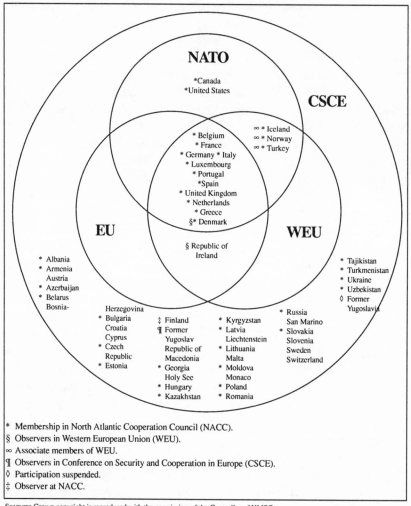

* Membership in North Atlantic Cooperation Council (NACC).
§ Observers in Western European Union (WEU).
∞ Associate members of WEU.
¶ Observers in Conference on Security and Cooperation in Europe (CSCE).
◊ Participation suspended.
‡ Observer at NACC.

SOURCE: Crown copyright is reproduced with the permission of the Controller of HMSO.

many, Belgium, Luxembourg, and the Netherlands. In the next circle are the less-willing western European partners and the new EU members to enter in January 1995. In the last circle come the candidate CEE members, especially the favored Visegrad states of Poland, Hungary, Slovakia, and the Czech Republic.

Again for the core states, the primary focus is economic and financial: a new effort to maintain a European monetary union, steps toward a common currency, the new dimensions of social policy integration, export controls, and many more issues. But security and defense will still be key, whether the issue is European cooperation in challenging the American dominance of advanced weapons production or in the basic structuring of forces and their training.

In sum, the European security landscape is still in a state of flux. But through it all, one thing seems increasingly clear: while they themselves are changing, the organizations of the past will, for the time being, continue to be the primary vehicles for meeting the challenges of the future for European security. NATO is clearly not perfectly suited to a security regime that does not revolve around confronting a Soviet menace. Still, it maintains primacy of place among sometimes competing, sometimes cooperating alternative security structures.

In part, NATO has retained this position by default. It is the most venerable, the most credible, and above all the most capable guarantor of European security. It is the channel preferred, managed, and underwritten by the United States—and it is likely to remain so. The CSCE may have a strong mandate, but it has no enforcement mechanisms and is in any event too susceptible to deadlock, given its broad and diverse membership. Similarly, the WEU is limited by a lack of a clear mandate independent of NATO, a widely perceived subordinate position to the transatlantic alliance, an underdeveloped (though improving) infrastructure, and some internal dissent between Atlanticist and Europeanist members.[45] Indeed, the tone of the Petersberg Declarations confirmed that even some important Europeanist states (such as Germany) prefer NATO as their security organization of first choice.

Until the EU is able to develop a significant degree of political cohesiveness, especially on foreign and security policy, it will probably be unable to muster sufficient levels of cooperation and commitment to make the WEU a credible alternative to NATO in Europe (though it may be a legitimate complement in the not-too-distant future). And though the field is somewhat more open with regard to a security regime for out-of-area concerns, NATO again has the inside track, owing to, if nothing else, its greater operational capabilities and already fully developed consultative forums. NATO may well choose to defer out-of-area authority to other institutions, but that right of first refusal remains firmly within NATO's purview. The questions of European security may be changing, but the answers, at least for now, are largely the same.

4

Outreach to the East, 1989–94

The revolutions in central and eastern Europe confronted the United States and its European allies with a different set of debates and dilemmas.[1] The need for Western outreach to the East was almost nowhere in doubt; nor was there lack of opportunity to promote true security through political, economic, and military reform. But there were critical differences almost from the outset with Russia and among the allies, the chief protagonists once again being Washington, Paris, and Bonn. What were possible and appropriate types and rates of assistance? Within what scope could external actors affect democratic change, and what criteria should ultimately define states as European, as potential candidates for inclusion within the transatlantic-European security framework? Was there in fact a meaningful definition of European security that did not include the close engagement of Russia as a partner?

The outreach issues were almost always framed in organizational terms: membership, extension, the acceptance of multilateral responsibility for assistance or progress. The core was multilateral cooperation and risk sharing, just as in the earlier NATO-EC partnership of the 1950s. It was assumed that leading states, the United States and Germany in particular, would pursue their bilateral programs and agendas and that private investment would flow once there was stability as well as opportunity. Myriad channels also existed to promote cooperation through cultural and educational exchanges and through the voluntary activities of private citizens and nongovernmental groups.

But the real focus was to seek through multilateral organizations, which were often overlapping and sometimes ineffective, to create a new legitimate framework for ensuring the compatibility, if not always the convergence, of security policies. The open practices and limited transparency measures achieved through the Conference on Security and Cooperation in Europe were no longer enough for the security reassurance of the newly democratizing states or for the West. From the perspective of both sides, what was to be sought was a legitimate framework for dialogue and debate about goals, policies, perceived threats, and problems of common concern.

Perhaps the only fundamental point of allied agreement in 1989 was on a broad division of labor. In accordance with the clear preferences of the Bush administration, the United States accepted principal responsibility for dealing in security issues with the Soviet Union and then, after the demise of the Soviet Union in December 1991, with the post-Soviet states. Western Europe in general, and Germany and the rest of the European Community in particular, took on the burden of political and economic reform in central Europe.

After five years the record of achievement reflects considerable CEE achievement and some Western success in direct outreach. But, more important, it shows the deep ambivalences that threaded through every phase of Western outreach efforts and Russian responses. Direct Western, particularly American, support was slow and fragmented and in many areas at far lower levels than expected. Some new programs, new organizational frameworks, and new instruments were tried, but few met with stunning success or satisfied the CEE countries.

Again and again, both the EC and NATO rhetorically accepted central European appeals for more direct security assurances while finding new reasons why direct membership was not possible or why it must be a question of time and demonstrated readiness. This response in part reflected the self-absorption and the policy caution bred of severe economic recession experienced first in the United States and then in western Europe. In part, too, it reflected the short-term reactive character of policymaking in a time of great uncertainty and constant change. That was certainly true in the many ad hoc responses to continuing political changes in central Europe, the shock of the attempted Soviet coup and the fall of Gorbachev in 1991, and the violent confrontation that capped the continuing struggles between President Boris Yeltsin and the Russian parliament in 1993.

But in the largest measure the jagged nature of Western security outreach to the East reflected the lack of consensus about the security outcome that was preferred or that was thought possible to achieve. The role that might or should be played by Russia was clearly the most controversial problem, in many respects directly paralleling the allied disputes in the first postwar decade about how to treat Germany and what role the defeated state should play in the West. But there were difficulties also with most, if not all, of the central European applicants. Few political elites in western Europe or North America were prepared to deal directly with these issues. Even fewer electorates were prepared for, or even engaged in discussions about, the new political and economic burdens that would surely be involved.

The result in late 1994 is a range of European and transatlantic mechanisms for extending stability to central Europe and the post-Soviet states and a set of still-conflicting national agendas of how, when, and why to accomplish the tasks foreseen. All approach the question of further expansion in gradualist terms: the European Community has promised eventual membership to the qualified; the question of NATO expansion is declared to be when, not whether. But there is little agreement on how to order what increasingly appears to be the establishment of different tiers of security relationships. There are converging expectations that whenever any full expansion occurs, the Visegrad states—Poland, Hungary, the Czech Republic, and (probably) Slovakia—will be the first to join the EC and NATO. But there is little agreement on the other applicants that will or should come in at the same time, or later in a second or third group. And there is no consensus on Russia's appropriate role, on how to get Moscow to play such a role, or on ways to meet Russia's legitimate security requirements.

Diverging National Agendas

This section examines the national concerns of the major European actors, the United States, and Russia that shaped the evolution of Western outreach efforts.

The United States

U.S. policy itself was initially somewhat jagged; the early 1990s was a time of rapid political change and short-term political fire fighting. Among the many items crowding the American political agenda were the distractions of the Gulf War in 1990 and 1991, the Bush absorption in elections and the pending change of administrations for most of 1992, and the hedging congressional constraints imposed on direct aid of any kind to the Soviet Union. The Bush administration was quick to define reform and stability in central Europe as too much for a deficit-ridden United States, given its global burdens and its special burden toward the other military superpower. Reform and stability were, therefore, a European problem and easily left to what Washington feared was a far too self-confident EC.

For most of the Bush tenure the United States was primarily concerned about the traditional security relationship with the Soviet Union. The agenda was an ambitious one: to implement and expand the scope of strategic nuclear reductions; to bring to full completion the Conventional Forces in Europe treaty; and to speed up the ongoing negotiations on chemical and biological weapons and open skies. Aid to Russia on other issues was far more limited; even direct security assistance under Nunn-Lugar was slow in implementation and hedged by cautious "buy American" provisions placed by a Congress not yet convinced of the lasting quality or perhaps even the ultimate benign orientation of Gorbachev's reforms.[2]

The fall of the Soviet Union in late 1991 brought new urgency to the American agenda, particularly in efforts toward denuclearization in the four successor states on whose territory Soviet weapons were based: Russia, Belarus, Ukraine, and Kazakhstan. Bush and Secretary of State Baker moved quickly to ensure an equivalent security dialogue and partnership with an increasingly uncertain Russia, above all to limit the chances of a reversion to Soviet or Russian imperialism. The democratizing states of central and eastern Europe also had to be brought into this dialogue, both to ensure political balance and to create channels that were sturdier and ultimately more stabilizing than those afforded through the CSCE. The mere explosion of the numbers of states involved made progress slow and often unpredictable. Arms control, and especially the CFE agreements that already included all the former Warsaw Treaty Organization (WTO) states, were extended to all the post-Soviet states. So too were bilateral and, above all, NATO-based efforts to promote military-to-military exchanges, aid and technical assistance, and organizational support.

Specifically, beginning in 1992 (and accelerating into 1993 and 1994) the United States took significant unilateral steps to provide real substance to offers of outreach to the east. A concept for intensified assistance to the militaries of the new democracies through traveling "contact teams" became a reality in July 1992. This program rapidly grew from an initial program for Hungary to an extensive system of exchange visits of military experts to CEE states by 1994. The program focused on advice in nonlethal areas such as legal, medical, budgetary, and similar matters that were of immediate usefulness to militaries attempting to establish themselves in democratic states. In June 1993 the United States also created a new academic institution in

Garmisch, Germany (fittingly named the George C. Marshall Center for European Security Studies), aimed at educating new civilian and military leaders from central and eastern Europe and the former Soviet Union.

The Clinton administration continued the effort to balance the needs of central Europe and Russia and the other FSU states, but at least initially gave primary attention to ensuring Russian engagement, given the deteriorating Russian political environment. It succeeded in concluding a number of critical cooperative agreements toward denuclearization, including a trilateral agreement in January 1994 with both Russia and Ukraine on warhead transfer back to Russian soil and ultimate dismantlement. Over time central European relations attracted more interest and attention, and by the fall of 1994 there was a conscious balance of Clinton visits and speeches to central Europe and the FSU. But the ongoing conflict in Yugoslavia and the continuing uncertainties about Russia left an atmosphere of unease and at times anxiety about future security.

Clearly, one of Clinton's triumphs was the NATO Partnership for Peace initiative, launched at the January 1994 NATO summit and immediately defended against all comers, first in Prague and then in Moscow and Kiev.[3] The PFP was a program to promote military cooperation to peaceful ends, an instrument both to stimulate democratic reform and transparency in national military institutions and to create options for greater cooperation and compatibility with the NATO countries. Its goal was to buy time and stability, particularly against a premature offer of membership in NATO or guarantees that could have shattered the Western security consensus. Moreover, it was a visible, positive channel through which to engage the "willing," those states that by their behavior would approach NATO standards and express similar values and goals. The PFP was designed neither to patronize Russia nor to antagonize it nor to allow it to set the terms of cooperation with CEE states. Not everyone in Washington was surprised, therefore, when Russia finally decided to participate at least in the PFP's initial phase, signing its Framework Document in mid-1994.

Russia

Russia's own ambivalence regarding Western outreach efforts only added to the turbulence. The Soviet approach under Mikhail Gorbachev was to stress openness to and cooperation with all potential partners. His strategy toward Europe tried to ensure both economic aid and market access for the

Soviet Union, as well as the embedding of German economic might. Toward NATO his tactics were in the short run to ensure the transformation of cold war doctrines and force structures, as had been promised, in return for Soviet acceptance of a unified Germany in NATO. In the longer run Gorbachev, along with other central European reform leaders, sought to effect NATO's demise as a symbol and obsolescent instrument of the cold war. Soviet statements usually suggested progressive NATO dismantlement in favor of a pan-European structure—the CSCE or perhaps something new—with both the Soviet Union and the United States assuming special security responsibilities commensurate with their status as superpowers.

Russia's role in a democratizing central Europe was the subject of intense debate in the waning months of Gorbachev's presidency. Many close to the Soviet military and the party hierarchy argued that the Soviet Union must preserve its influence and its leverage there, at a minimum to prevent the emergence of an "anti-Soviet" bloc, perhaps with German encouragement.[4] They favored the creation of a new "political" version of the WTO or a close substitute through a web of new bilateral relations.[5] The concerns of the military, facing withdrawal and the loss of critical intelligence and air defense assets, were more operational. Not only did Russia need assurance that it would still have a de facto central European glacis behind which to mount its homeland defense. It would also require the access it needed to cooperative military facilities and resources (such as radars and ports) essential to that task, at least until they could be replaced.

Others, closer to Foreign Minister Eduard Schevardnaze, argued that the Soviet Union had nothing to lose in closer relations between central Europe and the West. Both the West and the Soviet Union had a stake in stability and the new status quo; neither wanted any exceptions to the CSCE principle of no border change except by mutual consent. Indeed, central Europe's security might be the test ground for the Soviet-American strategic partnership that was crucial to the new international order outlined by Bush. Schevardnaze's resignation led to a harder Soviet line toward central Europe and a rash of proposals for treaties to reflect exclusionary bilateral relations with each of its former WTO allies. By then, however, central European independence was more clearly established and supported; only Romania assented.

Policies under Yeltsin showed a realistic Russian acceptance of much looser relationships with central Europe but were colored far more by the twists and turns of Russian domestic politics. General disappointment about

Western aid and disillusionment about market economic progress reinforced the increasing suspicion about Western plans to draw new lines of confrontation in central Europe. As Vladimir Zhironovsky later demonstrated, Russian nationalists saw in almost all the outreach efforts a plot to weaken Russia. Boris Yeltsin himself at times supported an eventual expansion of NATO membership and Russia's involvement in both the North Atlantic Cooperation Council in 1992 and the PFP in 1994.[6] Indeed, as early as December 1991 Yeltsin only half-jokingly asked for direct NATO membership for Russia as a protection for Russian interests at home, in the post-Soviet area, and abroad.[7]

But in each case, almost simultaneously, Yeltsin or his spokesmen backtracked or warned the central European states and the West about premature and precipitous moves against Russia's security interests. Yeltsin increasingly asserted Russia's legitimate stake in control, by right or because of the West's default, of the near abroad, the post-Soviet states. He at times pressed the West for recognition of the "emergence" of the Commonwealth of Independent States as an effective military or peacekeeping organization for former Soviet territory parallel or even equal to NATO. From time to time, indeed, he suggested that future European security architecture would see the incorporation of NATO and the nascent CIS security organization as "two pillars" under a reinvented umbrella CSCE.[8]

Western Europe

Britain and France (at least until 1993) took what might be called a limited Europe, or status quo stance. Both wanted outreach and support at moderate levels, principally through the Community, to central Europe and more selectively to the FSU states other than Russia. Both wanted to eliminate any serious attempt to engage with or include the central Asian states in the European domain. Security cooperation did not require special new efforts but could be left to broad discussions in a status quo CSCE, to stronger bilateral relationships, and to increasingly congruent practices. Any extension of the existing membership in NATO or in the EC would require a long transitional period and might even then put core goals at risk—for Britain, the transatlantic commitment; for France, the Franco-German-led European coalition.[9] Russia remained a separate issue, best dealt with directly through traditional great power arrangements and bilateral channels. Moreover, if they were ever achieved at all, more cooperative security links with the CEE states would follow long after economic integration based on free market criteria.

France's shift to a more conciliatory position reflected the political changes in France after the 1993 elections, which rejected socialist policy control.[10] The new line was more conciliatory toward dialogue with the East, more attuned to the "legitimate" security concerns of the central European states, and more in favor of an activist EC outreach under French and German leadership. The lessons of Yugoslavia weighed heavily in French concerns for stability in central Europe and in a greater willingness to accommodate to the more permanent American presence so desired by Germany and the central European states.

The key European state for outreach, though, was the Federal Republic, both because of its traditional economic ties to central Europe and Russia and its central concerns with stability to its east. Not surprisingly, Germany took a broader, more favorable approach than did the other European states toward the aspirations of the central European states for close association with, or integration into, economic and security Europe. Consistent with the strategy West Germany had followed toward its western neighbors in the 1950s and 1960s, a unified Germany favored a strategy of reconciliation, with paramount emphasis on reassurance in all aspects of security: political, economic, and military. Its preference also was to multilateralize the issue of central European reassurance, to allow for the eventual extension of both the European and transatlantic frameworks.

German leaders disagreed about whether, especially for the Visegrad states, full EC and NATO-WEU membership was a realistic goal even in the medium term. But all agreed that close security cooperation with the Soviet successor states, especially Russia, would be a constant priority, as would substantial economic assistance. Such cooperation was necessary at a minimum, given the history of German-Russian relations and the presence of Russian troops on former East German soil under the unification agreements until the end of 1994.

The Evolution of Outreach Efforts

All the national agendas just described contributed to shaping the evolution of Western outreach to the east. Because of a relative lack of a sense of urgency on the part of the West, however, advances in the outreach efforts were largely reactive to events in Russia. Outreach efforts can be separated broadly into three phases, each punctuated or initiated by events in Russia.

Phase One: Central Europe and Security Outreach, 1989–91

The first outreach phase is perhaps best described as the time of fundamental central European disappointment and Western disarray. To the central European reformers, the democratic wave of 1989 and 1990 that swept
first through Poland and Hungary, spilled over into a popular revolution in
East Germany and Czechoslovakia, and finally reached Romania and Bulgaria meant that there should be no further barriers to the Europe whole and
free that for so long had been the core of Western political rhetoric. Central
Europe, in the words of Vaclav Havel, could now "return home," could reclaim its European identity.[11] Democracy could emerge from the socialist
ruins; security was now to be pursued in common against a declining Soviet
threat; and CSCE principles toward political, social, and economic justice
could now be fully implemented.

Operationally, returning meant not only expectations of long-promised
Western economic and political assistance but, more important, claims for
membership in Western institutions. Most central Europeans saw EC membership as their primary goal, which translated into guaranteed access to their
first-order goal, economic security. Their initial calculus acknowledged the
economic disparity between their economic standing and that of the EC, but
they saw this as only more reason for large-scale assistance and direct EC
participation as soon as possible. With such aid, some asserted, the central
European economies, and especially the most advanced—Poland, Czechoslovakia, and Hungary—would be capable of paralleling the glittering successes of the EC in western European economic reconstruction in the 1950s
and 1960s, perhaps even by the end of the century.

Membership in a Western security organization was initially a less urgent
priority. The central European states had been among the most active in the
CSCE and continued for a while to see it as a natural forum. Most rejected
the prospect of direct NATO involvement, either because they preferred a
less-engaged role or because they saw little future for the organization.[12] As
hopes for a swift reinvigoration of the CSCE faded, there was increasing central European interest in a NATO security guarantee, if not in direct membership. Association with the WEU was also welcomed but was considered
less vital, given the increasing desire to be associated with a strong American military presence.

What the central Europeans clearly opposed was what at least some western European leaders preferred, the re-creation of the WTO on a more de-

mocratic but still isolated basis. In 1990, largely on Havel's initiative, Poland, Czechoslovakia, and Hungary launched the Visegrad group to expand cooperation among the three (later four, with the Czecho-Slovak divorce) states, including questions of security.[13] These states also participated in an Italian-sponsored effort, the Pentagonale, which emerged in 1990 and 1991 as a broader-based regional grouping for economic and environmental cooperation.[14] But a central aim of central Europeans' interest in both groups was to harmonize their approach to Western institutions, not to create a new military alliance or a substitute for direct EC membership.

Most of the initial Western outreach was focused on central Europe and was managed primarily by the EC.[15] The first steps were taken before the Wall fell, at the June 1989 G-7 summit in Paris, where the European Commission assumed responsibility for coordinating Western aid for the rapidly reforming Poland and Hungary.[16] By December the EC launched the PHARE (Pologne-Hongrie: actions pour la réconversion économique) initiative to offer concrete aid in sectoral restructuring.[17] More extensive assistance and market access were covered under the Europe agreements that the EC concluded in 1991 with almost all the central European states. In addition, in 1990, to funnel public money to private sector development in all these states, Europe founded and became the largest funder of the European Bank for Reconstruction and Development (EBRD).[18]

But two European assumptions about outreach quickly became evident. First, the central European states were virtually alone in envisaging even a mid-term timetable for their inclusion within the EC. Commission president Jacques Delors spoke for the majority of the EC membership when he declared that "deepening" within the EC had to take precedence over "widening" into central Europe for the foreseeable future.[19] Any expansion would favor the European Free Trade Association neutrals—Austria, Sweden, Norway, Finland, Switzerland, and Iceland—long in the EC waiting line.

The central European states also soon discovered that, even with the Europe agreements, market access to the Community was not going to be smooth or unproblematic. The resistance of the "little Europe" protectionist bloc led Hungary and Poland to threaten to walk out of negotiations on the Europe agreements unless some measure of equitable market access was allowed the central European states.[20]

Despite assurances, the EC itself limited full access to the common market by formal and informal means. The continuing recession in western Europe slowed the flow of private investment to the central European states, and each one struggled to maintain even a mildly negative trade balance with the Community. The winter of 1992–93, for example, saw continuing protests about the violation of EC rules through the "protected" import of cheaper goods from central Europe, including steel, textiles, and agricultural products.

Second, the Community clearly preferred to differentiate between the Visegrad states and the other CEE states. Outreach to the Baltics was a political, not an economic issue, one that increased in importance only as Baltic efforts to assert their independence from the Soviet Union increased. Most of the EC states were pleased to leave the primary support burden to the Scandinavian countries, especially Sweden, and to the EU Baltic neighbors, Denmark and Germany. Moreover, Bulgaria and Romania were clearly always in an inferior bargaining position compared with the Visegrad states. (See figure 4-1.) The Europe agreements, for example, were concluded with the Visegrad states in December 1991, whereas negotiations had barely begun with Romania and Bulgaria by that time.[21] In addition, the Visegrad countries enjoy a disproportionate share of G-24 aid,[22] and commitments to them accounted for 59.8 percent of all commitments by the EBRD through 1993.

Finally, European and EC relations with the Soviet Union were unquestionably in a separate category. (See figure 4-2.) Despite a total aid program that far exceeded the efforts of the Bush administration, few European leaders then or later foresaw immediate Russian progress toward either political or market reform.[23] The EC in particular showed more interest in leaving assistance to Russia to national initiatives, such as the substantial German aid and investment program, than on continuing high levels of general economic support.[24] The EU has announced no plans to negotiate an association agreement with Russia or other CIS members and in fact only recently completed a Partnership and Cooperation agreement with Russia.[25] Similarly, EBRD disbursements to CEE have consistently outpaced disbursements to Russia.[26] (See figure 4-3.)

But the EU's focus on the CEE is most apparent in the level of assistance provided through its two special economic aid programs for the regions, PHARE and TACIS (technical assistance to the Commonwealth of Independent States and Georgia). Following a trend begun in 1990, the EU allocated ECU 1.04 billion to PHARE for 1993, compared with ECU 510 million for TACIS (see figure 4-4). These economic efforts constituted the bulk of Western outreach efforts in the phase-one period. Formal security links in

Figure 4-1. Net Flows of Foreign Direct Investment into Eastern Europe and Russia, 1990-93

Millions of U.S. dollars

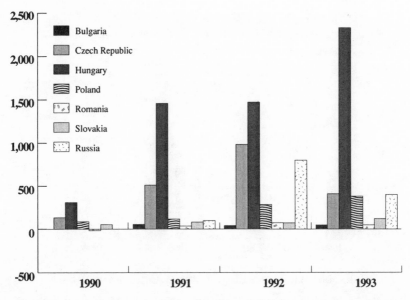

SOURCE: UN Economic Commission for Europe, *Economic Survey of Europe in 1993-1994*, New York and Geneva: United Nations, 1994. 1990 figure for Russia not available; 1993 figures for Bulgaria and Slovakia are estimates; 1993 figures for Czech Republic are Poland exclude December.

this period were only occasionally a primary focus of attention. NATO's outreach at the London 1990 summit and afterward was only to establish direct ties with the former members of the WTO, to promote exchanges and the representation of the Soviet Union and the other CEE states at NATO headquarters. There were also many bilateral contacts, as well as a coordinated rush to adapt the CFE treaty to enable independent central European voices and to arrive at a reallocation of the equipment levels that had been previously set for Soviet equipment and forces. The Western European Union was largely interested in the potential for later dialogue, which was on the edges of its organizing effort in western Europe. The CSCE was in some sense the default organization.

The growing nationalist pressures in the Soviet Union and the apparent failure of Gorbachev to mobilize against them did lead in mid-1991 to a clear

Figure 4-2. European Union Trade Flows with Central Europe and Russia, 1990–93[a]

A IMPORTS TO THE EU FROM CENTRAL EUROPE AND RUSSIA

Millions of U.S. dollars

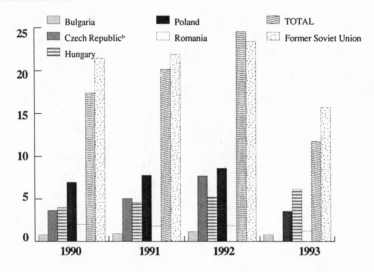

B EXPORTS FROM THE EU TO CENTRAL EUROPE AND RUSSIA

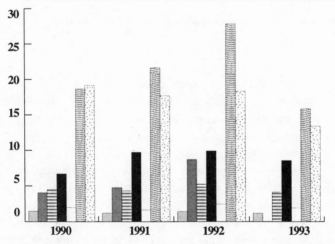

a. 1993 percent statistics are through September only.
b. The Czech Republic and Slovakia figure for 1993 is an estimate based on 0 percent growth in 1993.

SOURCE: International Monetary Fund, Directon of Trade Statistics (Washington, various years)

Figure 4-3. Commitment of the European Bank for Reconstruction and Development to Eastern Europe and the CIS and Baltic States, 1990-93

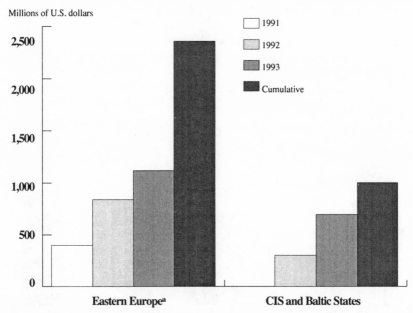

a. Includes Poland, Hungary, Czech Republic, Slovakia, Romania, Bulgaria, and Albania; excludes the former Yugoslavia.

SOURCE: UN Economic Commission for Europe, *Economic Survey of Europe in 1993-1994*, p. 139.

NATO warning against pressure on central Europe. At its June Copenhagen summit, echoing German and American national statements, the NATO Council declared that NATO security was "inseparably linked" to the security of the central European states.[27] Moreover, though the exact nature of NATO's response was not described, the alliance would from then on regard "any intimidation or coercion" against central Europe as an issue of "direct and natural concern to NATO." But, overall, security issues were subordinated to economic assistance (primarily to central Europe) in the early years.

Phase Two: The Issues of Institutional Expansion, 1991–93

The fallout from the failed August 1991 coup attempt in Moscow, however, brought the security issue to the fore in dramatic terms. Even after all the plotters were eliminated, central Europeans were anxious about what

Figure 4-4. Funds Allocated for the TACIS and PHARE Programs by the European Community, 1990-93[a]

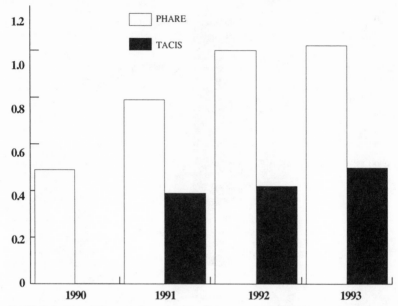

Billions of U.S. dollars

a. TACIS: Technical Assistance to the Commonwealth of Independent States; PHARE: Pologne-Hongrie: Actions Pour la Réconversion Économique.

SOURCE: © 1993 The Economist Newspaper Group, Inc. Reprinted with permission.

might have been, how reversible events in Russia might be, and how precarious their own security status was. More practically, the obvious end of the Gorbachev era led Washington and Bonn to push for a direct NATO initiative to expand the security transformation in the East, if possible to a point where the engagement of the East in a cooperative dialogue was assured. An October 1991 Baker-Genscher initiative for a new transatlantic charter was clearly designed to reassure the non-Soviet WTO members through the establishment of a North Atlantic Cooperation Council.

As adopted at NATO's December 1991 summit, the NACC was to involve the governments of the democratizing states as limited discussion partners in an ongoing security dialogue. It was not a new organization as such; it had no permanent organizational basis or rights to make presentations to the

North Atlantic Council or any other NATO bodies. Nor did the NACC participants receive any promise of full or even associate membership.[28]

True to French fears from the outset, however, the NACC's arrangements for formal liaison to NATO headquarters and the resulting discussions led to pressures for more substantive and operational interactions. The NACC soon evolved an ambitious seminar program and an even more ambitious work plan. By December 1992 cooperation in peacekeeping was added; by 1993 joint exercises were featured in the 1994 work plan.

Also, in keeping with cooperative security principles that rely increasingly on measures that transcend the military arena, the NACC developed economic and environmental components. The NACC's current economic priority is to promote defense conversion and in so doing increase civilian industrial output in central and eastern Europe. The NACC also incorporates a program of environmental cooperation that focuses on arms control technologies and environmental clean-up strategies, through a series of pilot programs under the auspices of the Committee on the Challenges of Modern Society.[29]

For all but its first few months, however, the NACC was principally a holding operation, a symbol of concern about security rather than an effective security dialogue.

The NACC's greatest challenge, and perhaps greatest barrier to becoming anything more than a useful forum, was the explosion in the number of participants. Adding Russia and the other FSU states meant that the NACC became almost as cumbersome as the CSCE. Yet the dialogue did not include all the states (most especially the EFTA neutrals) that could have helped its programs. Still, an unofficial NATO conference, NACC's seminars, formal visits, and demonstrations satisfied none of its most demanding participants. The Visegrad states, for example, complained about its "Asian " focus and lack of military substance appropriate to a true security dialogue, while the fledgling central Asian republics complained about the costs and difficulties of maintaining constant representation in Brussels.

Because the NACC is only an intergovernmental council, the effectiveness of the programs and exchanges is only commensurate with the enthusiasm of the governments. At a time of great uncertainty and talk of peace dividends, resources to strengthen East-West ties were far less plentiful than proposals to the same end. Consequently many of the suggested programs have languished in neglect. The NACC was in effect an interim solution to a long-term problem and has suffered because of that continuing orientation.

Efforts to reduce duplication were also countered by a new interest in a similar expansion of the WEU, largely fostered by Germany and France and clearly colored by the WEU-NATO organizational competition. Events in Russia, but also the delayed ratification of the Maastricht Treaty and a change in early 1993 in the French government, opened the way to reconsider links to central Europe. The WEU had already set up a special Forum of Consultation in June 1992, which was closely parallel to the NACC and was also to meet only twice a year as an intergovernmental conference. It had, however, initially only invited the five central European states (the Czech-Slovak divorce was not completed until January 1, 1993) and the Baltic republics, clearly closing the door on any further extension eastward. Should the threshold not have been clear, Prime Minister Edouard Balladur offered his "Pact on Stability in Europe" plan for a new, narrower pan-European forum on urgent security issues (see the discussion in chapter 3). Even the offer to central Europe seemed partial; despite continuing German interest, there was no firm offer of associate status or option for direct WEU participation before or without EC membership itself.[30]

On June 21, 1993, the EC at its Copenhagen summit offered an invitation for full membership at an unspecified future date to the four Visegrad states, as well as to Romania and Bulgaria if they also met the political and economic criteria.[31] Negotiations were to begin clearly after the admission of the EFTA states (presumably in 1995). There was neither promise nor real expectation that all six would enter at once. But the six were granted immediate trade concessions in critical export areas, which thus alleviated some of the pressures on economic development and reconstruction.

After the Copenhagen EC pledge on membership, pressure increased on NATO both to take a decision on expansion and to specify the criteria states would have to meet to become candidates for membership. Many, including leaders in Poland and Hungary, had come to the conclusion that they had equal or even better chances for accession to NATO because of the value the NATO countries would place on the military contribution the CE states could make from the start. The NACC was clearly not a framework to organize cooperative peacekeeping; this perhaps presented an opportunity to agree at least on the steps to both operational cooperation and formal membership in NATO. The involvement of Hungary as a base for AWACS surveillance of the Bosnian no-fly zone and the inclusion of Russian and Ukrainian troops in the UN Protection Force (UNPROFOR) both demonstrated the contributing role these states could play in what could well become NATO's primary peacetime mission.

Phase Three: The Birth of the PFP

Additional Moscow events, the Yeltsin-parliament standoff and the growing political mobilization of the Russian nationalists in the spring and summer of 1993, once again galvanized the discussion of organizational expansion and the criteria for the extension of membership. Once again the demands of the Visegrad states for reassurance were the most constant and the most intense, given further encouragement by the support of some of the German political class.

The Russian reaction to Visegrad demands was muddled at best. Interviewed in an August visit to Poland and to the Czech republic, President Yeltsin seemed to suggest that Russia would not have major objections to their NATO membership.[32] A retraction followed swiftly, coupled with various statements by Yeltsin, Foreign Minister Andrei Kozyrev, and others that either Russia should also and simultaneously join NATO, or there should be no NATO expansion but rather a continued reliance on Russian-American direction, the CSCE, the NACC, or collective cooperation only in specific areas such as peacekeeping.

The October 1993 confrontation in Moscow dramatically reinforced the clearest signal to emerge from this confusion of voices and messages: the danger that NATO expansion might leave Russia isolated and thus hasten the defeat of democratic leaders who supported continued cooperation with the West. Yeltsin himself emerged from the crisis measurably weakened and significantly indebted for his survival to a Russian military that generally opposed the extension of NATO membership to the former WTO states and wanted at most an equal relationship of Russia with the West.

The Western response came relatively quickly. The Partnership for Peace initiative, largely an American invention, was first floated by Secretary of Defense Les Aspin at the informal October 1993 meeting of NATO defense ministers at Travemuende, Germany.[33] The PFP initiative was instantly surrounded by controversy. Many, including some in the Clinton administration, saw it primarily as a means of not offending or isolating the Russians; indeed some saw it as a way to avoid further discussion of an expansion of NATO's membership. The secondary aim was accomplishing useful military cooperation, perhaps overtaking the level of the ongoing planning for the Bosnian settlement contingency and the operational coordination under UN-PROFOR.

The loudest voices, however, came from those who disapproved of the initiative. Perhaps the most dismissive were the "little Europe" backers, who saw it only as another public relations gimmick, the NACC by another name, or an American fad that would be useful only if it kept Congress somewhat more interested in retaining the American NATO commitment and the 100,000 troops in Europe. France feared that the PFP would be one more concession to the NATO integrated command and tried, without much support or success, to ensure that the PFP was directly controlled by the North Atlantic Council rather than by the NATO defense ministers. Critics in the United States dismissed it as too little, since it denied immediate membership to central European states or gave Russia a new veto right over the candidacies of the morally deserving Visegrad states.[34] Russian comments ranged from the outright rejection of Russian participation to those who saw it as too little for Russia's central security requirements.[35]

Officially approved at NATO's Brussels summit in January, 1994, the PFP was an invitation for military cooperation extended to the "willing" among the NACC membership and to other interested states in the CSCE. Its aim was not to draw new lines of confrontation but to allow alliance support for the transformation of nonmember military establishments interested in future joint military operations for peaceful purposes, especially in peacekeeping and humanitarian missions.[36] The channel was to be bilateral agreements between NATO and the candidate countries, outlining particular areas and levels of defense cooperation for an explicit period. There would also be regular military representation in a joint PFP planning and coordination cell, located ultimately in Mons, Belgium, near but not within SHAPE headquarters.

Secretary Aspin's argument was that in contrast to the all-inclusive approach of the NACC, the PFP was a self-paced and a self-selecting program. States whose ultimate goal was NATO membership would begin with the PFP, which would allow them to shape their doctrines and practices to NATO standards according to their own timetables and resources. Ultimately, converging or compatible policy choices and military organization might make the specifics of membership less urgent or represent a clear behavioral standard by which to judge among candidates for admission. Some countries might never meet the behavioral standards; others might choose not to go beyond PFP cooperation.

By the fall of 1994 twenty-three countries, including Russia, had signed initial PFP agreements.[37] Russia's participation was by far the most discussed and the most difficult. Russian policy interest waxed and waned all spring, with arguments by Russians about why membership was not desirable[38] and repeated official voices explaining why Russia would never be interested in joining the PFP.

One dramatic assessment was given by Sergei Karaganov:

> Russia already has many elements of the Weimar situation—a feeling of national humiliation due to the dissolution of the Soviet Union, high inflation, growing unemployment, and the low and falling living standards of large groups of the population. The only factor missing is the feeling of being unfairly treated by other countries. No one could question the right of NATO to widen its membership or of East Central European nations to apply for NATO membership. But the price could be the creation of a fully fledged Weimar syndrome in Russia.[39]

Dates for Russian accession were predicted and then withdrawn. Finally in May came a formal presentation at NATO headquarters by Defense Minister Pavel Grachev of proposals for additional functions or related bilateral cooperation to recognize Russia's special role and its particular needs.[40] He called for a "full-blooded strategic relationship with NATO," one that built on but went beyond the "usual" PFP framework and allowed especially for a broader consultative mandate on strategy, disarmament, and nuclear issues. Grachev also insisted on describing the future of the PFP as parallel to a possible future evolution of the CIS on former Soviet territory, with both eventually to be incorporated into a CSCE-like framework.

Grachev's proposals were immediately and publicly rejected by NATO leaders; Russia would have to sign the same type of PFP agreement as the other twenty states that had already joined. Further negotiations followed under the impending deadline of the Naples G-7 meeting and the EU summit at Corfu, at which the Yeltsin government hoped to present new evidence of cooperation and association.[41] Finally on June 22, 1994, Russia signed the PFP but with an accompanying NATO "conclusions" communiqué.[42] In areas where Russia has "unique and important contributions to make, commensurate with its weight as a major European, international, and nuclear power," there would be an "enhanced dialogue" through information sharing, political consultations, and cooperation, including in peacekeeping.

In the end, perhaps the greatest measure of formal outreach to the East came in the WEU. In May 1994, in the Kirchberg declaration, the WEU Council offered the CE states and the Baltics full associate status. Moreover, beginning in June most WEU Council meetings were to include both full members and associate members, with regular military consultation and exchanges through the permanent national military representatives in Brussels.[43] The WEU declared that these were part of the preparatory steps toward membership (acquis Européene) in the EU and promised speedy and comprehensive progress.[44]

The Partnership for Peace: Vehicle for Cooperation

In operational terms, most of the twenty-three states that have signed up for the PFP have now met the initial requirements for participation. All have signed the Framework Document, which outlines the rights, procedures, and requirements of PFP members vis-à-vis the alliance (the 16 + 1 formula, which provides for bilateral discussions between NATO [the 16] and the PFP applicant [the 1]) and that guarantees partner states the right of access to the North Atlantic Council if the partner perceives a direct threat to its territorial integrity, political independence, or security. More than half have already negotiated and submitted the national Presentation Document, which outlines the scope, pace, and level of participation in cooperative activities with the alliance, in such fields as peacekeeping, search and rescue, and humanitarian operations.[45] The final step, not yet completed by many in the months since the January 1994 summit, is the individual partnership program for which appropriate national personnel, assets, facilities, and capabilities are pledged to cooperative functions, again requiring approval of the 16 + 1.

Partner states are also taking up the invitation to establish liaison offices at NATO headquarters in Brussels for the PFP. They all may have permanent representation in the Partnership Planning Cell, established under a military director and located at Mons, Belgium, where SHAPE is headquartered and where presumably parallel Combined/Joint Task Forces planning will also take place. There have and will continue to be frequent national-alliance discussions, usually involving national defense establishments and the NATO international staff. There are also scheduled meetings for all the partner states, of necessity closely paralleling the NACC meetings at the intergovernmental level.

Five basic commitments enter into force on a signing of the PFP Framework Document.[46] First, as members of NATO have done since the alliance's inception, all members of the PFP will be trained and encouraged to comply with disclosure in military planning and in national military budgets, thus enhancing military and economic transparency across all of Europe. The standard will not be quite equal to that achieved by most NATO members in the defense planning questionnaire exercise, but it still represents a radical and somewhat uncomfortable departure for the CEE militaries. Second, PFP members are pledged to promote democratization of their militaries, which, in practical terms, will mean implementing reliable systems of civilian control over military decisionmaking, especially over planning and institutions.[47]

The remaining requirements are fundamental to future military cooperation. Eligible PFP participants must be constitutionally permitted to participate in multilateral operations, either through the CSCE or the UN. Operational compatibility will also be essential, although that has less to do with NATO's long-desired equipment standardization than it does with establishing compatible modes of communication and command structures and congruent equipment that will not impede side-by-side operations in joint missions. Finally, PFP states agree to produce forces to a military operational standard that will allow joint military exercises and planning with NATO forces in all appropriate areas of operations.

Many of the first-year PFP programs look similar, offering a series of seminars, activities, and joint exercises. Negotiations on the Presentation Documents themselves were an educational process, with the NATO international staff often having to help scale back overoptimistic programs for joint exercises or to prod countries to consider the range of capabilities beyond "parade units" that effective cooperation with NATO will require. Further evolution will now be tailored to the capabilities and the expectations of each partner state, especially as reflected in the defense planning and review strategy it works out with NATO Headquarters and the limits of domestic approval for cooperation with the alliance. As time passes and various states reach different levels of compliance, it will presumably be possible for NATO to distinguish between states that are genuinely eager and able to participate, having compatible interests, from those that are participating now but that have no realistic interest in or readiness for full NATO membership. (See table 4-1 for the PFP signatories.)

The initial exercises to include the PFP's expanded membership took place in the fall of 1994. The first was a field exercise in Poland, involving nearly one thousand troops from thirteen countries. More limited exercises were held at sea off the Norwegian coast and on the ground in the Netherlands. Not all partner states have participated. Russia, for example, took part in the naval exercise but proved far more interested in and sensitive to, both positively and negatively, the summer 1994 "Peacekeeper" exercise with the United States.

Table 4-1. PFP Signatories as of October 12, 1994

Country	Date	Country	Date
Romania	January 26, 1994	Georgia	March 23, 1994
Lithuania	January 27, 1994	Slovenia	March 30, 1994
Poland	February 2, 1994	Azerbaijan	May 4, 1994
Estonia	February 3, 1994	Finland	May 9, 1994
Hungary	February 8, 1994	Sweden	May 9, 1994
Ukraine	February 8, 1994	Turkmenistan	May 10, 1994
Slovakia	February 9, 1994	Kazakhstan	May 27, 1994
Latvia	February 14, 1994	Kyrgyzstan	June 1, 1994
Bulgaria	February 14, 1994	Russian Federation	June 22, 1994
Albania	February 23, 1994	Uzbekistan	July 13, 1994
Czech Republic	March 10, 1994	Armenia	October 5, 1994
Moldova	March 16, 1994		

Source: NATODATA, electronic mail transmission, October 13, 1994.

The actual exercise, though, may not be the principal benefit. As one official interviewed said, "By the time we get to the exercise we will already have gotten most of the benefit—just in all the steps we have had to take to plan and coordinate with one another. We all have to learn a lot about one another."[48]

There were, of course, a number of start-up difficulties. There is still, for example, disagreement within the United States interagency process on how to implement the PFP, with the Department of Defense and the Department of State having somewhat different agendas and versions of the PFP's purpose. Moreover, the division of labor between the previously established NACC work plan and the work plan for the PFP was not clearly established; indeed some of the earlier NACC projects reappeared as PFP activities.[49] Russian grumbling about eventual expansion of NATO membership out of the PFP has continued.[50]

The PFP would appear, however, to have achieved many of its short-term goals: it allows for the possibility of self-selecting membership and expands cooperation, stability, and transparency, and it has done all this without so far having to face a forced choice on membership or to alienate Russia. It operates within the NACC intergovernmental framework, which allows still for broad consultation, but it is more attuned to individual national capabilities and potential for membership and involves defense establishments directly. From the West's perspective at least, the PFP has managed the slippery balance between recognizing the progress and real contributions of the

CE states and allowing Russia sufficient room for maneuver and encouragement for participation.

But just like the NACC before it, the PFP faces serious political and operational impediments that NATO must resolve in order for the PFP to have the desired long-term effects. First, a clear discrepancy exists between proposals and resources. Although the signatories have been invited to set up their offices in Brussels and Mons to enhance military and political contacts, space and start-up funds were initial problems. Despite the self-starter emphasis, some participants clearly need funding even to carry out the initial schedule of activities. They surely need it to bring existing equipment or to buy new equipment—communications above all—to an operational standard that allows cooperation with NATO forces. President Clinton's offer of just over $100 million in Poland is only the first deposit.[51]

Second is the continuing Franco-American disagreement on how to structure particular PFP programs. France is ever fearful of increasing the influence of SHAPE and the American-dominated integrated command at the expense of the North Atlantic Council and any potential European effort. It wanted, for example, to limit the mandate of the Mons military planning cell, making it independent of SHAPE but subordinate to the NAC. Most other allies and certainly the United States favored having the cell closely associated with the SHAPE planning process. That particular dispute has been resolved through eventual compromise and some artful language, but the basic issues continue to reemerge whenever political control is in question.

Third, the PFP's implementation is further complicated by operational questions. One planning issue is how PFP activities should relate to the ongoing plans for the Combined/Joint Task Forces. There is still little agreement on the specifics of designing forces that can constitute a separable but not separate military capability under European or at least non-NATO command. The terms on which PFP troops and equipment might also be available have to be factored in, in terms both of peacekeeping and of humanitarian missions.

Fourth, and most important, are the outstanding political challenges. The PFP faces a difficult political agenda almost immediately. It is not just that the Visegrad countries are complaining bitterly about the slow pace of the PFP's evolution. They unquestionably will continue to push for membership; indeed, the PFP at its highest point of evolution will never satisfy what the CEE states see as their right to full article 5 security guarantees. It is rather that the PFP is in many respects an unstable hybrid, still seen as a clever compromise to buy time in the short term but under pressure from all sides regarding its longer-run evolution. NATO in many respects is also a cautious bureaucracy, committed to consensus and slow change, to a slow, steady pace of achieving agreement and detailed attention to all the items on which agreement is necessary. To be successful, the PFP must have a different timetable, one that shows significant change and measurable evolution in the very near term. This requires a full agenda of activities, major political pushes, and NATO-partner military interactions that lead to measurable effects and cumulative change. Equipment, training, exchanges, language instruction, budgetary standardization, and particularly NATO-like defense planning techniques are all required—and as soon as possible.

But the hurdles being set from the NATO side are many. The bureaucracy is slow to change, unaccustomed to dealing simultaneously with so many new tasks and responsibilities with so many states at different levels of development. They and certain member states are extremely sensitive to the expenditures of resources for the PFP that might have been used for NATO projects within the NATO area or for NATO's "real purpose," improved collective defense to fulfill article 5 guarantees. Moreover, some NATO members, especially those that are less enthusiastic about a rapid expansion of membership, want a continuous, rigorous demonstration of NATO standards, not just seminars and activities at the relatively introductory level favored so far in the NACC. The burden of proof in their minds lies with the PFP states themselves and the actions they take on their own in force structures, budgets, and planning to make themselves attractive partners and later perhaps membership candidates.

Finally, a consensus is clearly lacking on the specifics of the link, if one exists, between the PFP and eventual NATO membership, and the countries to which the membership option will be extended. The divergent viewpoints were sharply delineated in September in Berlin by German defense minister Ruehe and U.S. secretary of defense William J. Perry.[52] Ruehe spoke of membership for central Europe but not for Russia or other states on the territory of the former Soviet Union. Perry insisted that the door must be left open for Russia even if the Russians themselves decide they do not wish to join.

Conclusion

In late 1994 prospects for increasing Western security outreach to the east, while seemingly more improvised than planned, should be viewed with cautious optimism. The European Union process is under way, the commitment to membership for the qualified has been made, and broad security cooperation is clearly one of the areas for harmonization. The PFP has successfully walked a fine line between offering security assurances to central Europe and avoiding the isolation of Russia. It stops short of guaranteeing the security of central European states, which could well be viewed as a threat by Russian nationalists and military leaders, yet it still encourages those states to strive for Western security norms: transparency and cooperation. It points out a realistic path of achievement for those states that show the capability for eventual full membership, but it also has at least the potential of broadening practical military cooperation between partners and members in all phases of European security.

Yet even with the relative success of the EU and the PFP, the outreach program of the West, seen as a whole, cannot be considered a smashing success. The track record of Western assistance to date has been shaky at best, in form as well as in substance. From the beginning, Western powers took an evolutionary approach to outreach. Basking in the glow of having "won" the cold war, they were slow to recognize that perhaps the greatest challenge was (in the words of George Bush) to "win the peace." As a result, outreach programs were essentially reactionary. Instead of Western leaders taking the initiative and setting the pace of reform, their decisions were driven by events in Russia. Thus phase one of Western outreach, the PHARE and TACIS assistance programs and the Europe agreements, were tempered by a lack of interest and commitment and knee-jerk protectionism.

Events in Russia then forced the West to change tack to a phase two, which paid more attention to security concerns, but only at a consultative level. Once again, Western initiative stopped there (at the NACC and WEU consultations) until events in Russia—this time the Yeltsin-parliament conflict—again forced a change by highlighting the dangers of isolating Russia from European security regimes. The resulting PFP and WEU offers of associate status indicate another lurch forward in Western outreach to central Europe and Russia and the CIS. But even with this progress, it is felt that the West has given the minimum it could afford and that these measures will prove more than inadequate in the long run.

What, then, does the future hold? Future considerations for East-West relations must consider two overriding realities. The first is that central Europe is interested in security regimes only as a second best mechanism for reintegration into the West. Central European countries have consistently said that their first priority is and will be EU membership. They have pursued NATO or WEU membership only when the EU firmly shut the door to the "common European house" in their collective face.[53] Security concerns have become more important, as Russian reform proves far from certain. While CE states have undoubtedly benefited from the PFP and related programs, their long-term development is still predicated on economic and political stability, something EU membership, with its tighter standards of integration and its greater resources for cooperative economic support, would go much further toward securing. Thus it is imperative that the EU pay more attention and invest more political, not to mention financial, capital into eventually admitting central European states into the fold.

The second, and most important, concern is that sooner or later Russia may be in a position to reexert itself over its traditional spheres of influence. The Bear may be sickly at present, but it still has an image of itself as a military superpower, an image buttressed by the possession of nuclear weapons, if not of a cohesive ready conventional force equal to its former capability. A Russian need to regain influence is already being discerned by some in the West because of Russia's stronger statements about its rights and responsibilities in the near abroad and especially about its unique role in peacekeeping in the CIS. Although a more realistic fear seems the fragmentation of the Russian military and a subsequent descent into warlordism, it is critical that the West not isolate Russia from European security. The choice is essentially one of either isolating a Weimar-like Russia or rebuilding and including a renewed Russia in the manner of German rehabilitation after World War II.

The PFP is a good beginning. Yet as it stands, the PFP alone will be inadequate to the task of broadening collective security in Europe eastward. Already it is being overtaken by events. Poland, fresh from the success of the joint exercises held in September 1994, is calling much more forcefully for serious negotiations over full NATO membership. But there seems to be a real deficit of political will on the part of the West for widening NATO membership. In mid-1994 some in Washington made a significant effort to give substance to President Clinton's assertion that expansion was a question of when and how, not whether.[54] NATO protagonists on both sides of the Atlantic proved less than enthusiastic (to be charitable) over the prospect of enlargement in the short term; most indeed saw it first in parallel with EU expansion by 2003 or 2005, or for some candidate countries even later. Any serious effort to extend mutual defense arrangements will, they argued, mean more money and effort. These will be needed both to bring the partners up to NATO standards and to ensure that in the intervening period—perhaps a longer period than the decade it took West Germany to reach full capability—there is no further decrease in the present capabilities of the member states. To do less or require less of new members would mean turning NATO into a variant of a loose collective security arrangement with political, not military, guarantees and abandoning the true basis of security cooperation so hard won over four decades.

If NATO is unwilling to expand formal membership in the short then run, the best option would still seem the intensification of the PFP, especially in creating real opportunities for cooperation and growth for those countries, the Visegrad at least, with which the alliance foresees closer cooperation. It means having serious planning dialogues, cumulative exercise programs, joint discussions and training between the most powerful alliance members and the partner states. These would include, for example, taking steps to coordinate the ongoing U.S. joint contact team program to make it focus more effectively on helping the militaries of the CEE and FSU states to improve their capacity to operate alongside NATO forces in future operations, as envisioned in the CJTF concept. Other national assets, such as the U.S. Marshall Center in Germany, can also be used to foster greater understanding and habits of cooperation within Europe as a whole.

Probably the best approach would be to strengthen the overall Partnership for Peace program in and for itself. The PFP as a concept has great potential, but to succeed it means creating new opportunities for all the partners, the potential members, and those that will not become members. Above all else it means an enhanced security dialogue with Russia on all levels—16 + 1, multilateral, bilateral—to avoid Russia's isolation and to engage its identity publicly as an actor in European security operations. True cooperative efforts mean that this is not just a task for the United States alone but that national assets from NATO countries need to be pooled and applied in a more organized way.

If such changes can be accomplished, they would give the PFP more legitimacy as a cooperative organization in its own right. Further, the changes made (transparency, civilian control of defense budgets) and the linkages formed (joint training exercises, common command and communications structures, and institutionalized dialogue between militaries) could well obviate the need for formal NATO membership. The PFP is currently a halfway house, a marked improvement over the model of the NACC but of necessity only a pathway to potential membership and a framework to be filled in with cooperative security measures and greater transparency. The opportunity exists now to transform it into a new "common home" for mutual efforts to safeguard European security. That opportunity should not be missed.

5

Operational Choices: The Management of Conflict and Peacemaking Outside Europe

Another major issue of post–cold war politics of European security is considerably less positive: the inconclusive and often irresponsible debate over the management of conflict and peacemaking outside Europe. Since the Berlin Wall fell, two major crises have occurred—the Iraqi invasion of Kuwait and the exploding conflicts in the former Yugoslavia—to test the willingness of the NATO–European Community states to respond together to violence and threats to security outside Europe. Each has presented a different challenge to the conceptions and the decisionmaking patterns left over from the cold war concerning the response to out-of-area violence. Each too was a crucial probe of the will in the West for cooperative political and military action, with fairly discouraging results. Organizational capacity for collective action has meant little without the willingness to take action; elaborate procedures have remained hollow in the absence of joint decisions and commitments to joint risk taking.

In many respects this situation is a clear continuation of cold war patterns. Over its four decades of experience, NATO usually failed to reach a consensus on cooperative military action outside its geographic area. Despite significant pressure from the United States, NATO took no action on Lebanon in 1958, on Vietnam in the 1960s and 1970s, or on Lebanon or Libya in the 1980s. Each member state was free to take national action; all military operations and attempts at peacemaking took place outside the alliance framework. The experience of the EC was roughly similar. The major achievements were common declarations, not actions; consensus not to act, especially under pressure from the United States, was often easier to attain than a commitment to take or support military or diplomatic cooperation.

The pattern of decisionmaking, at least in the Iraqi case and in Somalia, demonstrated great continuity. In both instances, the United States made clear its willingness to act and to exercise leadership almost from the outset. It took the initiative to organize and lead an ad hoc coalition, eventually involving some of the principal European states but outside the NATO framework and with only minimal involvement of the Western European Union–EC framework as such. Perhaps the most striking change from the past was the decision in each case, at the beginning, to seek legitimacy through a UN mandate.

Conflict in the former Yugoslavia, which I focus on the most, represents a new, more mixed case: the greatest ongoing risk to Europe's stability and a dramatic challenge to post-Wall hopes for a new, more cooperative international environment. These difficult issues have arisen out of the savage violence and destruction and the spillover of three years of fighting on Europe's threshold, the lengthiest armed conflict in the region since World War II. Moreover, in 1990 the situation in Yugoslavia was a test of conflict resolution capacity that the EC sought for itself as evidence of its new-found solidarity in foreign and security policy. As the crisis in Bosnia has evolved, the situation has become an ever-increasing test of the possibilities and the risks of broader security cooperation under NATO's article 4. The lessons learned as well as the outcome of the conflict itself will cast shadows long into the future for the alliance, for the European Union and its major state members, and for the nascent post–cold war international order.

At the end of 1994 there are encouraging signs of organizational adaptation and military learning. But the political agenda is still daunting and unresolved. None of the major institutional frameworks—NATO, the European Union, or the UN—provide a present basis for anything more than case-by-case cooperation and the slow mobilization of capabilities, diplomatic as well as military. The search for a single "forcing" architecture, or even a single set of guidelines or criteria for action, seems misplaced or at least very premature. The experience of the past five years suggests a need for a wide range of instruments adaptable to a broad spectrum of crisis and conflict situations. Some of the unexpected successes indeed have been the limited crisis-dampening procedures applied through the Conference on Security and Cooperation in Europe and the Council of Europe. But what is needed most is the political will to act, to commit resources and influence to the process of conflict resolution.

Three years of failed cease-fires and political negotiations in the former Yugoslavia also make dramatically clear how difficult the management of conflict and peacemaking is, and will continue to be, compared with the patterns of the cold war. One decisive lesson has been learned: organizational capacity needs to exist to permit timely response but is no guarantee of action in the absence of strong political will or perceived national interest. Democracies are slow to act; coalitions of democracies may well be slower still. State decision remains paramount; the issue is how to secure a commitment to act together among at least "the willing," if not every EU or NATO member. Most important of all is the issue of leadership, a task that now falls to the United States by assertion but also by default. France is currently the only European source of leadership and strategic thinking. No other European government seems to have the resources or the enduring interest to exercise such a role or to commit the resources needed to sustain it.

But the critical question is still the goals to be sought and the burden to be shouldered and shared. Is the relevance of conflict outside Europe to the maintenance of European security to be sought in its proximity, in its capacity for spillover in terms of both violence and refugees? Does it turn on a core set of values and interests, or is it a function of the "CNN factor," the direct mobilization of public sympathy and involvement that forces governments to respond cooperatively? And what share of the burden is to be borne by Europe? The United States? Russia? Under what cooperative conditions and constraints?

The Gulf War and Its Lessons

Before turning to the former Yugoslavia, it is instructive to look at an earlier case of cooperative action. The Iraqi invasion of Kuwait in 1990–91, the first instance of U.S.-European cooperation in a post–cold war military crisis, saw the largest mobilization of military force in several decades. The United States was clearly in the lead, cooperating with a few willing allies and orchestrating both the diplomatic and the relatively brief military phases of the mission to expel Iraq from Kuwait. This case illuminates critical problems in the U.S.-European relationship and the parameters set for cooperative action in response to crisis and war outside the formal NATO area covered by article 5 guarantees.

Actions in the Gulf War represented what President Bush liked to call a "defining moment" of the post–cold war era.[1] At stake in realpolitik terms were oil supplies and the denial of the fruits of aggression to Saddam Hussein, who had threatened a regional balance perceived as favorable or at least not unfavorable to the West. Perhaps more important in the long run were the war's demonstration effects about what Bush had called the new world order. Whether valid or not, the decisions in the Gulf War became the measure against which foreign ministries and defense departments judged the need to adapt and transform. What were the specific roles dictated by the new post–cold war power hierarchy? Who would lead and who would follow? Whose participation was crucial and whose was merely status enhancing? What were the relative merits of sanctions versus the use of force to ensure compliance? What was the concrete value of the UN option? And what was the legitimate outcome to be sought in Iraq with respect to present punishment and constraints on future behavior?

The course of the Gulf War is so well known as to need little retelling here beyond a focus on the respective roles claimed by the United States, the European powers, and Russia. From the first days of the Iraqi invasion of Kuwait, the United States took the lead in organizing collective responses, initially with declarations, then with economic and political sanctions, and finally with the use of military force. The division within the Atlantic alliance, and especially French resistance and German unwillingness to take part in decisionmaking, led the United States to put particular reliance on the legitimizing power of the UN Security Council. Not only did Britain and France support the process resolution after resolution; they also provided the bulk of the largest and most effective non-U.S. forces that invaded Iraq and won Iraqi withdrawal.[2]

European efforts to exercise influence as the Community were generally unsuccessful, particularly in the attempts in the fall of 1990 to avoid the use of military force.[3] Without question, Europe had an overfull agenda: the unification of Germany just completed, the initial outreach to the East, the critical internal debates in the Intergovernmental Conference on Political Union that would ultimately lead to the Maastricht Treaty and the commitment to develop a European common foreign and security policy. But the Community was unable to act either to modify American decisionmaking or to use its own economic power to gain Iraqi compliance in withdrawal from Kuwait. Germany's self-absorption and its perceived political constraints against the use of force constituted a clear policy drag. But so too did the resistance of many other states to any involvement beyond economic sanctions, as well as their unwillingness to see this as a case in which Europe could or should act as a single entity.

To many observers it was the Gulf War experience as a whole that was ultimately the goad for Maastricht's emphasis on the creation of an effective

European defense identity.[4] There were some Community influences on the outcomes, especially in the postconflict decision to extend humanitarian assistance to the Kurds and to place aid activities under military protection. But this decision came largely as a result of British (and some German) pressure arising out of domestic political agitation. For the rest, there were only American choices and European responsibilities both to acquiesce in the conduct of the war and to pay for its costs. Europe expressed as the Community was unable to translate its political and economic status into effective influence over the United States, over the Iraqi-Kuwaiti protagonists, or even over the Turkish-Kurdish dispute. Moreover, the political cohesion that the EC and WEU did achieve in the prewar months rapidly broke apart once force was used. German elites, but also others, challenged the use of force as an instrument even of last resort in such a crisis, at least for Europe.

The Gulf War unquestionably demonstrated the relative military incapacity of the European allies. The only form of European military involvement consisted of British, French, and Italian national forces acting under the UN command and the WEU's coordination of a naval blockade to enforce the embargo imposed on Iraq. In almost every military dimension, the United States showed the "crushing superiority of its military power, its technological excellence."[5] European capabilities were simply not appropriate or quickly adaptable for this mission. In force structure, in their dependence on conscripts, and in their equipment, these were militaries still reflective of cold war patterns and assumptions of large-scale cooperative action on NATO's central front.

Britain and France were without question more capable and more flexible.[6] But the American military assets that dominated the war—long-range transport, communications, intelligence, and even antimissile defense—were not in European inventories or perhaps within its realistic grasp for budgetary reasons alone. France, in particular, emerged from the Gulf War with a new appreciation of how badly it had neglected its conventional capabilities to meet the budgetary demands of its nuclear force. Its military also came to understand how difficult it was ad hoc to achieve the command coordination that came so easily to British and American forces accustomed to NATO operations.

What the Europeans did achieve was a fairly rapid and inclusive ad hoc system to support a naval embargo. They built on the experience they had gained in an analogous embargo in 1987–88 during the Iran-Iraq conflict; the WEU indeed was coordinating the activities of more than twenty ships in the Gulf less than a month after the invasion of Kuwait and before a similar NATO force was introduced.[7] Europeans made decisions in common on rules of engagement, on logistical support for the national forces that were engaged, on support actions of all kinds immediately outside the conflict area, and on financial support for the war itself. They also set up coordination channels with the NATO commands that were involved in the redeployment of allied forces, in logistical support, and in communication and intelligence support. But these actions only highlighted the limitations of ad hoc structures and the lack of interoperability within the WEU, as well as the political divisions over outcomes.

The transatlantic disagreements were also clear but somewhat contradictory. American elites were also divided about the relative utility of sanctions versus the use of force to secure the withdrawal of Iraq. But they were somehow less tolerant of European debates and more inclined to downgrade European capacities to take action. The Bush administration, however, was also increasingly agitated about even the discussion of the demonstrated need for greater European autonomy, especially the outlines of the CFSP then being discussed. Indeed, only two days before the ground offensive in Desert Storm, the Bush government officially warned its European allies about the negative security consequences of too close an identity between the WEU and the Community.[8]

The Yugoslav Case

The relative lack of European initiative and leadership in the Gulf goes some way to explain Europe's prompt response to the emerging conflict in Yugoslavia and perhaps also its ultimate failure to deal with both crisis and then war in that country. The war in the former Yugoslavia embodies many unhappy firsts: the first test after the Maastricht Treaty of the European Community's CFSP, the first war in Europe since the early 1950s, the first postwar return to claims for ethnic purity as the legitimate basis for national state organization, the first atrocities committed systematically in post-Wall Europe, the first shots in anger fired by NATO, and the first WEU-coordinated mission in European space. All these firsts underscore the continuing inability to contain the crisis, mitigate conflict or its consequences, or end the war resulting from the fragmentation of the former Yugoslavia. (See figure 5-1 for a map of the former Yugoslavia; see the appendix to this chapter for a chronology of the crisis and conflict.)

Figure 5-1. The Former Yugoslavia, 1993

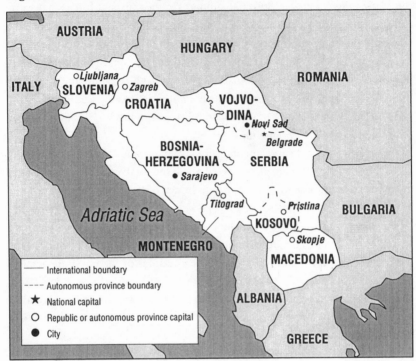

The Problems in Dealing with the Crisis

Yugoslavia is in the first instance a failure of European attempts at crisis management and dispute resolution, although there is enough blame for all parties to share after three years of violence, ethnic conflict, and massive human rights abuses.[9] The resolution of strife in Yugoslavia was a test that western Europe, particularly the states of the EC, set for themselves explicitly. The recognition of Slovenia and Croatia constituted the first united foreign policy acts of post-Maastricht Europe; unfortunately, they were also not only the proximate cause of intensified Serbian attacks against Croatia but also the progenitor of a repetition of the cycle of European recognition, intensified fighting, ethnic cleansing, and political stalemate in Bosnia that followed shortly.

In 1991 and 1992 the EC vision of European political cooperation impelled efforts to mediate the conflict, to arrange cease-fire after cease-fire,

to impose economic sanctions, to provide humanitarian assistance to inno-
cents caught in the bloodshed, and to manage the flood of refugees. All efforts were in vain and probably even exacerbated the level of violence and
destruction.[10] By early 1993 the EC finally turned to the UN for the establishment of global sanctions and to the establishment of the UN Protection
Force to provide monitoring and protection for humanitarian aid. By 1994
NATO had become an agent of increasingly harsh UN measures and the safe-
guarder of tenuous safe areas throughout Bosnia.

The reasons why western Europe accepted, and even sought, such a role,
were many.[11] In many senses the European states were victims of a special
kind of hubris. The flush of the achievement at Maastricht, the successful
completion of German unification, and the wave of democratic revolution in
central Europe were perhaps at their high points. The European insistence
on being the sole mediator in 1991–92 was founded in the self-confidence
and self-assertion that these achievements produced—and the unwillingness
to accept failure or admit inadequacy. Jacques Poos, the Luxembourg foreign minister, after the first seemingly successful cease-fire in Slovenia in
June 1991, summed up this Europhoria in grand fashion: "This is the hour
of Europe, not the hour of the Americans."[12]

Other causes were more usual or more predictable. Europe had failed to
achieve a common stance on the Gulf War; the situation in the former Yugoslavia would give the EU a chance to recoup and to demonstrate what the
CFSP, then in formation, could achieve. Also, there was a sense of indirect
threat: the possibility of Russia's intervention on the part of its traditional
ally Serbia, and the possibility of fracturing Europe along the fault lines of
traditional Balkan patronage—France and Britain with Serbia, Germany with
Croatia. And there was a genuine outpouring of humanitarian outrage. This
was especially prevalent in a unified Germany, sensitive as perhaps never
before to the need to recognize legitimate rights to self-determination.

In the United States, many were clearly willing to let Europe handle the
Yugoslav crisis on its own, and some felt a certain level of Schadenfreude
at the degree of European failure. The initial efforts of the Bush administration (already inadequate and tardy by some accounts) had been unsuccessful attempts to shore up the Yugoslav federation. Thereafter, the George
Bush–James Baker team condemned the violence and delayed formal recognition of the emerging states as long as it dared. Then it declared that the
United States had no vital national interest at stake that would require direct
American involvement in either conflict resolution or military intervention,

beyond that of assisting in the provision of humanitarian aid through airlifts. A policy against the introduction of American ground forces remained a constant, and though the Bush administration in 1992 did make a direct threat of retaliatory air strikes against Serbia in the event of aggressive action in Kosovo, the focus was on containment rather than military intervention. At the same time, while candidate Clinton's rhetoric promised some hope for more U.S. activism and leadership, President Clinton had discovered by early 1993 that few good options were left for either a peaceful or an interventionist solution.

On a more theoretical level, the Yugoslavia crisis raised questions about the future of Europe's cooperative security system in three crucial respects. First, for most of the early phases, concerns about the breakup of the unified Yugoslav state were fueled by far greater anxieties about the future of the then Soviet Union. Dramatic parallels were drawn between Yugoslavia and the Soviet Union. At issue were the degree of ethnic hostility, the role of the conservative excommunists, and the precedents the international community was setting regarding intervention into the domestic affairs of a state still formally sovereign.

Second, by the end of 1991 and the collapse of the Soviet Union, these fears were replaced by new worries about Yugoslavia as the first of an unending string of ethnic conflicts, especially along the periphery of the former Soviet Union. There were exaggerated arguments about cascading fragmentation throughout eastern and central Europe, the collapse of the "artificial" states constructed after World War I and World War II, and the exploitation or manipulation of the potentially explosive diasporas that had been created: Russian, Hungarian, Polish, and Ukrainian, to name only a few. The Yugoslav crisis seemed to legitimate once again the right to self-determination for all groups, however small, able to organize politically and to call into question the accepted CSCE tenet of no border changes without political agreements on all sides. Finally, concern was expressed in some circles in western Europe (notably Spain and the United Kingdom) that the improper handling of the Yugoslav crisis might lead to unacceptable precedents for international oversight of or intrusion into violent ethnic separatism within their own minority communities. Although this concern was probably more theoretical than actual, it still colored policymaking within some states (contributing later to friction over the recognition issue, among other things).

The Role of the European Community

All these concerns compelled the EC to act in a situation for which neither it nor any of the existing European security structures—beyond perhaps NATO—were equipped. The first action of the EC, mediating the Slovenian divorce from Yugoslavia, was fairly painless and created false hopes that Europe would be easily capable of handling ethnic and territorial conflict in post–cold war eastern Europe. The relative bloodlessness of the process (less than fifty dead on both sides) and the relative ease with which the Yugoslav army was convinced to "pack it in" led EC leaders to believe they could manage similar crises in Croatia and elsewhere. Yet what they failed to realize was that the situation in Slovenia was fundamentally different from that in Croatia and, later, in Bosnia. Slovenia was in the main ethnically homogeneous, whereas Croatia (and Bosnia to an even greater extent) had large Serbian minorities understandably fearful of a reduced political status and economic marginalization in a nationalist Croatian state and thus easily mobilized behind Serbian president Slobdan Milosevic's campaign to create a Greater Serbia. Similarly, although Slovenia could be split without necessarily threatening the dissolution of the entire Yugoslav federation, Croatia was the linchpin holding the federation together, the only counterweight with Bosnia to Serbian domination of the federation.

Mindless of these realities, in 1991 the EC accepted the burden of working for a cease-fire in the Serb-Croat conflicts and was (understandably) disappointed time after time. The Community under Lord Carrington organized a peace conference that met for several months. EC diplomats also tried to devise an arbitration mechanism for the settlement of disputes, to draw together ideas for the reconstitution of Yugoslavia on a more acceptable basis, and to develop more effective reporting and monitoring regimes.

Perhaps the most controversial Community decisions came late in 1991, when the EC extended full diplomatic recognition to Croatia and Slovenia. The principal impetus came from Germany, where domestic political outrage over nightly television reports on the violence in Yugoslavia and at least some of the feelings of helplessness of the Gulf War period led to a popular campaign for immediate recognition of Slovenia and Croatia.[13] This campaign moved forward, however, without any real recognition that force might be required to bring ultimate resolution and that German preferences would have to be weighed against the constraints on German involvement in the region, owing to the memories of Nazi occupation and alliance with a fascist

Croatian state fifty years earlier. Foreign Minister Genscher, himself a late convert to the recognition strategy pressed by domestic political forces, argued in the end that recognition of Slovenia and Croatia would allow comprehensive Community oversight over the pace and costs involved in the disintegration of the former Yugoslavia. This would not be true if the conflict remained simply a civil war. In what one account described as "a tortuous compromise to avoid an embarrassing rift within days of the Maastricht summit," the Community announced recognition by January 1992, only to have Germany move to independent recognition before Christmas 1991. That, in the view of some observers, made conflict over the division of Bosnia virtually inevitable.

Whatever the unanticipated consequences, the EC at least took action in the face of deafening silence from the Bush administration. Other institutions, especially the CSCE, could not even discuss the crisis until quite late, given Yugoslav membership and the unanimity procedures still in effect, as well as Soviet (after December 1991, Russian) opposition. But to paraphrase James Goodby's conclusions, EC actions in 1991–92 revealed both a Community deeply divided over whether to use armed force under any conditions and a Community that chose to deny itself most of the very few instruments of coercion it had had throughout most of the crucial period from July through October 1991.[14]

Europe's response in 1992 to the outrages in Bosnia reflected those divisions and were particularly ineffective. Despite popular outcries and increasing public pressure for European action, the general response within the EC and from member governments was an expression of grave concern and the imposition of economic sanctions, always with great operational diffidence and constant delay. The EC was most engaged, with only intermittent success, in monitoring a series of unsuccessful cease-fire attempts or in emergency humanitarian measures. The London peace process that started during the fall of 1992 included new cooperative elements for bringing about an end to the hostilities, such as the no-fly zone, the stationing of more European monitors under the UN, the use of NATO AWACS resources to provide greater information about compliance, and finally the Cyrus Vance–David Owen blueprint for the reconstitution of Bosnia drawn up under EC-UN auspices. Yet the few operational achievements paled in comparison with the magnitude of the crisis in human terms, and most EC leaders acknowledged that prospects for a peaceful resolution or even the mitigation of the war's effects on civilians were slight.

Perhaps the strongest stance in the crisis was taken by two national leaders, Presidents Bush and Mitterrand, who declared in December 1992 that any new or overflow "ethnic cleansing" military incursion into Kosovo would prompt a military response, presumably against Serbia itself.

These direct national threats of retaliation and pledges of support, coupled with the eventual stationing of U.S. troops in Macedonia in 1993 (and before violence erupted there) as part of a UN trip-wire force, may well have been instrumental in containing the spread of the conflict.[15]

NATO Involvement

In any event, it was a combination of Europe's inability to press a resolution to the crisis and the advent of a new administration in the United States that led to an increasing NATO involvement. The Yugoslav crisis has been a watershed both for NATO as an organization and for some of its members individually. For NATO itself, the crisis produced not only the first instance of NATO military actions but also the first instance of NATO participation in out-of-NATO conflicts. Also, NATO involvement provided Germany with firsts of its own; the participation of German naval forces in the Adriatic blockade, the use of German planes to airdrop supplies into besieged Bosnian towns, and the use of German personnel in AWACS patrols over Bosnia to enforce the no-fly zone were bold steps forward in German military participation.

The NATO response to the Yugoslav crisis initially took a hands-off approach. NATO secretary general Manfred Woerner said in November 1991 that NATO felt the EC should handle the crisis. At that time some serious debate was taking place about the appropriate post–cold war mission for NATO, with "activists" promoting a role for NATO in peacekeeping and "conservatives" advocating a more traditional, defensive role for the alliance. Even when it became clear that the EC was not up to the task, Woerner claimed that the UN, not the alliance, was the logical successor for the peacekeeping operations.

Woerner's position, however, had changed radically by the end of 1992. The June 1992 North Atlantic Council conference agreed to support the CSCE, and in December, UN peacekeeping missions. By October 1992 Woerner had changed his tack, saying NATO should be considering not only peacekeeping but also "creating the conditions for peace."[16] With that, the way was made clear for NATO involvement in the Yugoslav wars.

NATO's involvement, though, started with very low profile tasks. NATO's first operation was a sanctions monitoring operation conducted jointly with the WEU in the Adriatic.[17] This mission was coordinated through a headquarters unit set up in Zagreb with Northern Army Group assets and personnel earlier in the year. The headquarters also supported UN-PROFOR operations, which signaled the first use of NATO assets to support UN peacekeeping.

To these actions NATO added conflict prevention activities, two of which were prominent. First, NATO sent a group of verifiers to Bulgaria (on invitation from the Bulgarian government) to assure the Serbian government that there were no Bulgarian troop movements occurring on the Serbo-Bulgarian border. Second, NATO began overflight and surveillance missions in Hungarian airspace (again, on the invitation of the Hungarian government) in 1992. Primarily designed to collect intelligence for potential missions to support UNPROFOR, one consequence of the overflights was to deter further bombing raids by the Yugoslav People's Army forces on border towns in Hungary. These conflict prevention measures were by and large successful, though of course very limited in scope.

NATO activism in the crisis increased throughout the last part of 1992 and all of 1993. In August 1992 NATO completed plans to protect aid delivery in Bosnia should the UN request it, and in December Secretary General Woerner pledged NATO support for UN military action in Bosnia if requested, including possible enforcement of a no-fly zone created by the UN in October.

In February 1993 NATO initiated a major planning effort for providing an implementation force in the event of a successful political agreement. The Clinton administration gave the impetus for the effort with Secretary of Defense Aspin's offer of U.S. ground troops in the event of a settlement acceptable to all sides. NATO planners produced a plan for a force about 50,000 strong, with half expected to be American. Although President Clinton placed many caveats on U.S. participation, including congressional approval, this offer still represented a significant step toward greater possible U.S. involvement in a potential NATO peacekeeping force.

In April 1993 enforcement was authorized for the no-fly zone, and NATO began its first flights over Bosnia—and thus its first "live" combat operations. In August NATO again increased its visibility, endorsing a U.S. plan for retaliatory air strikes to halt the shelling of Sarajevo. The endorsement stipulated that air strikes would be initiated only with UN approval.

NATO's profile in the region became much more visible in February 1994, when NATO fired its first shots ever in a combat mission, downing four Serbian bombers that had violated the UN-mandated no-fly zone.[18] Finally, NATO began its most assertive engagements in April, launching air strikes against Serbian targets that violated weapons-exclusion zones or shelled safe havens in defiance of UN resolutions.[19] The decision to authorize air strikes was initially the UN's, and was prompted by the shelling of a Sarajevo market that killed sixty-eight civilians. After the initial UN authorization, UNPROFOR commanders on the ground were given primary authority to call down air strikes if they deemed it necessary. Thus by early 1994 NATO was actively involved in peacemaking operations in many areas of the former Yugoslavia.

The NATO response to the crisis was at first muted, growing in intensity into 1994 but always (ostensibly) under the political control of UNPROFOR. While NATO has had some operational success—especially in forcing compliance with weapons-exclusion zones—it has remained essentially a tool of the UN and has not drafted much policy itself, though member nations have of course encouraged various courses of action. The NATO countries contributing air power have grown increasingly frustrated with the pace and nature of UN decisionmaking, particularly with what they see as the taking of real risks to strike against single, symbolic targets while giving prior warning to Serb forces in place. Sometimes even different national opinions have been expressed on the same issue; for example, voices from the national military forces under UN command in Bosnia versus the more traditional national diplomatic actors at the UN in New York. The role of the United States remains ambivalent. On the one hand, it is the most "activist" power in terms of arguing for the lifting of the arms embargo against the Bosnian government; on the other, it remains adamant against any American military involvement on the ground before a successful peace settlement.

The Reasons for the Failure to Resolve the Crisis

European and transatlantic actions regarding Bosnia in 1993 and 1994 revealed even greater divisions and greater levels of frustration and indecision. The Community increased its sanctions, and Community members, through the WEU, put in place a fairly effective monitoring and control system on the Danube. Shortfalls have occurred in almost every other area, including promised support and access for refugees, provision of humanitarian aid supplies and equipment for use in Bosnia, and the financing of the UN effort. Most important, there is no consensus or process of consensus building on what to do next, on how to bring to the end the attacks on civilians or the enforced flight of refugees under ethnic cleansing.

Further, the addition of America to the mix, while providing leadership lacking in Europe, has tended to strain political cooperation and slow the peace process. Arguments within the alliance over air strikes, the lifting of the arms embargo against Bosnia, and the easing of sanctions against the rump Yugoslavia have worked against a united Western effort to bring an end to the crisis.

Finally, although NATO has undoubtedly shown some operational successes (three air strikes since April 1994 to enforce UN resolutions and four planes downed in enforcement of the no-fly zone), it has had little effect on overall progress toward what must be a political settlement of the problem. Thus the current situation shows bleak prospects for peaceful resolution or even the mitigation of the war's impact on civilians, at least for the near future. Why?

The explanations for such a poor showing are myriad. Among the most plausible are (1) the Yugoslav crisis occurred before any institutional structures and procedures for peacekeeping or peacemaking assistance were ready in Europe and when the United Nations was overburdened; (2) the neutrality and operational insights the UN had to offer the EC mission were initially ignored, so the EC had to learn peacekeeping from square one, which limited its effectiveness; (3) the complex internal politics of Yugoslavia hinder attempts by outsiders to influence the situation; (4) the physical terrain of Yugoslavia is too intractable to permit intervention or even selective application of military sanctions; (5) the instruments for restraining or punishing incidents of civil war are simply still too rudimentary at this stage; and (6) the Western powers early on lacked political will or commitment and cooperation.

Yet the breakdown was not in the strict sense a failure of either cooperative or collective security. The EC had no direct link, although Yugoslavia had applied for entrance under EC associate status in 1989.[20] Yugoslavia was outside the NATO area subject to article 5 guarantees, and no state had proposed consultation under article 4. There was no firm pledge under the CSCE to preserve unity or to achieve an international assessment of blame and to impose, by force if necessary, a collective solution. The measure of failure stemmed from a less binding test: the standards of international behavior cooperatively set by the CSCE states themselves. Moreover, CSCE Europe had proclaimed it had an ability for the early invocation of conflict resolution mechanisms: prompt decisions to intervene on behalf of human rights, including those of minorities; the timely imposition of credible political, economic, and military sanctions; and a commitment to use all possible efforts to ensure a war-free Europe. In Yugoslavia few of these were tried, and those that were have enjoyed only limited success.

The critical fault, in fact, has been both the lack of political will and the failure to find multilateral agreement on direct, remedial action. There has never been a European decision taken within the Community or elsewhere to commit the time and resources—political, economic, and military—to resolve the crisis. Indeed there have been no European decisions toward peacemaking, only the unwillingness of a number of member governments and their populations to risk the lives of their military forces in direct intervention and the inability to devise political and military incentives to induce an early end to the fighting or to the horrifying process of ethnic cleansing. These were particularly evident in the 1992 debates within the European Community, just after the proponents of Maastricht had proclaimed the will to develop a common foreign and security policy and to proceed eventually to majority voting.

The Basis of Cooperative Security in Europe

Quite apart from these specific failures, the unfolding of the Yugoslav tragedy underscored critical assumptions that had been the basis of the cold war system, in the West as well as across Europe. All existing European and transatlantic institutions involved in cooperative security tasks presuppose the existence or emergence of state actors. For the system to work, member states must be capable of providing for the basic security and human rights of their populations, of ensuring minimal political order, and of ensuring respect for clear state boundaries. The definition of European cooperation under the CSCE accords formal equality and inclusion to all states that acknowledge CSCE principles, even to states that clearly bring with them great burdens of instability, such as refugees, ethnic strife, and repressive or undemocratic governments.

Less obviously, western European and transatlantic commitments to NATO's collective security system presupposed strong state organizations, capable of keeping civil violence to a minimum level. The promise of all states to defend one another against civil violence was therefore to be invoked rarely, and the most probable contingency was a communist-led attempt at overthrow or revolution, in the style of Greece in the late 1940s. In its pan-European efforts the West indeed approached the socialist central European states as illegitimate in their origin and in their exercise of power but as still capable of preserving boundaries and civil order.

The European cooperative security system was therefore state based and not really capable of dealing directly either with emerging civil societies in the cold war period or nonstate actors like ethnic or minority groups in the present. Moreover, states experiencing severe problems of economic decline, political disintegration, or an inability to form an effective government pose intractable difficulties for a cooperative framework. This lack of effective government is not remedied by Western actions that focus on the formal tenets of democratization, on marketization, and on austerity programs, oblivious to the harsh political damage to reform governments that ensues. The only instrument of censure for the regime against a state that is violating collective norms is exclusion. This is a limited penalty in weak institutions like the CSCE, and it is only slightly more effective in a stronger organization like NATO. With states that have experienced political and economic disintegration, the only formal way to cooperate is to wait until a statelike entity emerges from the current disorder.

In stronger, more powerful cooperative institutions such as NATO and the EC, the response to disintegration or political heterogeneity is simply not to extend equal benefits, guarantees, or membership. Turkey, for example, is not "European" enough to be a member of the EC. Similarly, NATO has had difficulties with the idea of membership expansion to the neutral and nonaligned countries, as well as to the Baltics. There are gradations made among associated states; Poland, Hungary, the Czech Republic, and perhaps the Baltics are seen as somehow more "European" than the rest. These states are considered more likely to share the goals and the core activities of cooperative security and to be able to limit not only military capabilities but the sources of civil violence in a democratic manner. The rest of eastern Europe and many of the CIS states are, by contrast, still viewed largely as aspirants; they will have looser ties and will require a substantial transition period before core members grant them inclusion in the tighter circle.[21]

The question is whether cooperative security in Europe can be pursued at all among states that have highly unequal levels of economic development, a disparity likely to remain for a long period in Europe. The experience of the Marshall Plan in the late 1940s and early 1950s suggests this is possible; so too does the incorporation—albeit with some difficulty—of Greece and Spain into EC membership. Proponents of cooperative security tend to argue that the most acute threats to European stability have an economic cause and thus an economic solution, whether these be ethnic conflicts, irredentist border disputes, tensions over the protection of national minorities on the territory of others, or unchecked flows of refugees searching for security and economic prosperity. In the oft-repeated formulation of former German foreign minister Genscher, the primary long-term security task must be an economic restructuring in the East to establish, with massive economic assistance from the West, the base conditions of democracy and peaceful stability.[22] That must be done, however, in such a way as to not promote economic development at the expense of political stability and democratization. Ignoring the effects on political stability invites the politics of nationalism, which preys on unemployment, inflation, and xenophobia—all short-term effects of austerity.

Skeptics are more likely to argue that ethnic conflicts, except perhaps for those that overflow existing borders or involve clear genocide, are probably beyond settlement through external influence, particularly once fighting has begun. Most ethnic disputes, they argue, are not amenable to the pressure of economic or political sanctions. They foresee at most the need to intensify cooperative security actions to stem state disintegration for "damage limitation," that is, to ensure the security of neighboring states, to redress the problems of refugees, and to design options for long-term resolution of political disputes once the fighting stops.

Conclusion

Maximalists claim that if peacemaking is to be one of the critical security functions in the future, the Gulf and especially the Yugoslav cases emphasize the need for greater integration and new authority within the EC and within NATO. Without that, there can be no assured or even timely response and no assurance of decisive action. The fundamental requirements are political choice and the commitment of states willing to jointly incur a range of risks in the interests of peace and able to act jointly toward specific crisis or conflict goals.

The maximalists may well be right, although the present failures in Yugoslavia probably unduly color present assessments of what can be achieved through interstate cooperation alone. Whether old or new, none of the present European or transatlantic institutional arrangements ensure that cooperative action toward restoring or righting the peace will occur. NATO and the WEU go the furthest, but theirs are hedged guarantees, dependent on circumstance and state action and limited to automatic cooperation only in the defense of alliance territory and according to case-by-case decisions in everything else. And no European (or American) state is willing now to make a binding commitment to future cooperation in peacekeeping, to limit its sovereign decisionmaking on issues over which lives will be risked and great costs incurred.

The most acceptable and plausible form of joint action at an early stage of (especially out-of-area) conflict or crisis would be cooperation toward crisis prevention, toward the management of conflict and the limitation of scope and damage, and toward conflict resolution. The classic instruments involved are almost all nonmilitary: fact finding, mediation and arbitration, "good offices," and negotiation brokerage or leverage. Preventive military deployments may also be a valuable instrument in conflict prevention. The example of U.S. deployments to Macedonia, though only a single case, demonstrates the possible role of military forces both in containing crises and deterring their start.

Once a direct conflict begins, however, few peacekeeping moves can be made at any level without the trust or the exhaustion of the belligerents. Humanitarian aid missions, as Bosnia has once again proved, almost always constitute political intervention on one side. Assistance cannot be neutral, since, for example, it clearly involves military benefits (for instance, food aid for a besieged population delays surrender) or it implies an international ascription of blame. And the forces that provide aid become appealing targets for an adversary that sees there is little still to be lost internationally, that is determined to demonstrate resolve, or that may simply want the aid for itself.

Furthermore, cooperative intervention by only a few self-selected states (that is, without legitimation through the UN, NATO, the CSCE, or the EC-WEU) would seem of little lasting political value. That would be particularly true in the most probable and problematic crises in the post–cold war European order: ethnic conflicts that escalate, ethnic conflicts that involve the protection of ethnic diasporas outside national boundaries, and the resulting border fights or refugee streams. Intervention for the objective protection of minorities from internal repression is not yet a European norm, despite the formal commitments to CSCE principles. Several states oppose any early action because they feel vulnerable to the setting of any precedent: Britain, Romania, Russia, and Slovakia, to name only four. The prospects for success may well be few. All that outside parties and institutions can provide is a framework for settlement and peacekeeping once the fighting stops.

But in those cases in which there is a chance for early action, the key is to organize the broadest possible cooperative agreement on early nonmilitary intervention. That means early consultation and information sharing, early offers of mediation and nonmilitary incentives toward peace, and cooperative, credible resolve against conflict. These are precisely the steps that require political choice for multilateral involvement, in which organizational frameworks become relevant and necessary only after the decision to cooperate. It is a second-order consideration whether the EC-WEU or the NATO framework is used to implement the decision, though it will be important to involve those organizations early on to ensure more timely and effective use of their resources.

Figure 5A-1. Chronology: The Crisis and Conflict in Yugoslavia, 1991-94

1991 *Mar. 28:* President George Bush tells Yugoslav prime minister Ante Markovic that the United States will not encourage separatism from any of the Yugoslav republics.

May 24: The United States resumes aid to Yugoslavia. Aid had been cut off to protest repression in Kosovo.

June: EC president Jacques Poos (of Luxembourg) declares, "If anyone can do anything [in Yugoslavia], it is the EC. It is not the United States or the USSR or anyone else."

June 21: U.S. secretary of state James Baker travels to Belgrade and warns Slovenia and Croatia that the United States will not recognize either state's independence.

June 23: EC officials warn Slovenia and Croatia that neither state will be recognized.

June 25: Croatia and Slovenia declare independence from Yugoslavia. The United States says it will ignore the declarations. The Yugoslav federal assembly orders the Yugoslav People's Army (YPA) to intervene to protect Yugoslavia's borders.

June 28: EC foreign ministers Poos, Gianni DeMichelis, and Hans van den Broek negotiate a cease-fire in Slovenia and call for the withdrawal of the YPA and a three-month suspension of declarations of independence. U.S. State Department officials call for an end to the fighting.

June 30: EC threatens to suspend $1 billion in aid if YPA attacks on Slovenia and Croatia do not stop and reemphasizes its support for "Yugoslavia."

July 2: EC cease-fire crumbles. Yugoslav air force bombs Ljubljana, Slovenia.

July 3-4: CSCE holds its first emergency meeting to discuss the war; recommends sending EC mission to monitor and facilitate negotiations.

July 5: EC and United States impose an arms embargo on Yugoslavia. EC suspends financial aid.

July 8: EC negotiates a truce among three parties (Slovenia, Croatia, Yugoslavia) in Brioni (Brioni agreement). Agreement calls for release of prisoners of war, negotiations on future relations, withdrawal of the YPA, demobilization of Slovenian forces, and dispatch of EC observers to Croatia and Slovenia.

Aug. 7: Germany threatens to impose sanctions on Serbia and recognize Croatia and Slovenia if truce in Croatia is not respected.

Sept. 5: EC and CSCE send 200 monitors to Zagreb.

Sept. 7: Slovenia and Croatia formally secede. Croatia shuts off oil pipeline supplying Serbia. EC-sponsored peace talks begin in The Hague under Lord Carrington.

Sept. 8: 95 percent of voting Macedonians approve sovereignty and independence. Ethnic Albanians boycott the referendum.

Sept. 12: The Hague peace conference ends with a declaration preserving existing borders and respect for minority rights.

Sept. 19: EC foreign ministers reject a proposal to send peacekeeping troops to Yugoslavia.

Sept. 25: UN Resolution 713 is approved, instituting arms embargo to Yugoslavia. United States accuses YPA of supporting the Serbs.

Oct. 6: EC approves a plan for economic sanctions on Yugoslavia.

Oct. 8: Three-month waiting period agreed to at Brioni ends. Slovenia and Croatia secede from Yugoslavia.

Nov.: NATO secretary general Manfred Woerner declares that the Yugoslav crisis is best handled by the EC.

Nov. 8: EC suspends trade, aid, and investment in Yugoslavia. United States supports and calls for oil embargo.

Nov. 18: WEU ministers propose establishing a "humanitarian corridor" for refugees.

Nov. 27: UN Resolution 721 authorizes 10,000 peacekeepers for Croatia, contingent on success of Nov. 23 cease-fire (the fourteenth to date). Germany promises recognition of Slovenia and Croatia before Christmas.

Dec. 4: Germany cuts air and road links with Serbia.

Dec. 12: Ukraine recognizes Croatia and Slovenia. UN warns Germany not to recognize either country.

Dec. 15: UN Resolution 734 establishes embargo on Yugoslavia and approves monitors.

Dec. 16: EC decides to recognize Croatia and Slovenia after January 15, 1992.

Dec. 23: Germany recognizes Croatia and Slovenia and offers economic aid to Croatia. Bosnian president Alija Izetbegovic requests dispatch of UN peacekeepers to Bosnia.

Dec. 24: Bosnia, Croatia, Slovenia, and Macedonia apply to EC for recognition.

Dec. 31: Vance plan is agreed to, calling for a cease-fire, deployment of UN peacekeepers, and withdrawal of YPA and Serb irregulars from Croatia. Establishes UN protected areas" in Croatia.

1992 *Jan. 2:* Croatia accepts the Vance plan.

Jan. 7: Five EC peacekeepers are killed when the YPA shoots down their helicopter.

Jan. 8: UN Resolution 727 authorizes a multinational observer team for Macedonia.

Jan. 9: Bosnian Serbs declare autonomy. EC peace talks resume in Brussels.

Jan. 15: EC recognizes Slovenia and Croatia. Bulgaria recognizes Bosnia and Herzegovina.

Jan. 30: CSCE gives Slovenia and Croatia observer status.

Feb. 7: UN Resolution 740 urges Serbia to accept the Vance plan.

Feb. 21: UN Resolution 743 establishes UN Protection Force of more than 14,000 peacekeepers.

Feb. 29: In a referendum that saw a 63 percent turnout, 99.4 percent of voters vote for independence in Bosnia. Most Bosnian Serbs boycott the referendum.

Mar. 9: Secretary of State Baker suggests the United States may be ready to consider recognizing Slovenia and Croatia, contingent on the EC decision on recognition of Macedonia and Bosnia.

Mar. 18: The three major factions in Bosnia agree to an EC plan (the Cutilheiro plan) to divide Bosnia into three ethnic cantons that would form a loose confederation.

Mar. 24: CSCE grants membership to Slovenia and Croatia.

Mar. 25: Izetbegovic rejects Cutilheiro plan after returning to Sarajevo.

April 4: First 1,200 UNPROFOR peacekeepers arrive in Croatia.

April 7: The EC recognizes Bosnia. The United States recognizes Bosnia, Slovenia, and Croatia. Macedonia is not recognized. UN Resolution 749 recommends full UNPROFOR deployment.

April 27: Serbia and Montenegro proclaim the formation of a new Yugoslavia. The United States and EC withhold recognition.

April 30: CSCE grants membership to Bosnia.

May 11: EC pulls its ambassadors out of Yugoslavia.

May 12: EC monitors are pulled out of Sarajevo. United States recalls Ambassador Warren Zimmerman.

May 22: UN admits Bosnia, Croatia, and Slovenia.

May 24: At a conference in Lisbon, Baker attacks EC members for not being more forceful in confronting the Yugoslav crisis.

May 30: UN Resolution 757 calls for sanctions against Serbia and Montenegro.

June 5: Bush signs an executive order to block trade with Serbia and Montenegro.

June 22: The General Agreement on Tariffs and Trade suspends Yugoslavia's membership.

June 30: U.S. defense secretary Richard Cheney says the United States is prepared to use air power to protect aid missions.

July 10: WEU, NATO, and CSCE announce that warships will help monitor the trade embargo.

July 25: Candidate Bill Clinton criticizes President Bush for lack of leadership; recommends selective bombing.

July 27: EC-sponsored peace talks reopen in London.

Aug.: NATO completes plans for potential protection missions for aid delivery.

Aug. 4: Russia recognizes Macedonia.

Aug. 6: Deputy secretary of state Lawrence Eagleburger calls for war crimes investigations in Yugoslavia.

Aug. 10: Clinton says the United States should consider using force to liberate prison camps.

Aug. 13: UN Resolution 770 allows for "all necessary measures" to ensure delivery of humanitarian aid. Resolution 771 condemns ethnic cleansing and promises to prosecute war crimes. Yugoslavia recognizes Slovenia.

Aug. 26: Joint UN-EC peace conference opens in London.

Sept. 22: UN General Assembly expels Yugoslavia. United States requests establishment of a war crimes tribunal.

Sept. 28: U.S. Joint Chiefs of Staff chairman Colin Powell opposes any military intervention in Yugoslavia.

Oct.: Woerner calls for NATO to consider peacekeeping missions as well as missions designed to create "conditions for peace."

Oct. 2: Bush calls for the implementation of a no-fly zone over Bosnia.

Oct. 6: UN Resolution 780 authorizes the establishment of a war crimes tribunal.

Oct. 9: UN Resolution 781 bans all combat flights over Bosnia but does not authorize enforcement.

Nov. 5: CSCE supports creation of a war crimes tribunal.

Nov. 16: UN Resolution 787 authorizes a naval blockade on Yugoslavia, including stop-and-search authority.

Nov. 22: NATO and WEU ships begin implementation of Resolution 787.

Nov. 25: UN Security Council endorses a plan to send observers to Macedonia.

Dec.: President Bush warns Serbia against aggressive behavior toward Kosovo, threatening U.S. retaliation. Woerner pledges NATO support for UN military action if requested.

Dec. 20: Bush and U.K. prime minister John Major release a joint statement calling for military enforcement of the no-fly zone. European leaders reject Eagleburger's proposals for lifting the arms embargo on Bosnia.

1993 *Jan. 2:* Peace talks begin in Geneva, centered around the Vance-Owen plan to separate Bosnia into ten ethnically mixed provinces (each of the three groups—Serbs, Muslims, and Croats—to have majorities in three provinces), slated to have autonomy within a decentralized Bosnian state.

Jan. 12: Bosnian Serb leader Radovan Karadzic accepts the Vance-Owen plan; pledges to submit it to his parliament.

Jan. 20: Bosnian Serb parliament accepts Vance-Owen plan. Croatia and Slovenia accede to International Monetary Fund.

Jan 29.: Peace talks in Geneva break down when all three parties fail to agree on all parts of the Vance-Owen plan.

Feb. 3: France and Britain voice opposition to lifting the arms embargo. United States continues to avoid endorsing the Vance-Owen plan.

Feb. 9: Clinton administration announces it is willing to put U.S. troops on the ground as peacekeepers but only if all three sides freely accept the Vance-Owen plan.

Feb. 28: U.S. planes drop twenty-one tons of emergency relief in the first unilateral U.S. action in the crisis. Other drops follow later in the year.

Mar. 17: NATO approves a plan to send 50,000 peacekeepers to Bosnia once the Vance-Owen plan is signed by all sides.

Mar. 18: France joins the United States in calling for enforcement of the no-fly zone.

Mar. 28: Secretary of State Warren Christopher describes Yugoslavia as a historic "problem from hell."

Mar. 30: Clinton administration refuses to sign a UN Security Council endorsement of the Vance-Owen plan.

Mar. 31: UN Resolution 816 authorizes enforcement of the no-fly zone.

Apr. 3: Bosnian Serb Assembly rejects the Vance-Owen plan.

Apr. 6: President Clinton describes the Yugoslav conflict as "the most difficult, most frustrating problem in the world."

Apr. 7: UN Resolution 817 admits "the Former Yugoslav Republic of Macedonia" into the UN.

Apr. 12: NATO forces begin enforcing the no-fly zone in Bosnia.

Apr. 13: Denmark recognizes Macedonia. It is the first EC state to do so.

Apr. 15: Clinton administration releases a report recommending the establishment of "safe havens" in Bosnia for Bosnian Muslims.

Apr. 17: UN Resolution 820 tightens sanctions on Serbia, including freezing of assets, a maritime exclusion zone, and a total embargo on all trade in or transport of goods.

Apr. 28: WEU offers visitor status to Macedonia.

May 2: Karadzic signs on to the Vance-Owen plan, which will still require the approval of the Bosnian Serb Assembly.

May 5: Bosnian Serb Assembly rejects the Vance-Owen plan. Karadzic calls for a referendum on the issue.

May 19: Results of the May 15-16 referendum indicate 96 percent of voters opposed the Vance-Owen plan.

May 22: Western leaders warn Croatia that continued support for Bosnian Croats could cause the West to include Croatia as a sanctions target.

June 18: Clinton expresses willingness to examine a peace plan based on ethnic canonization of Bosnia.

June 29: UN Security Council defeats resolution to lift the arms embargo.

July 13: UN mediator Thorvald Stoltenberg says he will recommend that UNPROFOR withdraw from Bosnia unless the situation improves there.

July 16: NATO begins deployment of sixty aircraft to Italy to support any future UN missions.

July 27: Peace talks begin again in Geneva, based on the Owen-Stoltenberg plan on ethnic canonization of Bosnia.

July 28: Clinton says United States is ready to take part in protective or punitive air strikes as soon as UN requests them.

Aug.: NATO endorses U.S. plans for retaliatory air strikes to halt the shelling of Sarajevo (pending UN request).

Aug. 20: U.S. troops begin patrolling Macedonia as part of a UN monitoring mission.

Sept. 9: Clinton says he will seek congressional approval before sending U.S. troops into any peacekeeping mission in Bosnia.

Oct. 17: NATO planes fly low-level sorties over Serb gun positions. No shots are fired.

Nov. 17: War Crimes Tribunal opens; begins compiling data.

Nov. 22: EC recommends suspending sanctions against Serbia if it supports the international peace plan and stops aiding the Bosnian Serbs.

1994 *Jan. 7:* France presses the United States to get more active on the ground in Bosnia.

Feb. 5: More than sixty-one people are killed in a mortar attack on a Sarajevo market.

Feb. 6: UN secretary general Boutros Boutros-Ghali tells NATO to prepare to launch air strikes on his command.

Feb. 7: European Union calls for the immediate lifting of the siege of Sarajevo.

Feb. 8: United States recognizes Macedonia.

Feb. 28: NATO planes down four Serb war planes violating the no-fly zone over Bosnia.

Apr. 10: NATO planes attack Serb gun positions around Gorazde.

Apr. 11: NATO attacks continue. Serb shelling of the city ceases.

Apr. 16: British jet is shot down over Gorazde.

Apr. 17: Concern is voiced in Britain over the continuation of involvement in the peacekeeping mission in Bosnia.

Apr. 25: Secretary of State Christopher and U.K. foreign minister Douglas Hurd announce the formation of a Contact Group of U.S., EU, UN, and Russian delegates to begin work on a new peace plan for Bosnia.

May 12: U.S. Senate passes resolutions asking Clinton to seek a lifting of the arms embargo on Bosnia within the UN Security Council.

May 17: France announces plans to pull out 2,000 of its approximately 6,000 troops from UNPROFOR.

June 9: U.S. House of Representatives votes to order Clinton to unilaterally lift the arms embargo.

June 29: Contact Group agrees on a peace plan based on a territorial settlement.

July 1: U.S. Senate votes no on ordering Clinton to lift the arms embargo in a close vote.

July 18: Bosnian parliament agrees to Contact Group's peace plan.

July 19: Bosnian Serbs delay accepting peace plan but do not reject it.

July 31: Serbian president Slobodan Milosevic urges Bosnian Serbs to endorse the peace plan.

Aug. 5: Milosevic cuts ties to Bosnian Serbs for not accepting the plan. U.S. planes again attack Serb gun positions.

Aug. 11: United States sets deadline of October 15 for Bosnian Serbs to accept the peace plan, at which time the United States will lift the arms embargo against the Bosnians. France supports the move.

Aug. 29: In a referendum, Contact Group peace plan is overwhelmingly rejected by the Bosnian Serbs.

Sept. 7: Contact Group recommends easing of sanctions on Serbia in exchange for allowing monitors on the border with Bosnia.

Sept. 22: NATO planes attack Serb targets outside Sarajevo.

Sept. 23: UN Security Council votes to ease sanctions on Serbia if Milosevic continues to support the peace plan.

6

What Is to Be Done?

What is to be done in the next decade to preserve and expand security co-operatively in Europe now seems clear in outline, but one central question must still be answered. Is the United States willing to lead in the creation of a new transatlantic consensus on the goals and instruments of a cooperative security regime in Europe? The magnitude of the conceptual and political effort is at least equal to the one the United States successfully undertook in 1947–52.[1] The resource demands on time, money, and attention will be no less; the prospects for success will again turn on the capacity to persuade and cajole. Above all else, there must be a willingness to lead, rooted in a commitment to stay the course that spans administrations, that garners support from Congress and the electorate as well as from the president.

The parallels to the great challenges of the immediate postwar era, to the efforts to create NATO and the European Community, are striking. The United States again must deal with European allies that are self-absorbed and focused on the critical economic and social transitions they must make at home to restore economic viability. With governing coalitions that are weak or deeply divided, the Europeans have a limited horizon, a penchant to do less rather than more, and a preference for incremental, cautious steps. At home, the Clinton administration faces a public and a Congress that increasingly ask about the present and future rationale for American involvement in Europe, that question the nature of the future military mission and the justification within a smaller military establishment to maintain 100,000 troops in Europe. There are also fundamental concerns, in light particularly of continuing European-American disagreements over cooperation in Bosnia, about the willingness of the Europeans to provide for their own defense and to share burdens and risks even at their own doorstep.

Other facets of the policy environment are a mix of advantages and disadvantages. Clearly, the level of immediate threat has drastically diminished; this allows more time but makes action far less urgent than in the early 1950s. Also, despite declines, far more assets are already sunk in military capability by all the allies. (See figure 6-1.) But there is also great popular pressure to reap a "peace dividend" and a retreat into greater national or Community protectionism in a number of policy spheres. Past investments and past patterns of cooperation will help enormously but may also be barriers to the flexibility and the creativity needed to meet new challenges. Without question, these will require political and economic cooperation as well as integrated military capabilities and the traditions of four decades of doing military business together.

This chapter looks at some of the principal challenges the United States as leader must meet and bring to resolution in the near and medium term. These cut across the organizational realignment and transformations already discussed in terms of the American and European security partnership, the outreach to the East, and the peacekeeping mission in and beyond the present crisis in Yugoslavia. The focus first is on the crucial political variables, the transition in both Russia and a united Germany to new European roles. Fostering conditions for both states to be cooperative, constructive partners in the stability of Europe must be a primary goal for the United States, even though American efforts will be neither exclusive nor necessarily determining. Attention then shifts to more functional categories, including the steady improvement of the existing arms control–arms reduction process, the creation of an ongoing framework for cooperative peacekeeping, and the implementation of new common projects, especially in the area of arms production and export control.

Russia: The Cooperative Imperative

Russia clearly presents a most difficult set of choices for the United States and its allies. What seems to be emerging is a consensus to make every effort to keep a turbulent Russia engaged in European security and taking an active partnership role. That must, however, be on mutually acceptable terms and by arrangements within existing European and transatlantic frameworks. No agreement exists yet—in Europe, in the United States, or in Russia—on what the boundaries are for Russian engagement.

Many influential Americans and most Europeans see the present NATO-Russia agreement within the Partnership for Peace and the European Union's

Figure 6-1. Force Levels in EC Countries, 1985, 1994, 1997

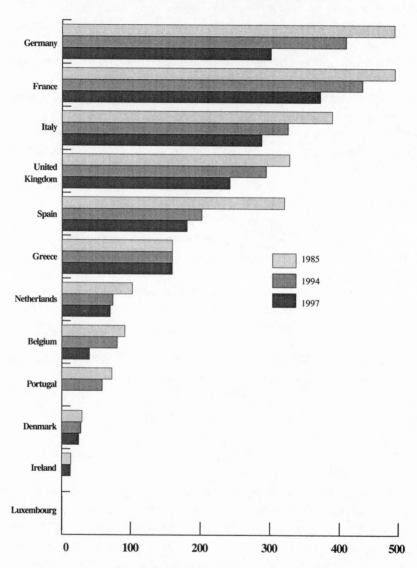

SOURCE: NATO Press Release, M-DPC-2(93)76, Brussels, December 8, 1993.

Partnership and Cooperation Agreement with Russia as the limits of formal inclusion. Anything more, it is argued, would mean accepting Russian claims for a special status or for a veto over eventual central European membership. Russia may be able to assert special interests and try for de facto reintegration of the military and economic resources of many of the former Soviet republics, the Russian-defined near abroad. The instrument used for such reintegration may be the skeletal Commonwealth of Independent States framework, or a revived Russian protectorate if it can be financed. But the time for a Russian sphere of influence in central Europe must be defined as long past, in the Visegrad and southern European states as well as in the Baltics.

Less discussed is the fear that Russian inclusion would overwhelm the present European security institutions just as they are beginning to transform themselves to meet the post–cold war agenda. Guarantees of even the most limited nature would mean involvement in the preservation of civic order in Russia, perhaps under very adverse conditions and perhaps even in a cascading series of regional and ethnic conflicts to draw new boundaries or to back rival factions. The magnitude of the steps necessary to support civic order seems enormous, as evidenced by the steps required simply to help prevent fragmentation of Russian defense structures and arrangements. In this view even long-term cooperation in broad political-military programs must be carefully designed, given the uncertainties of Russia's present political and economic status.

A quite different argument is central to this monograph: there can be no security for Europe—west, central, or east—if Russia is not an integral part of the cooperative framework within which security is preserved in western Europe and extended eastward.[2] To be sure, some short-term gains can be achieved without Russia's participation or its direct agreement; the immediate extension of NATO membership to certain central European states, for example, will mean gains in the perception of their security at home and abroad. There may even be some superficial advantages if Russia withdraws into itself, as a hostile though not aggressive Fortress Russia.

But these gains count little compared with the long-term benefits of active Russian engagement now in a transformed European security regime. No greater threat exists than a Russia that reverts to an autocratic, expansionist regime, especially when it retains large stocks of nuclear weapons and advanced conventional arms. Perhaps no single state can contribute more to future European security and to a new global security regime than a Russia that adopts a policy of cooperation with the United States and the major European allies on key diplomatic and military agendas. A Russia moving toward democracy, committed to stability, willing to assume security responsibilities in Europe and outside in accord with Conference on Security and Cooperation in Europe principles—that must be the long-term and overriding goal for American and European policy.

As was argued earlier, this objective does not necessarily involve Russian membership in NATO either now or in the future. Some other states may well take part in various forms of association and commitment that do not include either NATO or European Union–Western European Union membership: Sweden and Finland, for example, will almost certainly remain only participants in the PFP for the foreseeable future. What matters in the West's relationship to Russia is demonstrated respect for, and responsiveness to, legitimate Russian security concerns and stakes, particularly at this time of heightened perceptions of turmoil and vulnerability. Only thus can the United States and western Europe demand reciprocation and the implementation of Russia's CSCE pledges on the use of military force, the respect for existing borders without prior political agreement on change, and the dimensions of transparency and reassurance in military operations of all kinds.

There is, of course, no guarantee of Russian agreement or satisfaction. Choices in Moscow may simply be otherwise. Reversion to past authoritarianism now seems a less likely outcome in the short term than does further disintegration and fragmentation within the Russian Federation, and perhaps political decisions that retreat further into truculent nationalism and fundamental suspicion of the West. To meet Russian interests, the West will have to offer incentives: material ones but perhaps more important a chance for greater real partnership. No overt attempt should be made to gain at Russia's expense, to exploit or even, if possible, to amplify the weakness that Russian political and military leaders necessarily feel after the turmoil of the last five years. The door to cooperation must be demonstrably and genuinely kept open.

Russia's seat on the UN Security Council provides a crucial Russian lever so long as the transatlantic community and the world feel the need for a UN mandate to legitimize multilateral security actions beyond border defense. So too does the web of interlocking roles President Boris Yeltsin put in place before the 1994 G-7 summit in Naples: assurances through NATO's PFP, a cooperation agreement with the EU, further bilateral agreements on denuclearization with the United States, and a key role in the Contact Group bargaining over the Bosnia peace settlement. But every effort must also be made to reinforce a new European security network including Russia that makes the issue of formal organizational membership less relevant and that ensures dialogue and at least compatibility in the fundamentals of security policy.

The overcoming of Russian resistance to German unification through a generous political and economic formula offers one cause for hope. So too does the model of open, equal, and progressive cooperative action used in the earlier Western strategies to transform a defeated enemy, Germany, into a fully engaged cooperative alliance partner. Further, the achievements of the recent PFP negotiations, particularly the relatively supportive role taken by some leading Russian military in defining common European tasks, suggest that there are opportunities still to be found and channels still to be exploited.

It is here that the United States has perhaps the greatest leadership role to play in the short term. No other state can provide the reassurance, the resources, and the political attention that the engagement of Russia requires. It will take great skill to affect this engagement, given the Russian sense of vulnerability and political loss, the military's paranoia about imposed inferiority, and Russia's uncertain search for a new political and military equilibrium. It will also take persuasive powers to convince some more short-sighted allies and the American neoconservatives that drawing new lines at the westernmost Russian border, if it results in the alienation of Russia, is of little benefit to fundamental, long-term European security.

How to engage Russia is a question for careful cooperative calculation and the commitment of a wide range of American and European resources. There are and can be more special arrangements to reflect Russia's legitimate status as a key security "player" and to deepen the American-European-Russian cooperation that already exists outside formal security institutions: peacekeeping in Bosnia, U.S.-Russian exchanges over arms control and denuclearization, and the emerging G-8 (the G-7 plus Russia) forum on economic coordination and stabilization. At the practical level, PFP suggests an expandable operational menu: seminars, exercises, exchanges, and training in the democratic accountability of military leadership and of transparent military choices. A host of other conceivable measures, all designed to build confidence and ensure openness and communication, can be put into operation if Russia is willing.

The specific issues on which to engage Russia seem fairly clear. Close to the top of the Russians' "wish list" presented with their PFP application were proposals for three special relationships, all important to the United States and western Europe. The first was in the field of nonproliferation and counterproliferation and the detailed challenges of denuclearization and the handling of fissile materials in every phase from storage to export. The second was essentially an institutionalization of the Bosnia Contact Group (the quad-plus-one formula) and an expansion of its agenda to include broader diplomatic consultations on issues of peace and security in Europe. In essence, what Moscow proposed was a right of automatic consultation and a de facto guarantee of no surprises in either diplomatic or military action. The third was recognition of Russia's special peacekeeping burden within the CIS.

These demands can be (and were) read from one perspective to constitute a Russian demand for a veto right (droit de regard) over the highest levels of NATO decisionmaking. But the North Atlantic Council's decisions at Istanbul in the spring of 1994 reflect a broader and what is clearly a more constructive reading.[3] Shorn of the details, these constituted a request by the Russians to be brought into the general process of security decisionmaking on a level that recognizes them as different from the other aspirants, because of their size, geographic position, and potential contribution. The procedural transition will be difficult, and recent experience suggests specific diplomatic interchanges may well be irritating. But there can and should now be joint agreement on the operational standards for a NATO–Russian partnership in Europe. Terms must be mutually set; this must be a clearly marked two-way street. Also, it should be recognized from the outset both that disagreements are probable and that a commitment to attempt to resolve them exists within a cooperative framework based on mutual interests in stability in Europe.

One type of Western outreach that would dramatically increase political reassurance would be the initiation soon of several large military support projects that will both increase mutual transparency and require NATO–Russian–central European cooperation. The model is the infrastructure projects under the Marshall Plan, funded only if they involved cross-border participation and mutual end use on the basis of equality and guaranteed access. The incentive for Russia will be to replace military capabilities lost in the withdrawal from central Europe or to gain help in the reconstruction of infrastructure required for the defense of its new borders. Projects now under discussion include a Europewide air traffic control system (military and civilian), new information-sharing and communication networks, and joint monitoring centers for the integration and sharing of satellite data. Many others are possible.

Important too in the short run are the creative cooperative steps that can be taken to help limit the risks of fragmentation and disaffection within the Russian military and military-scientific community. There are the pressing problems of insufficient housing stock and the need to build new facilities for forces returning from central Europe, an obvious need that, despite the Nunn-Lugar initiatives, has yet to receive the attention and the resources required for a full-scale cooperative program. There should also be a more vigorous effort to demonstrate to Russian military and political leaders just what is involved in NATO. Exchanges, frequent consultation, and a commitment to transparency about NATO practices will overcome some of the attitudes and perceptions of many of the military derived from old thinking, if not the outright anti-NATO propaganda that survived well into the 1980s. Another useful tactic—again drawn from the German experience—might be the direct twinning of some NATO units with specific Russian units. There could also be an investment in common communications equipment as well as stepped-up language training, both to allow reinforcement of mutual professional standards and to increase the potential for regular contact and special exercises.

The German Connection

For the United States, one of the harder post–cold war adjustments has been, and will continue to be, forming a new relationship with the Federal Republic of Germany, the key country in all future European enterprises. The postwar German-American relationship has gone through several phases: Germany as pupil; Germany as key NATO ally; Germany as America's strategic partner in ending the cold war. But unification signals the end of informal as well as formal political constraint and an ultimate reduction of security dependency, leaving Germany less affected in the long run by American choices and preferences. A united Germany has a larger agenda, a more assertive, confident tone, and a more critical approach to the United States and its western European partners.[4] It has strong political and economic interests in stabilizing eastern Europe, if only to guard against a security vacuum in the east or migrations westward. It also has had a special relationship with the former Soviet Union, not just because of the presence of Russian troops on German soil through August 1994 or the much discussed "ransom payments" for unification. In largest measure, the special relationship reflects fundamental German interest in stability to its east and an extension of its traditional love-hate relationship with Russia.

Much American adaptation to this new Germany will take place in familiar channels: through NATO, through the NATO-EU-WEU nexus, and through bilateral U.S.-German military cooperation. With the question of constitutional constraints on the use of German military forces abroad at least formally settled, and the day-to-day burdens of unification lessening, the potential gains are enormous. Of all the European states in the postwar period, Germany has been the most receptive to the concepts and the techniques of multilateral security cooperation. It benefited directly from that approach in the past and made major contributions to its application within the EU and in the effort to bring Spain into NATO. Germans are still skeptical about the utility of military force for missions of conflict resolution or peacekeeping; they are still ambivalent about the appropriate scope of European or NATO actions outside Europe. But whether in the Eurocorps or in NATO's rapid reaction force, they remain committed to as high a degree of multilateral integration as their partners are willing to accept. It is in Germany's interest to demonstrate that there has been no renationalization of its defense, to act with the United States to prevent any other renationalization in western Europe, and to keep renationalization in central and eastern Europe within bounds that do not create new lines of division or prevent cooperation.

German unification itself has transformed NATO and German military capability. Now is the time for major changes in structure and personnel—far fewer forces even as a ceiling, perhaps a German supreme commander for NATO—as well as in strategy. The shift in emphasis is from larger active forces and static forward defense at the inter-German border to smaller, highly mobile, multinational units (and involvement in the Combined/Joint Task Forces and the Eurocorps) and a policy of force regeneration should an attack (almost totally unlikely) against NATO's borders actually threaten. There may be few, if any, nuclear weapons on German soil in the future, given the expressed preferences of at least the former East Germans and the inevitable calculations of cost versus objective military utility that may emerge from the American downsizing of the military establishment in Europe.[5] And over the next decade NATO forces stationed in Germany will certainly shrink further, with an American contingent perhaps at the level of 50,000 to 75,000 troops, depending primarily on how the overall security situation in Europe evolves.

Many in Germany and Europe in the initial months after the Wall fell saw the American role in Europe diminishing even further in the medium term, largely because of American domestic pressures and congressional demands for a return to "normalcy." Some still hold that position and accept the attenuation of the American operational commitment in the interest of building a credible European capacity. In this view the United States may come to act as a guarantor of European choices and the nuclear protector of ultimate resort, but not as the leader or shaper of European security. But the percentage of German political elites that take this position is far smaller than before, as the party positions in the 1994 German federal and state elections well demonstrated.[6]

The present majority view is that for the foreseeable future the United States will still be the primary reassurer of a new Germany against a gathering of its enemies and, through its NATO leadership, the guarantor of security, given a volatile security environment to the east. However desirable, a credible European capacity for the second mission does not yet exist. Germany does not see itself as suited to or capable of performing either function on its own. Many German leaders fear that if no NATO or other multilateral solution proves feasible, the level of its own anxiety might well force Germany toward national efforts (for example, to preserve stability in central Europe), with all of the disadvantages and historical burdens involved. Together with the Franco-German alliance, the American connection provides insurance in the face of a now more dominant Germany that all Europeans, East and West, seem to want for now. In the longer term, if the EU broadens and deepens significantly, the United States may become less central. It will be more an available partner, an honest broker, and only occasionally a counterweight in a German-led Europe.

To many in the United States, American images of Europe have always been too German-centric, at the expense of greater popular and elite identification with France or Britain. Some Americans too have played up the competitive nature of the Franco-German tie to American NATO interests, or have tried—without much direct success—to play the German card to gain French assent or back-channel cooperation in line with American preferences. President Clinton's warm embrace of a united Europe in partnership with the United States brings that era essentially to an official end; so too do the warming relations between France and its NATO allies more generally. But vestiges of the past remain. Moreover, criticism of Germany for tripping the Yugoslav crisis or of its absence from the critical debates over Bosnia often reflects more fundamental concerns about Germany's continued reliability and willingness to accept the political-security burden appropriate to its clear dominance of the European future.

It is therefore more necessary than ever that the United States reinforce a democratic Germany, the new kind of democratic Germany, as the new leader of democratic as well as economic Europe. A continuing American military presence, so long as it is wanted by Germans and other Europeans, remains extremely useful. Nuclear weapons should not be an item of theology but should remain as long as they are wanted, have value as symbols of political reassurance, and truly reinforce a commitment to no further nuclear proliferation in Europe. American leadership, with Germany in NATO on more equitable terms and in more cooperating or coordinating modes, will be essential.

It may not be easy to sustain a constructive relationship with a newly assertive Germany. That country will undoubtedly be more self-absorbed than before, less willing (and able) to contribute to the transatlantic common good, and determined to stabilize its central European neighbors, whatever the U.S. position.[7] Mutual irritation will grow, and there will be temptations to rehearse the German past to constrain the German future.

The United States, though, will still have a unique facilitating role to play despite policy differences and diverging areas of primary economic commitment. The German government and German public opinion need support in the transition to greater security responsibilities and to more direct involvement in military operations short of border defense or deterrence. They will need even greater help in stepping up to the international political role that is commensurate with their economic power. The EU is clearly a primary framework for some of this help. But the United States alone can do for Germany what Britain did for the United States in the late nineteenth century: help without obvious support or direct interference and consult at the grand level with tolerance and flexibility for the inevitable clashes and irritations—for the country's own long-run benefit.

The Agenda for Arms Control and Arms Reductions

Clearly, the most straightforward scenarios would mean broadening and deepening the fundamental provisions of the intersecting frameworks set in place under the Conventional Forces in Europe, CSCE, and Open Skies agreements in 1992.[8] The goal would be not only to rationalize efforts but also to use these unique frameworks to help shape the short- and longer-term outcomes in Russia and the newly independent states in ways eventually consistent with NATO-CSCE standards.[9]

Taking these steps requires new strategic concepts and renewed political leadership, spearheaded by the United States but including at least Russia and Germany in key roles. Essential is a widening political awareness throughout Europe and most especially in the United States that the present security regime has critical holes and vulnerabilities that may grow in significance in the face of repeated crisis. Without the extension and reinforcement of the present regime now, there may be more crises and fewer chances for the gradual evolution of the cooperative security regime in the post-Yugoslav environment in Europe.

Broadening the scope of the existing frameworks is an obvious first step once the political turmoil, especially in Russia, diminishes. Already some unofficial broadening has occurred—the informal sharing of information, for example, among CFE and non-CFE states in the CSCE context. Far more advantageous for long-lasting security, however, would be reporting measures to go beyond the present CFE boundaries of the Atlantic-to-the-Urals area. These should also move away from mere counting rules toward measures that ensure greater transparency and monitoring of intentions. Critical to meeting Russian concerns about symbolic equity with the United States would be an immediate global data exchange: reports on all national holdings, Vancouver to Vladivostock, and thus for the first time on all American forces outside Europe and on all Russian forces east of the Urals.[10]

Neither the American nor the Russian military is currently prepared to go beyond data exchange to talk about limitations on or verification of these total holdings or about constraints on naval forces. Indeed, they may never be prepared to do so without critical strategic changes that convince each side that the other will never harbor military ambitions against it. But there seems little reason not to begin annual data exchanges on selected categories of military equipment, and very soon, to include more detailed reporting on equipment, national manpower levels, locations, and general force organization. Doing so would provide both a new baseline for the dissemination of information within and outside the CFE-CSCE, and perhaps a foundation for eventual expansion to reporting on major national holdings in Asia, especially Chinese forces of concern to both Russia and the United States.

It would seem at least as worthwhile to try to expand the CFE regime, with its critical limits and verification provisions, to the non-CFE members of the CSCE: the remaining republics of the former Soviet Union, the neutrals and nonaligned states, and any emerging states in the CSCE region. Although that alone would not have a notable impact on the risks of internal conflict, it would contribute to the further lowering of interstate conflict. The optimal solution would be adaptation and adoption of the full CFE measures: limits in terms of national ceilings, constraints on transfer and force generation, and the full program of monitoring, inspection, and verification. The nonmember states so far have offered many reasons for delay or for partial implementation, perhaps even for a differing reporting basis. Sweden and Finland have argued, for example, that they have particular problems with full transparency, given their reliance on large numbers of reserve forces and on what are often secret, dispersed equipment stocks. But their mobilization would presumably be at a slow pace in times of crisis. Immediate steps toward reporting at least a portion of existing stocks would be a critical icebreaker and would provide reassurance and validation to neighboring states, in effect raising the standard of information flows within the CSCE arrangements for arms control, confidence- and security-building measures, and disarmament to that of the CFE in both scope and level of detail.

Deepening the existing regime involves a greater number of options and is undoubtedly of more importance in the short run to the implementation of cooperative security principles than the territorial extension to any particular non-CFE state. One set of actions falls within the Forum for Cooperative Security charge to "harmonize" all arms control arrangements. Of clear advantage to the smaller states, but also to the Russian skeptics, would be an integration and consolidation of the regular inspection and reporting requirements of the CFE, the CSCE, and Open Skies when it enters into force. The smaller states have already complained about the economic and manpower burdens; indeed, in the widespread budget-driven cuts, states are reducing their trained inspection personnel sometimes by as much as half. The Russians, on the other hand, need evidence to persuade domestic critics, in the military and on the right, that such integration reflects a coherent, equitable set of rules and obligations that yield information and new instruments of reassurance against all their neighbors.

Cooperation in Peacekeeping: The Long-Term Test

Cooperation in peacekeeping poses far more fundamental and difficult challenges to the emerging European security system than does the arms control agenda. Under the impact of Bosnia and some of the possible peace settlements in the former Soviet space, substantial planning and development is currently under way, but no amount of cooperative strategizing among leaders can create the political will necessary to build a cohesive and credible security regime. The Gulf crisis and the Yugoslav debates show how difficult it is to ensure that even all EU members simultaneously recognize a threat and agree upon a response.

There are more options for collective security if the European Community moves to more coordinated political choices and therefore to a more integrated security and foreign policy. Belgium and Spain have said they would contribute forces to the Eurocorps, which will now reach 40,000 troops by 1995. Spearheaded by France and Germany, the Eurocorps will operate under NATO command, specifically in out-of-area NATO actions, and as a part of the Western European Union, ultimately subject to EC decisions as well.[11] The strategic objective is to have specially trained troops that Europe could call on to react rapidly, to provide humanitarian assistance before and during conflicts, or to ensure high-technology, real-time monitoring of cease-fire and conflict functions. A functioning CJTF will help; so too might coordination with willing nonmembers like Poland.

Some argue that Europewide cooperation might be easier if a clearer differentiation were made between crisis and conflict intervention, or at least clearer distinctions established among the quite different functions and risks now loosely defined as peacekeeping. Only a small number of these actually fit within the framework of the classic, UN-style peacekeeping operation involving monitoring of a negotiated peace or a cease-fire agreement. The CSCE seems at least at present to have responsibility for conflict prevention and might well assume responsibility for these postconflict tasks as well, always on a case-by-case basis.

The debate over relative power and responsibility in action to meet direct military and security threats outside of the NATO-EC area illustrates the changing nature of peacekeeping and the role of European security organizations in it. In the Gulf War the United States took the initiative to organize and lead an ad hoc coalition including principal European states but outside either NATO or the WEU-EC framework. In Yugoslavia the EC has taken some initiatives and provided intermittent leadership, but with increasing interconnections to the UN, the CSCE, the WEU, and even NATO itself.

At present, though, the European Community and NATO seem neither prepared politically nor equipped militarily to deal with Yugoslavlike aggression or similar conflicts that have erupted within the former Soviet Union. Security decisions, particularly those requiring the deployment of troops, are still made at a national level. NATO and the WEU have succeeded in articulating some common objectives through political debate and in conducting some preliminary planning for possible contingencies as well as support operations. But even in those cases the initiatives consist of hedged guarantees, dependent on circumstance and state action, limited primarily to alliance territory, based on case-by-case decisions, and requiring unanimity. For now, no European state—East or West—is willing to make a binding commitment to future cooperation in peacekeeping in a way that would significantly limit its sovereign decisionmaking. And after the debate on peacekeeping in Somalia in the fall of 1993 and the disputes over action in Haiti in the fall of 1994, the United States is clearly unwilling to undertake any noncontingent guarantees beyond NATO itself.

The lessons of the Yugoslav crisis suggest that the demands on European security organizations and European states themselves are more likely to be for joint action at an early stage for crisis prevention and then for conflict management and resolution. As is currently being practiced under the CSCE, the classic peacekeeping instruments are almost all nonmilitary, including fact finding, mediation and arbitration, and helping to press for and negotiate a settlement. These have been the hallmarks of the CSCE "missions of long duration" and the negotiating teams that have been deployed, with some success, to Moldova, Tajikistan, and the Baltics.

Quite separate, the argument runs, would be those political and military functions at the core of a collective security regime: joint action to achieve conflict management or the containment of horizontal or vertical escalation. A more demanding requirement would be for forces and policies to support peacemaking or enforcement of an international decision against warring parties. This function clearly would require a NATOwide commitment to act within a specific region (as in article 5) and with clear structures for decisions and command, with the United States most likely in a leadership role. States that are participants in a broader cooperative security regime could and probably would want to take far more limited roles, perhaps ones involving only attempts to ensure transparency and humanitarian assistance.

From the vantage point of late 1994, there seems little reason to expect the rapid evolution of a Europewide system that includes joint standing forces dedicated to peacekeeping or other collective security missions. As Bosnia has demonstrated, even in the simpler, nonmilitary aspects and in the initial stages of a conflict, cooperative peacekeeping requires the ability to identify, and to react jointly to, risk on the basis of broad political agreement on goals and outcomes and with mutual confidence and trust. Democracies and states with conscript forces require the tolerance or, better, the political support of populations both for action in the present and for that which may be needed if the conflict widens or deepens or if the political and military costs mount. Without those elements, cooperation is achieved only through negotiation, which is often protracted and subject to the distractions and delays of democracies and sometimes disrupted by the demands or intransigencies of several powerful states.

What this means in most cases is that there is a limit to the essentially functionalist integration argument inherent in the present European cooperative security regime, at least for the present. If at all, action will be taken by individual states (alone or perhaps in various coalitions on a per-case basis), making decisions founded on national security interests (as, most recently, the French government acted to establish the safe zone in Rwanda). This mode of action may not necessarily ensure timely crisis intervention or effective peacekeeping, given the stringent demands cooperation will impose on the maintenance and performance of interstate coalitions. European leaders should continue developing cooperative security structures, but without raising expectations that go beyond the political mandate established jointly. What is needed is leadership to mobilize support for cooperation within an agreed framework, not automatic or organizational predisposition to a set of fixed responses or unrealistic expectations about undertaking "exclusively" humanitarian missions. Military operations are still inherently national and, however labeled, require in democratic states a legitimate political mandate before citizen lives will be risked.

But even in the absence of present political will, much can be done to prepare for the peacekeeping cases for which a coalition of the willing can be found. The available instrument is the NATO Partnership for Peace, which has as a minimum goal the inventorying of the forces and resources that the twenty-three partner states plus the NATO sixteen will be willing to consider bringing to a cooperative effort. Plans also exist for cumulative exercises that will give more operational reality to the individual partnership programs, supplemented by the usual array of bilateral and multilateral military exchanges, seminars, and advanced officer training.

But much more can and should be done with PFP. Whatever its status in the past, PFP can now be expanded to a framework for the fullest possible preparation for peacekeeping. It can be the framework for forward planning for a range of contingencies, planning within the guidance of SHAPE, but with increasing roles and responsibilities for the partner states. Some, like

152   THE FUTURE OF EUROPEAN SECURITY: AN INTERIM ASSESSMENT

Sweden and Finland, have considerable experience and resources to contribute. PFP can also oversee a web of bilateral relationships, with each
NATO member contributing directly to the efforts of partner states to develop mature capabilities. Some partnering might be done through simple
measures like the twinning of units; others might involve a full-scale program of cooperation at every level of military education and training and at
every level of political-military decisionmaking. And there is no reason not
to begin now to educate parliaments and publics about the types of possible
situations to be faced, the risks and the benefits that may arise, and the usefulness of a multilateral approach.

The largest questions may well turn on the availability of resources for
what may be dismissed by most ministries of defense as nontraditional defense and therefore not their responsibility. PFP thus must be sure to encourage the active involvement of political leaders, present and possible, in
the various activities toward peacekeeping. There seems little virtue in res-
olutely keeping the partnership relationships as only a channel between a
state and the alliance or as a matter of concern only for the United States.
Whether it is called the North Atlantic Cooperation Council or a Partnership
Forum, a policy-political forum must be developed that can go beyond the
ceremonial and establish the kinds of regional and subregional cooperation
on which PFP will continue to thrive.

Arms Industry Restructuring: A Potential Tool for Security Internationalization

An only somewhat less complicated area for preserving and extending the
European security regime is cooperation in the management of arms production and export. Now, as in the past, this is a subject of great sensitivity,
colored by national economic and technological stakes and susceptible to the
currents of domestic politics. Yet in an environment of lowered threat and
planning for essentially multilateral missions, both efficiency and economy
suggest that joint management of production is a critical next step. And export control in common flows both from this step and from the logical implications of increasing policy coordination and commitments to cooperative actions outside the European area.

Moreover, this policy argument for joint management is reinforced by
trends occurring throughout the global arms industry, largely for economic
reasons. The keynotes are industry consolidation and internationalization.

There are far fewer firms in a far smaller, still declining market, both domestic and international. Those that do exist are already major cross-border collaborators, or themselves multinational firms. And there is a move to further disentangle government-industry links, leading to new privatization in France and Britain, for example, or to lessened subsidies and preferential treatment as in Germany and the United States.

Both European and American arms industry consolidations are now at a crucial turning point. The post–cold war budget cycle is in sight, and the next round of defense appropriations will be far less generous than the last. Although the search for new markets is currently expedited by relaxed exports controls,[12] even aggressive marketing will be thwarted by low oil prices and diminishing domestic defense budgets.[13] Defense firms, having had little success with efforts to convert to profitable civilian products,[14] are opting to either acquire the competition or get out of the business altogether.[15]

These trends toward consolidation and globalization should make cooperation easier, but that has not been true in the U.S.-European relationship. Although most international collaborative arms efforts are within NATO, intra-European projects are twice as common as transatlantic ventures.[16] Part of the reason is that European governments traditionally view collaborative procurement and production projects as politically and economically advantageous, whereas the United States also emphasizes the military and operational benefits of such cooperation.[17] The common objectives of European states has led to far more agreements on the Continent, while the United States, enjoying a large domestic and overseas market, has been able to maintain a semblance of autarky and has been unable to press its agenda of transatlantic interoperability on the Europeans, who often see it as a buy-American campaign. Moreover, since the Gulf War in particular, the United States has dominated the export market, in 1992 exporting some 70 percent of all arms sold.[18]

Exacerbating this problem has been the U.S. proclivity to engage in collaborative projects on only a limited scale, hindering development of integration that might facilitate transatlantic defense interdependence. The United States has normally favored licensing agreements and coproduction but has avoided codevelopment projects that require U.S. companies to share technological know-how or potential dual-use applications. Consequently, many attempted transatlantic ventures have failed, such as those initiated under the Nunn amendment.[19] In other instances, the U.S. government has prevented foreign acquisition of U.S. companies in order to bolster defense self-sufficiency and domestic employment opportunities. In 1992, for example, the French company Thomson-CFS tried to purchase the missile division of the U.S. steel and industrial group, LTV. Congressional consternation ensued, and fears of litigation under Exon-Florio legislation eventually pressured Thomson-CFS to drop the deal altogether.[20]

Prospects for cooperation with the central and eastern European states appear even more unfavorable. Arms production was a cornerstone of the socialist economies; in the slow economic transformations of the present, it remains a sector with which to earn hard currency and, in the eyes of the hard-liners at least, restore national pride. Initially, just as the cold war was coming to an end, the optimism in central Europe led progressively minded leaders like Czechoslovak president Vaclav Havel to declare an end to arms exports.[21] This position has now been replaced by a more permissive, if not cynical, attitude toward continued sales.

The situation in the former Soviet Union is also discouraging. In particular, Russia has experienced a severe drop-off in orders from cold war clients such as Afghanistan, Angola, and Ethiopia, resulting in a dramatic cut in the value of arms exports. Whereas the Soviet Union exported $20 billion worth of arms annually in the mid-1980s, Russia, by far the largest exporter in the former Soviet Union, sold only $2.5 billion worth of weapons in 1992,[22] reflecting both shrinking markets and diminished CIS production in most sectors. Many workers in Russian industry see the West, and in particular the United States, as being the major gainers in market share at Russian expense.

Russian production capabilities will most certainly increase as time passes and economic recovery takes hold. As early as April 1993 the Russian foreign economic relations minister Sergey Glazyev announced that Russia would "strive to the maximum to trade arms,"[23] in everything from ships to atomic power–engineering equipment, probably scoping out new markets in developing countries, particularly in Asia and the Middle East.[24] Like other industrialized powers, if Russia has the capacity to profit from arms exports, it will certainly do so in the absence of an expansive and powerful multilateral export control regime.

Some factors, though, favor cooperation with the East. The collapse of the former socialist economies and the dependence of the emerging democracies on both international funds and external goods for economic reconstruction have meant little continuing investment in military industry. Owing to the general post–cold war drop-off in global sales and to the inability of the eastern European firms to offer either special trade incentives or high-technology alternatives, many of the previous trading arrangements have collapsed, as in the Russian case. Also, reform has meant a shrinking domestic market, one that no longer supports even half the previous scale of typical eastern European production.

Despite this mixed picture, there would still seem to be great benefits in pursuing at least the first steps toward joint management of arms production and arms export in both the transatlantic and the pan-European domain. Consolidation of industry enhances not only the economic attraction of cross-border collaboration but also the chances for transparency about plans and output. Gone will be most of the "national champions," which are now able to command exclusive defense investment to protect national technological competitiveness.[25] Export and collaborative production decisions will of necessity mean more international consultation, at both the firm and governmental levels.[26] And the incentive for implementing two traditional military goals, standardization and a reduction of duplication and wheel reinvention, will be greater.

What is to be done? Whatever the logic of rationalization or the economics of consolidation, collaborative management of even a portion of planned arms production or export will not occur without concerted government intervention and cooperation. The crudest vehicle might be a negotiation on transforming current market shares and ensuring a five-year share in defense goods, divided according to total value or perhaps sectoral specialization as in high-performance aircraft. Such an agreement seems highly unlikely in either the transatlantic or the pan-European forum, given the hard-won commitment to free trade under the General Agreement on Tariffs and Trade, the North American Free Trade Agreement, and the European Union.

Institutional arrangements might prove the point of present entry. There is widespread consensus throughout Europe that the United States is largely, though not solely, culpable in the current arms collaboration drift within NATO. Creation of a formal transatlantic forum in which cooperative ventures are promoted, coupled with U.S. willingness to share heretofore protected military technology, could potentially increase defense interdependence and a greater sense of equity. This might be a way to restore public confidence in major new projects or to find a more objective basis for a new joint approach to reconfiguring the arms industry itself.[27] The forum could also address the problem of maintaining a "hot" technology base and of avoiding "technological surprise" even though actual production runs might be small or even halted at the prototype stage. Far more incentives would be needed than currently exist, both for the firms that are competitive to seek the benefits of scale and for the overcapacity firms to retreat and reconsider.

The danger still exists, however, that the defense industry will dig in its heels, resist prevailing economic forces, and call for greater government protection in the interest of jobs and research advantages. The pressure is becoming intense. In aerospace, for example, there are now nine producers of medium-distance or regional transport aircraft in the world, but, according to experts, this number must be cut to three in a fairly short time, with only one European producer.[28] Although free market forces may encourage further internationalization and rationalization of the arms industry, there is no guarantee that a reduction in arms production will result. In conspiracy with idiosyncratic and protective governments, arms industries in Europe and the United States may market their products more aggressively both domestically and abroad, and in the worst-case scenario, inadvertently foster regional arms races by facilitating continued arms accumulation.[29]

It is not clear which institution will take the responsibility for coordinating arms industry consolidation. In western Europe and perhaps beyond, the EU, in concert with a Partnership for Peace adjunct, would be a favorable locus of such efforts. The obvious start would be to plan for major new systems or even to improve progressively those already in place or received from allies. EU oversight would allow comprehensive regulation and encourage cross-border cooperation. It would provide the basis for later extension and expansion, especially in the thornier aspects of dual-use technologies. Over the last several years there has also been considerable European Commission and popular support for making Community oversight in the defense sector comparable to that now in place over purely civilian production. The move toward establishing common export controls for EC members is explained by the fact that "the application of 'export controls' on intra-EC trade in certain goods and technologies which can be used for both civilian and military purposes poses a problem for the completion of the internal market."[30] Such oversight will allow regulation at the firm level, whether the firm is national or multinational. The Community has also begun to work on common export-control procedures and the training of national and company officials in overseeing declared end use.[31]

There would clearly also be a need for parallel constraints on American production and sales, and eventually on eastern European and Russian sales as well, if only to ensure a level playing field. Inward-looking states outside the EU might still choose to protect their industries rather than to act cooperatively. Should sound strategic planning prevail, however, every country in Europe stands to benefit from equipment standardization, comprehensive export controls, and a more efficient, less costly defense industry, all of which would contribute to greater cooperation and security.

Epilogue

Five years after the fall of the Berlin Wall, the cooperative security regime that has evolved in Europe and across the Northern Hemisphere faces challenges and opportunities greater than at any time in the postwar era. After a period of misplaced euphoria and dismissal of all cold war definitions of security, a new appreciation of the risks and dangers to peace and stability has emerged, especially in a time of revolutionary political and economic transition. After much jostling and debate, a complex, interwoven system of institutions and capabilities is now in place which can meet most of the security requirements that can be foreseen in this era of relative peace in Europe. Short of massive civil unrest in Russia or global conflict, parts of the system in place can now be used to organize the limitation of offensive capabilities, provide mechanisms of reassurance against fears of surprise attack or fast-moving hostile action, and achieve transparency and verification in real time. The core is from Vladivostock to Vancouver; the periphery, from the borders of Florida to those of Anatolia.

What is lacking at present is the sustained political commitment to the tasks of cooperative security both for now and for the decade to come. Politicians and people are weary, ready to turn inward to domestic concerns and private prosperity. In the absence of a single common enemy, in the face of continuing uncertainty or low-level conflict, or even in the face of the horrors of Bosnia, the great temptation is to delay, to put aside, to temporize, or to ignore. The political will to maintain and extend cooperation, to share the obvious cooperative burdens in the preservation of peace and the extension of democracy, seems wanting. There is no clarion call to a new overarching definition of security that justifies actions short of war or prepares publics for contingencies and casualties beyond state borders.

The goal now must be to build the political consensus behind such a new definition of the nature and requirements of post–cold war security. Without political consensus, risking and possibly losing the lives of a multinational force, even in monitoring or extended humanitarian missions, could undermine the credibility of cooperative security efforts as a whole. Under present conditions the ultimate challenge from the former Yugoslavia to Tajikistan is to take early preventive action in a crisis and, if possible, to build on economic and cooperative military relations to provide options for peaceful conflict resolutions.

Once again, the critical factor is leadership. It is a role, a task, a burden that many believe is now uniquely that of the United States. Events in the Gulf, Somalia, and Bosnia suggest now even more strongly that where the United States does not lead, Europe, East and West, does not follow.[32] And the chance that this allocation of burden will change, in at least the foreseeable future, seems slim.

Yet at the same time, when others do not follow, the United States cannot lead. Just as the United States must continue to provide leadership in the near term, the nations of western Europe must continue to develop European—even pan-European—institutions to complement the current alliance structure. Europe must show more initiative in addressing issues of its future security. It must do so not only to protect its own self-image and security but also to better support stabilization to the east and to keep the United States involved in Europe by relieving some of the political and financial pressures of leadership.

At the basic level, the choices to be made are remarkably parallel to those open at the end of another war, the hot conflict of 1939–45. The arguments for action and inaction are the same; the resources, political and economic, needed for success are of comparable magnitudes. The preferred instruments are also similar: international and multilateral institution building, cooperation rather than competition, democratization and economic prosperity as the lodestones of security. Few states in history have had the luxury the United States now has of confronting the same choices twice, and perhaps on even more favorable terms the second time. The key this time is to maximize the opportunities of the present situation both to deepen cooperation with current allies and to widen the area protected by the security umbrella to the deserving and willing of the newly emerging democracies.

There is every reason to support and to extend the present cooperative security regime in Europe. All involved states must take robust action that reflects the belief that the benefits of cooperative security continue to outweigh the risks and that the time has come to confront the increasingly sensitive issue of harmonizing unilateral prerogatives with multilateral processes of consultation and decision. The available alternatives—the loss of transparency and confidence, the threat of widespread renationalization of security and defense policy, especially in Germany and the East—are hardly attractive. The deadline for developing an extended cooperative security strategy is not fixed, but allowing more time will not make the tasks smaller or easier. The path to the future is by no means an easy one, but it must be traveled. The time to begin is now.

Appendix A: Selected European Security Chronology, 1948–94

1948 *March:* Britain, France, Belgium, Luxembourg, and Netherlands create Brussels Treaty Organization. Essentially a mutual defense pact, the treaty also calls for cooperation in social, economic, and cultural areas.

1949 *April:* North Atlantic Treaty is signed in Washington by 12 original allies.

1951 *April:* NATO sets up first integrated military command, SHAPE. European Coal and Steel Community established by 6 European partners.

1952 *February:* Greece and Turkey join NATO

May: European Defense Community (EDC) Treaty signed

1954 *August:* France fails to ratify EDC

October: Paris Agreements signed. Germany to join NATO and, together with Italy, the transformed Brussels Treaty Organization, the new Western European Union.

1957 *March:* Rome Treaty signed by the 6 European partners establishing European Economic Community and EURATOM

1966 France withdraws from NATO integrated military structures; SHAPE and NATO headquarters leave Paris for Mons and Brussels.

1973 Opening of Conference on Security and Cooperation in Europe (CSCE) in Helsinki and of negotiations on Mutual and Balanced Force Reductions (MBFR) in Vienna.

1975 *August:* Helsinki Final Act signed by 35 European and North American states to set standards for human rights within countries, establish economic cooperation, recognize existing borders, and establish confidence-building measures.

1982 *May:* Spain joins NATO.

1984 In response to widening NATO rifts, Reagan's announcement of SDI to cover only U.S. territory, and the failure to effectively convert the European Community, the WEU is "revived." The French government leads the way as members call for a harmonization of views on defense, security, and military issues.

1987 Accession of Spain and Portugal to WEU.

October: WEU platform on European security; focuses on the "major responsibility" of the Europeans in conventional and nuclear defense against the Soviet threat. The platform further sets out the primary goal of developing a security dimension to European integration and attempts to define the conditions and criteria for the WEU's role in Western defense issues such as arms control and disarmament and East-West dialogue.

November: French Prime Minister François Mitterrand and German Chancellor Helmut Kohl plan for Franco-German brigade.

1987–88: During the Iran-Iraq war, Operation Cleansweep, a minesweeping operation, is initiated by the Netherlands in an attempt to secure free navigation in the Gulf region. French, British, Italian, Belgian, and Dutch mine hunters are sent to the Gulf to clear the waters. West Germany provides replacement naval forces in the Mediterranean, and Luxembourg makes a financial contribution to the operation. Operation Cleansweep provides the first example of a military operation coordinated by the WEU.

1988   France and Germany announce formation of a joint Franco-German military brigade to be fully operational in 1995.

1990   Franco-German brigade, with its headquarters in Muellheim, Germany, becomes operational with 4,200 troops.

French President Mitterrand proposes a European Confederation, a continentwide organization for Europeans intended only to replace CSCE.

August: WEU ministers strongly condemn Iraq's military invasion and annexation of Kuwait and insist on the application of UN Security Council Resolutions 660–62. To this end, the WEU helps coordinate European participation in the naval embargo against Iraq. By the end of 1990, forty-five vessels (destroyers, frigates, corvettes, mine hunters, and auxiliary and amphibious vessels) belonging to WEU member states (except for Luxembourg and West Germany) are deployed to the Gulf region.

October: German unification takes place.

November: United States and EC sign the Transatlantic Declaration, which establishes a formal process of consultation. CSCE adopts the Vienna document on expanded confidence- and security-building measures (CSBMs). The document builds on the 1986 Stockholm document, stipulating a strengthened verification regime, a greater amount of information, improved conditions for military observers, and lower thresholds for the number of troops in exercises that require advance notice. Paris CSCE summit meeting establishes the Charter of Paris for a New Europe. The G-22 (NATO and former Warsaw Treaty Organization states) sign the Treaty on Conventional Armed Forces in Europe and publish the Joint Declaration on Nonaggression.

1991   WEU headquarters is moved from London to Brussels, bringing WEU organizational structures closer to those of NATO.

February: German submission to the Intergovernmental Conference on Political Union proposes wide new powers for the European Parliament. In March these proposals receive only limited support from other member states.

April: WEU organizes Operation Safe Haven, the EC airlift of humanitarian relief to Kurdish refugees.

June: NATO foreign ministers' meeting in Copenhagen results in statements on Partnership with the Countries of Central and Eastern Europe, NATO's Core Security Functions in the New Europe, and the resolution of problems concerning the Conventional Forces in Europe (CFE) Treaty. Discussion of a "European pillar" for NATO. Chancellor Kohl and Prime Minister John Major of Britain meet and agree to slow down the European Monetary Union (EMU) process. EC Council of Ministers meeting at Vianden, Luxembourg. Ministers confirm their desire to be fully part of the process of European integration while enhancing WEU's role within the Atlantic alliance. Three levels of security are delineated: a European level centered on the WEU; an Atlantic level under Atlantic alliance; and a pan-European level under the CSCE.

October: Expansion of Franco-German brigade announced. Participation in the brigade (now dubbed the Eurocorps) is opened to all European member states. The Eurocorps is, according to the Eurocorps initiative, to be the backbone of an eventual common European army. France and Germany send letter to the Dutch president of the EC proposing speed-up of progress toward European union, including the eventual creation of the Eurocorps, to be cornerstone for a future European army as part of an EC-wide defense organization. Dutch presidency issues a final draft EMU treaty in the run-up to Maastricht summit.

November: Summit meeting of the North Atlantic Council in Rome. Heads of state and government publish the alliance's new strategic concept and issue the Rome Declaration on Peace and Cooperation. Discussion of future relationship between NATO, the EC, and the WEU in European defense. Council of Ministers meeting in Bonn; declaration on Yugoslavia issued, whereby WEU declares its willingness to give practical support in efforts to secure a cease-fire. NATO approves MC 317, the Future Force Structure, which recategorizes NATO forces as reaction, main defense, and reinforcement; establishes new standards of availability to reduce NATO active forces; and emphasizes multinational formations to prevent renationalization of defense requirements. EC foreign minister's meeting at Noordwijk. Further negotiations to reach an agreement on the details of a new political union treaty in the run-up to the Maastricht European Council.

December: European Council convenes in Maastricht, Netherlands; agrees to develop deeper political, social, economic, and defense integration among members of EC. Central issues include political union, economic and monetary union, and harmonization of social, economic, and military cohesion. Council endorses WEU as vehicle for stronger European pillar in NATO and development of common foreign and security policy. Declaration on the Role of the Western European Union and Its Relations with the European Union and with the Atlantic Alliance annexed to the Maastricht Treaty. The declaration explicitly acknowledges organic link between WEU and European Union; invites all EC states to join WEU; limits non–EC-NATO states to associate membership status; sets up a planning cell to be located in Brussels; declares WEU's intention to be developed as the defense component of the EU.

1992 *February:* Treaty of European Union signed at Maastricht by EC foreign and trade ministers. Economic Finance Council meets in Brussels, where French criticism of German monetary policy and discussion of Irish conversion plan take place.

April: Declaration on implementation of UN sanctions on the former Yugoslavia issued at an extraordinary meeting of the Council of Ministers in Luxembourg.

May: At the La Rochelle summit, France and Germany pledge to set up a joint army corps, the Eurocorps, by 1995 and invite other European states to join. NATO defense ministers approve a peacekeeping role for NATO and endorse the command structure.

June: At Oslo North Atlantic Council meeting, foreign ministers approve peacekeeping as a NATO responsibility in conjunction with CSCE. In ministerial meeting in Petersburg, Germany, Forum of Consultation is created by WEU to establish a dialogue with eastern Europe. Danish electorate rejects Maastricht Treaty in referendum. La Rochelle communiqué is issued, defining three basic tasks for Eurocorps: (1) joint allied defense under either the Brussels or NATO treaties; (2) "maintaining or reestablishing peace"; and (3) "humanitarian missions." Referendum in Ireland on Maastricht Treaty.

July: Referendum campaign in France on Maastricht. Former Yugoslavia is suspended indefinitely from membership in CSCE. At Helsinki Review Conference, CSCE claims the status of a regional organization for political and cultural cooperation (as opposed to a self-defense organization), according to UN criteria. Furthermore, a mandate for the Forum for Security Cooperation (FSC) is laid down in the "Program for Immediate Action." FSC's main task is the negotiation of CSBMs. Extraordinary meeting of WEU Council of Ministers on the situation in Yugoslavia takes place in Helsinki. Operation Sharp Vigilance, involving the monitoring of sea operations in accordance to UN resolutions 713 and 757, is established under Italian coordination. The surveillance is to be carried out in international waters, in the Otranto Channel and off the Montenegro coast.

August: Growing crisis in the former Yugoslavia inspires the EC-UN peace conference in London. Extraordinary meeting of WEU Council Ministers takes place in London, where foreign and defense ministers reaffirm the necessity of securing a cease-fire in the Yugoslav crisis and agree to strengthen Operation Sharp Vigilance.

September: Monetary crisis in Europe. Necessitates realignment of currencies in the European exchange rate mechanism (ERM) and reduction in German interest rates, September 13–14, 1992. Sterling is suspended within the ERM on September 16, while franc, krone, and punt all experience increasing pressure. September 20 meeting of EC finance ministers in Washington to discuss implications of the monetary crisis. French electorate narrowly accepts Maastricht Treaty on European Union. Forum on Security Cooperation meets for first time. Created by the CSCE under chapter 5 of the 1992 Helsinki document, the forum meets weekly and consists of two working groups addressing the six topics set forth in the "Programme for Immediate Action" of the Helsinki document.

October: The four Visegrad countries—Poland, Hungary, Czech Republic, and Slovakia—make a proposal to CSCE regarding development of a code of conduct for security matters. Danish government issues white paper on Denmark's future relations with EC following the Maastricht referendum. WEU Forum of Consultation meets for first time on an ambassadorial level. The participating countries are the members of WEU, Bulgaria, Czech Republic, Estonia, Hungary, Latvia, Lithuania, Poland, Romania, and Slovakia. NATO issues its proposal to CSCE regarding the development of code of conduct for security matters. It proposes that all CSCE member states adopt CFE standards and also focuses on information exchange, verifications, and national ceilings. General Agreement on Tariffs and Trade talks break down in Brussels.

November: Council of Ministers meeting in Rome. Greece becomes a full member of WEU, Denmark and Ireland attain observer status, and Norway and Turkey become associate members. Danish political parties agree to proposals to secure citizens' acceptance of Maastricht Treaty. A paper entitled "Practical Measures with Regard to Cooperations between NATO and the Western European Union" is published, outlining operational links between NATO and WEU. The paper lays framework for ironing out future relations between WEU and NATO, with the goal of avoiding rivalry and duplication. The paper calls for regular meetings between the NATO secretary general and the WEU secretary general and sets out procedures for information exchange between the two staffs. U.S.-EC trade talks fail in Chicago, and the United States threatens trade sanctions. Later, EC and United States agree to a deal in the long-running oilseed subsidy dispute.

December: United Kingdom presents proposals to allow Denmark to ratify Maastricht Treaty. French and German governments and NATO's supreme allied commander, Europe (SACEUR) reach agreement on the relationship among Eurocorps, NATO, and WEU. Meeting of CSCE Council of Foreign Ministers in Stockholm creates new meeting group known as the Vienna Group. Vienna Group is to meet weekly and recommend action on violent conflicts to the Committee of Senior Officials (CSO). Stockholm Convention on Conciliation and Arbitration is signed by twenty-nine participating states.

1993   WEU establishes the Centre for Interpretation of Satellite Data in Torrejon, Spain.

French Prime Minister Edouard Balladur proposes the Pact on Stability in Europe, a broader, more inclusive concept than Mitterrand's European Confederation.

January: Agreement signed between NATO and WEU regarding the use of Eurocorps under the auspices of SACEUR. Eurocorps can be used for collective defense, crisis management, and humanitarian intervention. First meeting of Vienna Group. North Atlantic Council informs UN secretary general that NATO is willing to carry out military operations in the no-fly zone over Bosnia and Herzegovina.

February: Maastricht Treaty ratification progress in United Kingdom. Meeting of CSO in Prague. Joint CSCE-EU Office of Sanctions Coordinator is established to support CSCE teams based in nations bordering Serbia and Montenegro. Later, CSO decides to double the number of monitoring missions in Kosovo, Vojvodina, and Sanjak. Russia introduces global information exchange proposal to FSC. Proposal includes all forces, both ground and naval, of CSCE states. UN Security Council unanimously votes to establish an international tribunal for the prosecution of war crimes in the former Yugoslavia.

March: Fact-finding mission sent to Slovakia and Czech Republic by CSCE. First meeting of the CSCE Economic Forum (established at Prague meeting of CSCE Council of Foreign Ministers in January 1992). CSCE meeting on Nagorno-Karabakh in Rome. Representatives of eleven member states (Armenia, Azerbaijan, and the nine states of the informal Minsk Group: Belarus, Czech Republic, France, Germany, Italy, Russia, Sweden, Turkey, and United States) and of Armenians and Azeris from Nagorno-Karabakh participate. They approve a document setting forth a draft mandate for an advance group of observers. Russia issues its proposal to CSCE for development of a code of conduct for security matters. UN Security Council authorizes member states to take all necessary measures to enforce the no-fly zone over Bosnia and Herzegovina.

April: Wilhelm Hoynck is selected as first secretary general of CSCE. NATO formally approves use of NATO aircraft in enforcing the no-fly zone over Bosnia and Herzegovina. U.S. President Bill Clinton and Russian President Boris Yeltsin hold their first summit in Vancouver, Canada. They reach agreements on a comprehensive nuclear test ban, the Nuclear Nonproliferation Treaty, and exploration of joint missile defenses. WEU Council of Ministers agrees to participate in enforcing 1992 UN embargo against Serbia and Montenegro through patrols and monitoring along the Danube. France proposes an EC-sponsored European Peace Conference in FSC. Observers from CSCE Minsk Group arrive in Armenia and Azerbaijan. On April 21 another group of CSCE representatives visits Nagorno-Karabakh. Macedonia is admitted to CSCE as an observer. CSCE Emergency Committee meets in Paris. Participants urge Armenia to pull its forces out of the Kelbadzhar corridor.

May: Annual Implementation Assessment for the Vienna document meets in Vienna. Danish electorate accepts Maastricht Treaty in a second referendum in Denmark. In response to the worsening situation in the former Yugoslavia as well as to a general call for strengthening the security arm of the European Union (EU), the concept of forces answerable to the WEU (FAWEU) is introduced. Belgium, Britain, the Netherlands, and Germany (the Multinational Division Central and the UK-Netherlands Amphibious Force) all agree to make units or equipment available for military tasks under WEU auspices. Eurocorps is also officially designated as a FAWEU. Third Reading of the bill to ratify Maastricht Treaty is passed in House of Commons in London. Through an exchange of letters, CSCE and UN agree to a framework of cooperation between them. CSCE representatives meet with North Ossetian Council of Ministers to get information about the situation in South Ossetia. Creation of Office of Free Elections in Warsaw of Office of Democratic Institutions and Human Rights (ODIHR).

June: Belgium joins Eurocorps. High Commissioner for National Minorities Max van der Stoel visits Romania. Operation Sharp Guard begins. Joint NATO-WEU operation replaces separate NATO and WEU efforts to enforce the UN embargo on Bosnia and Herzegovina.

The operation includes coordinated enforcement by surface ships, maritime patrol aircraft, fighter aircraft, and NATO airborne warning and control systems (AWACS). Operation Sharp Guard is coordinated with NATO Operation Deny Flight, which enforces the Bosnian no-fly zone. CIS Joint Armed Forces High Command is formally abolished; it is scheduled to be replaced by a more limited Joint Staff for Coordinating Military Cooperation. Balladur plan is unveiled at a Copenhagen meeting of the European Council. This plan of the French prime minister would address relations between western and eastern Europe, immigration and minorities, coordination between existing institutions in Europe, political stability in Europe, and development of military security in Europe.

July: Second session of the Parliamentary Assembly of CSCE is held in Helsinki.

August: Yugoslavia expels a dozen CSCE monitors from Kosovo and other areas of the former Yugoslavia. North Atlantic Council decides to prepare the use of stronger measures, including air strikes, in support of UN Security Council resolutions on Bosnia and Herzegovina. Consultations of CSCE Minsk Group with representatives of Azerbaijan and Armenia in Rome. While visiting Warsaw, President Yeltsin states that Poland's desire to join NATO is not counter to the process of European integration or to Russian interests. FSC resumes meeting in Vienna after summer break. Members focus on crisis stabilization, military contacts, conventional arms transfers, and defense planning information exchange in order to complete the issues before Rome meeting. High priority is still placed on arms control harmonization and "code of conduct."

September: CSCE Minsk Group starts its talks on Nagorno-Karabakh in Moscow. President Yeltsin objects to a possible enlargement of NATO to include central and eastern European nations. In a letter to western alliance governments, he proposes a common security guarantee for central and eastern Europe. President Clinton makes his first address to UN General Assembly. First Human Dimension Implementation meeting in Warsaw.

October: Election monitoring in Azerbaijan by observers from CSCE states, coordinated by ODIHR. Franco-German talks on joint armaments agency for Eurocorps take place. Franco-German brigade is formally assigned to the Eurocorps. General Secretary Hoynck admits that CSCE is not ready to send 500 monitors to Nagorno-Karabakh to monitor the cease-fire agreement, because of a general unwillingness on the parts of the Western member states to participate in such a mission. Partnership for Peace proposal is first raised by the U.S. secretary of defense at an informal NATO defense ministers' meeting in Travenmunde, Germany.

November: Treaty of European Union, signed at Maastricht, enters into force. CSCE Minsk Group meets in Vienna. A mutual-concession solution of the Nagorno-Karabakh conflict is proposed. Eurocorps is installed in Strasbourg, France; according to estimates, it will be fully operational by October 1995. CSCE decides to send a four-person mission to Latvia to reduce tensions between the government and the Russian speakers located there. Some reductions have been met by both NATO and the former Warsaw Treaty Organization as the first phase of CFE treaty implementation ends. Council of Ministers meeting in Luxembourg; period of WEU presidency is reduced to six months; conditions for the use of Eurocorps within framework of WEU are established.

November–December: CSCE Council meeting is held in Rome. CSCE decides to send four-person mission to Tajikistan to maintain a dialogue between regional forces in ongoing civil war between Islamic rebels and the Tajik government. Macedonia is denied full membership because of the objections of Greece.

December: Meeting in Vienna, CSCE establishes Permanent Committee. Meeting at least once a week, this committee has become the central forum for consultations and dialogue among member states. The U.S. proposal for the Partnership for Peace is supported by North Atlantic Council. Six hundred CSCE observers are sent to Russian Federation to monitor elections.

1994 *January:* Summit meeting of North Atlantic Council in Brussels. European Union and Maastricht Treaty are hailed as strengthening the

European pillar of the alliance. Greater cooperation between NATO and WEU is also applauded. NATO leaders formally invite former Warsaw Treaty Organization nations to join Partnership for Peace. Tensions among the allies continue over NATO activities in Bosnia. Georgian-Abkhaz talks in Geneva are brought to a successful close. The final communiqué is signed by a CSCE representative. Romania and then Lithuania join the Partnership for Peace initiative.

February: Poland and then Estonia, Hungary, Ukraine, Slovakia, and Latvia join the Partnership for Peace initiative. Chairman in Office Beniamino Andreatta (foreign minister of Italy) calls for resumption of blocked CSCE missions in Vojvodina, Kosovo, and Sanjak. France issues defense white paper calling for shifting resources from nuclear forces to conventional arms. The paper carefully avoids the issue of nuclear testing. Albania joins the Partnership for Peace initiative. Parliamentary elections are held in Moldova. The elections are monitored by representatives of ODIHR, the Parliamentary Assembly, and the CSCE Mission to Moldova; observers declare the elections to have been free and fair.

March: CSO calls for the early, unconditional return of missions to Vojvodina, Kosovo, and Sanjak. CSO does not accept an initiative to form a permanent CSCE forum for military stability in the former Yugoslavia. Parliamentary elections are held in Kazakhstan; the observer delegation of the Parliamentary Assembly concludes that the elections were not free and fair. The Czech Republic and then Moldova, Georgia, and Slovenia join the Partnership for Peace initiative.

March–April: Parliamentary elections are held in Ukraine. Representatives of the Parliamentary Assembly and of ODIHR are present as observers. After the run-off on April 10, they raise concerns about the fairness of the elections.

April: Germany issues defense white paper calling for the development of a rapid reaction force for deployment in peacekeeping missions and military crises. Russia requests that CFE treaty be amended or rewritten to accommodate redeployment of Russian troops in the region of the Caucasus and in other areas of the former Soviet Union to serve as peacekeepers and to protect Russian security interests in the region. Approval for redeployment of Russian troops requires the approval of CSCE or UN Security Council. CSCE monitors in the Ukraine express doubts about fairness of Ukrainian elections. In the Uruguay round of negotiations on the General Agreement on Tariff and Trade (GATT), 109 countries sign an ambitious and broad accord on liberalization of trade. The process of ratifying the accord begins in many countries, including the United States.

May: Negotiations concerning Spain's participation in Eurocorps begin. Azerbaijan and then Finland and Sweden join the Partnership for Peace initiative. Kirchberg declaration is issued at Council of Ministers meeting in Luxembourg. Status of association is granted to the republics of Bulgaria, Estonia, Hungary, Latvia, Lithuania, Poland, Czech Republic, Romania, and Slovakia. Turkmenistan joins the Partnership for Peace initiative. Azerbaijan insists that a multinational peacekeeping force operating under the mandate of CSCE be sent to its soil instead of an exclusively Russian force. Russian Defense Minister Pavel Grachev visits NATO headquarters in Brussels and pledges that Russia will join the Partnership for Peace but does not say when or under what specific terms. Negotiations over Russian positions regarding expansion of NATO and strengthening of CSCE prove to be obstacles to an immediate Russian signing. Russia also demands that special protocols be established between Russia and NATO because of Russia's special status. West rejects these demands. Kazakhstan joins the Partnership for Peace initiative. Nine east European nations agree to hold talks on territorial disputes and internal differences with the help of the European Union. The effort to resolve their disputes was based on the Balladur plan and builds on CSCE principles of "good neighborliness." Joint U.S.-Russian military training exercises, originally scheduled for July 1994, are delayed until September because of right-wing Russian opposition. In a largely symbolic gesture, U.S. Defense Department and Russia confirm that their respective nuclear missiles are no longer targeted on each other. The agreement to retarget their nuclear forces was made in January 1994.

June: Kyrgystan joins the Partnership for Peace initiative. President Clinton addresses National Assembly of France. Russia joins the Partnership for Peace initiative after a protracted negotiation with NATO. Agreement on Russia's participation in PFP had been delayed by Russian objections to the possible integration of eastern European nations into NATO before Russia, insistence on a veto over NATO actions and operations, and its proposal to subordinate NATO to CSCE. While acknowledging the special relationship of Russia and NATO in a separate document, NATO refuses to accede to Russian demands. European Union summit is held in Corfu, Greece. The twelve member states deadlock in efforts to name a successor for outgoing EU president, Jacques Delors. Overriding the support of the eleven other member nations, Great Britain blocks the choice of Belgian Prime Minister Jean-Luc Dehaene to the ten-year term as president of European Union. Prime Minister Major finds him "unacceptable," and the British fear that he would move the EU too quickly toward a more federalist union. President Yeltsin signs a far-reaching agreement with the European Union at the EU's summit meeting. The agreement provides for freer trade and closer ties between Russia and the EU. Greece ends its six-month chairmanship of the EU presidency; the rotating position passes to Germany. President Clinton addresses the Polish Sejm in Warsaw and later speaks at the Bradenburg Gate in Berlin.

July: Uzbekistan joins the Partnership for Peace initiative. Eurocorps, including 200 German officers and men, marches in the Bastille Day parade down the Champs-Elysées in Paris; Spanish and Belgian troops also participate. Jacques Santer, prime minister of Luxembourg, is elected commission president of the European Union in a special summit to select a new EU president, held in Brussels. Santer is praised by Prime Minister Major as a "decentralizer." The former candidate, Belgian Prime Minister Dehaene, and German Chancellor Kohl both suggested that changes in the procedure for electing the commission president might be discussed in the future.

August: NATO Secretary General Manfred Woerner dies.

September: "Peacekeeper '94," a joint U.S.-Russian military training exercise, is conducted in the southern Urals.

October–December: CSCE Review Conference meets in Budapest.

Appendix B: Partnership for Peace
Invitation

Issued by the Heads of State and Government participating in the meeting of the North Atlantic Council held at NATO Headquarters, Brussels, on 10–11 January 1994

We, the Heads of State and Government of the member countries of the North Atlantic Alliance, building on the close and longstanding partnership among the North American and European Allies, are committed to enhancing security and stability in the whole of Europe. We therefore wish to strengthen ties with the democratic states to our East. We reaffirm that the Alliance, as provided for in Article 10 of the Washington Treaty, remains open to the membership of other European states in a position to further the principles of the Treaty and to contribute to the security of the North Atlantic area. We expect and would welcome NATO expansion that would reach to democratic states to our East, as part of an evolutionary process, taking into account political and security developments in the whole of Europe.

We have today launched an immediate and practical programme that will transform the relationship between NATO and participating states. This new programme goes beyond dialogue and cooperation to forge a real partnership—a Partnership for Peace. We therefore invite the other states participating in the NACC and other CSCE countries able and willing to contribute to this programme, to join with us in the partnership. Active participation in the Partnership for Peace will play an important role in the evolutionary process of the expansion of NATO.

The Partnership for Peace, which will operate under the authority of the North Atlantic Council, will forge new security relationships between the

North Atlantic Alliance and its Partners for Peace. Partner states will be invited by the North Atlantic Council to participate in political and military bodies at NATO Headquarters with respect to Partnership activities. The Partnership will expand and intensify political and military cooperation throughout Europe, increase stability, diminish threats to peace, and build strengthened relationships by promoting the spirit of practical cooperation and commitment to democratic principles that underpin our Alliance. NATO will consult with any active participant in the Partnership if that partner perceives a direct threat to its territorial integrity, political independence, or security. At a pace and scope determined by the capacity and desire of the individual participating states, we will work in concrete ways towards transparency in defence budgeting, promoting democratic control of defence ministries, joint planning, joint military exercises, and creating an ability to operate with NATO forces in such fields as peacekeeping, search and rescue and humanitarian operations, and others as may be agreed.

To promote closer military cooperation and interoperability, we will propose, within the Partnership framework, peacekeeping field exercises beginning in 1994. To coordinate joint military activities within the Partnership, we will invite states participating in the Partnership to send permanent liaison officers to NATO Headquarters and a separate Partnership Coordination Cell at Mons (Belgium) that would, under the authority of the North Atlantic Council, carry out the military planning necessary to implement the Partnership programmes.

Since its inception two years ago, the North Atlantic Cooperation Council has greatly expanded the depth and scope of its activities. We will continue to work with all our NACC partners to build cooperative relationships across the entire spectrum of the Alliance's activities. With the expansion of NACC activities and the establishment of the Partnership for Peace, we have decided to offer permanent facilities at NATO Headquarters for personnel from NACC countries and other Partnership for Peace participants in order to improve our working relationships and facilitate closer cooperation.

Framework Document

1. Further to the invitation extended by the NATO Heads of State and Government at their meetings on 10–11 January 1994, the member states of

the North Atlantic Alliance and the other states subscribing to this document, resolved to deepen their political and military ties and to contribute further to the strengthening of security within the Euro-Atlantic area, hereby establish, within the framework of the North Atlantic Cooperation Council, this Partnership for Peace.

2. This Partnership is established as an expression of a joint conviction that stability and security in the Euro-Atlantic area can be achieved only through cooperation and common action. Protection and promotion of fundamental freedoms and human rights, and safeguarding of freedom, justice, and peace through democracy are shared values fundamental to the Partnership. In joining the Partnership, the member States of the North Atlantic Alliance and the other States subscribing to this Document recall that they are committed to the preservation of democratic societies, their freedom from coercion and intimidation, and the maintenance of the principles of international law. They reaffirm their commitment to fulfil in good faith the obligations of the Charter of the United Nations and the principles of the Universal Declaration on Human Rights; specifically, to refrain from the threat or use of force against the territorial integrity or political independence of any State, to respect existing borders and to settle disputes by peaceful means. They also reaffirm their commitment to the Helsinki Final Act and all subsequent CSCE documents and to the fulfilment of the commitments and obligations they have undertaken in the field of disarmament and arms control.

3. The other states subscribing to this document will cooperate with the North Atlantic Treaty Organization in pursuing the following objectives:

(a) facilitation of transparency in national defence planning and budgeting processes;

(b) ensuring democratic control of defence forces;

(c) maintenance of the capability and readiness to contribute, subject to constitutional considerations, to operations under the authority of the UN and/or the responsibility of the CSCE;

(d) the development of cooperative military relations with NATO, for the purpose of joint planning, training, and exercises in order to strengthen their ability to undertake missions in the fields of peacekeeping, search and rescue, humanitarian operations, and others as may subsequently be agreed;

(e) the development, over the longer term, of forces that are better able to operate with those of the members of the North Atlantic Alliance.

4. The other subscribing states will provide to the NATO Authorities Pre-

sentation Documents identifying the steps they will take to achieve the political goals of the Partnership and the military and other assets that might be used for Partnership activities. NATO will propose a programme of partnership exercises and other activities consistent with the Partnership's objectives. Based on this programme and its Presentation Document, each subscribing state will develop with NATO an individual Partnership Programme.

5. In preparing and implementing their individual Partnership Programmes, other subscribing states may, at their own expense and in agreement with the Alliance and, as necessary, relevant Belgian authorities, establish their own liaison office with NATO Headquarters in Brussels. This will facilitate their participation in NACC/Partnership meetings and activities, as well as certain others by invitation. They will also make available personnel, assets, facilities and capabilities necessary and appropriate for carrying out the agreed Partnership Programme. NATO will assist them, as appropriate, in formulating and executing their individual Partnership Programmes.

6. The other subscribing states accept the following understandings:
- those who envisage participation in missions referred to in paragraph 3(d) will, where appropriate, take part in related NATO exercises;
- they will fund their own participation in Partnership activities, and will endeavour otherwise to share the burdens of mounding exercises in which they take part;
- they may send, after appropriate agreement, permanent liaison officers to a separate Partnership Coordination Cell at Mons (Belgium) that would, under the authority of the North Atlantic Council, carry out the military planning necessary to implement the Partnership programmes;
- those participating in planning and military exercises will have access to certain NATO technical data relevant to interoperability;
- building upon the CSCE measures on defence planning, the other subscribing states and NATO countries will exchange information on the steps that have been taken or are being taken to promote transparency in defence planning and budgeting and to ensure the democratic control of armed forces;
- they may participate in a reciprocal exchange of information on defence planning and budgeting which will be developed within the framework of the NACC/Partnership for Peace.

7. In keeping with their commitment to the objectives of this Partnership for Peace, the members of the North Atlantic Alliance will:

- develop with the other subscribing states a planning and review process to provide a basis for identifying and evaluating forces and capabilities that might be made available by them for multinational training, exercises, and operations in conjunction with Alliance forces;
- promote military and political coordination at NATO Headquarters in order to provide direction and guidance relevant to Partnership activities with the other subscribing states, including planning, training, exercises and the development of doctrine.

8. NATO will consult with any active participant in the Partnership if that Partner perceives a direct threat to its territorial integrity, political independence, or security.

Appendix C: The North Atlantic Treaty, Washington, D.C., April 4, 1949

The Parties to this Treaty reaffirm their faith in the purposes and principles of the Charter of the United Nations and their desire to live in peace with all peoples and all governments.

They are determined to safeguard the freedom, common heritage and civilisation of their peoples, founded on the principles of democracy, individual liberty and the rule of law.

They seek to promote stability and well-being in the North Atlantic area.

They are resolved to unite their efforts for collective defence and for the preservation of peace and security.

They therefore agree to this North Atlantic Treaty:

Article 1 The Parties undertake, as set forth in the Charter of the United Nations, to settle any international dispute in which they may be involved by peaceful means in such a manner that international peace and security and justice are not endangered, and to refrain in their international relations from the threat or use of force in any manner inconsistent with the purposes of the United Nations.

Article 2 The Parties will contribute toward the further development of peaceful and friendly international relations by strengthening their free institutions, by bringing about a better understanding of the principles upon which these institutions are founded, and by promoting conditions of stability and well-being. They will seek to eliminate conflict in their international economic policies and will encourage economic collaboration between any or all of them.

Article 3 In order more effectively to achieve the objectives of this Treaty, the Parties, separately and jointly, by means of continuous and effective self-help and mutual aid, will maintain and develop their individual and collective capacity to resist armed attack.

Article 4 The Parties will consult together whenever, in the opinion of any of them, the territorial integrity, political independence or security of any of the Parties is threatened.

Article 5 The Parties agree that an armed attack against one or more of them in Europe or North America shall be considered an attack against them all and consequently they agree that, if such an armed attack occurs, each of them, in exercise of the right of individual or collective self-defence recognised by Article 51 of the Charter of the United Nations, will assist the Party or Parties so attacked by taking forthwith, individually and in concert with the other Parties, such action as it deems necessary, including the use of armed force, to restore and maintain the security of the North Atlantic area.

Any such armed attack and all measures taken as a result thereof shall immediately be reported to the Security Council. Such measures shall be terminated when the Security Council has taken the measures necessary to restore and maintain international peace and security.

Article 6[1] For the purpose of Article 5, an armed attack on one or more of the Parties is deemed to include an armed attack:

- on the territory of any of the Parties in Europe or North America, on the Algerian Departments of France,[2] on the territory of Turkey or on the Islands under the jurisdiction of any of the Parties in the North Atlantic area north of the Tropic of Cancer;
- on the forces, vessels, or aircraft of any of the Parties, when in or over these territories or any other area in Europe in which occupation forces of any of the Parties were stationed on the date when the Treaty entered into force or the Mediterranean Sea or the North Atlantic area of the Tropic of Cancer.

Article 7 This Treaty does not affect, and shall not be interpreted as affecting in any way the rights and obligations under the Charter of the Parties which are members of the United Nations, or the primary responsibility of the Security Council for the maintenance of the international peace and security.

Article 8 Each Party declares that none of the international engagements now in force between it and any other of the Parties or any third State is in conflict with the provisions of this Treaty, and undertakes not to enter into any international engagement in conflict with this Treaty.

Article 9 The Parties hereby establish a Council, on which each of them shall be represented, to consider matters concerning the implementation of this Treaty. The Council shall be so organised as to be able to meet promptly at any time. The Council shall set up such subsidiary bodies as may be necessary; in particular it shall establish immediately a defence committee which shall recommend measures for the implementation of Articles 3 and 5.

Article 10 The Parties may, by unanimous agreement, invite any other European State in a position to further the principles of this Treaty and to contribute to the security of the North Atlantic area to accede to this Treaty. Any State so invited may become a Party to the Treaty by depositing its instrument of accession with the Government of the United States of America. The Government of the United States of America will inform each of the Parties of the deposit of each such instrument of accession.

Article 11 This Treaty shall be ratified and its provisions carried out by the Parties in accordance with their respective constitutional processes. The instruments of ratification shall be deposited as soon as possible with the Government of the United States of America, which will notify all the other signatories of each deposit. The Treaty shall enter into force between the States which have ratified it as soon as the ratifications of the majority of the signatories, including the ratifications of Belgium, Canada, France, Luxembourg, the Netherlands, the United Kingdom and the United States, have been deposited and shall come into effect with respect to other States on the date of the deposit of their ratifications.

Article 12 After the Treaty has been in force for ten years, or at any time thereafter, the Parties shall, if any of them so requests, consult together for the purpose of reviewing the Treaty, having regard for the factors then affecting peace and security in the North Atlantic area, including the development of universal as well as regional arrangements under the Charter of the United Nations for the maintenance of international peace and security.

Article 13 After the Treaty has been in force for twenty years, any Party may cease to be a Party one year after its notice of denunciation has been given to the Government of the United States of America, which will inform the Governments of the other Parties of the deposit of each notice of denunciation.

Article 14 This Treaty, of which the English and French texts are equally authentic, shall be deposited in the archives of the Government of the United States of America, Duly certified copies will be transmitted by that Government to the Governments of other signatories.

1. The definition of the territories to which Article 5 applies was revised by Article 2 of the Protocol to the North Atlantic Treaty on the accession of Greece and Turkey and by the Protocols signed on the accession of the Federal Republic of Germany and of Spain.

2. On January 16, 1963, the North Atlantic Council heard a declaration by the French Representative who recalled that by the vote on self-determination on July 1, 1962, the Algerian people had pronounced itself in favour of the independence of Algeria in co-operation with France. In consequence, the President of the French Republic had on July 3, 1962, formally recognised the independence of Algeria. The result was that the "Algerian departments of France" no longer existed as such, and that at the same time the fact that they were mentioned in the North Atlantic Treaty had no longer any bearing.

Following this statement the Council noted that insofar as the former Algerian Departments of France were concerned, the relevant clauses of this Treaty had become inapplicable as from July 3, 1962.

Selected Bibliography

Asmus, Ronald D., Richard L. Kugler, and F. Stephen Larrabee. "Building a New NATO." *Foreign Affairs,* vol. 72 (September–October 1993), pp. 28–40.

Borawski, John, ed. *Avoiding War in the Nuclear Age: Confidence-Building Measures for Crisis Stability.* Boulder, Colo.: Westview Press, 1986.

Borawski, John, and Bruce George. "The CSCE Forum for Security Cooperation." *Arms Control Today,* vol. 23 (October 1993), pp. 13–17.

Buchan, David. *Europe: The Strange Superpower.* Brookfield, Vt: Dartmouth Publishing, 1993.

Buzan, Barry, and others. *The European Security Order Recast.* New York: Pinder, 1990.

Carter, Ashton B., William J. Perry, and John D. Steinbruner. *A New Concept of Cooperative Security.* Brookings Occasional Papers. Washington, D.C.: Brookings Institution, 1992.

Chayes, Antonia Handler, and Abram Chayes, eds. "International Organizations in Conflict Prevention." *Preventing Conflict in the Postcommunist World.* Brookings, forthcoming.

Cromwell, W., *The United States and the European Pillar.* New York: St. Martin's Press, 1992.

Daalder, Ivo H. *The CFE Treaty: An Overview and Assessment.* Washington, D.C.: Johns Hopkins Foreign Policy Institute, 1991.

Dembinski, Matthias, Alexander Kelle, and Harold Mueller. *NATO and Nonproliferation: A Critical Appraisal.* PRIF Reports, no. 33. Frankfurt: Peace Research Institute Frankfurt, April 1994..

Deutsch, Karl W., and others. *Political Community and the North Atlantic Area: International Organization in Light of Historical Experience.* Princeton, N.J.: Princeton University Press, 1957.

Dinan, Desmond. *An Ever Closer Union? An Introduction to the European Community.* Boulder, Colo.: Lynne Rienner, 1994.

Donfried, Karen. "European Community Enlargement." In *Europe and the United States: Competition and Cooperation in the 1990s,* Hearings before the House Committee on Foreign Affairs, 102 Cong., 2 sess. Washington, D.C.: Government

Printing Office, June 1992.

___. *The Franco-German Eurocorps: Implications for the U.S. Security Role in Europe."* CRS Reports for Congress, no. 5. Washington, D.C.: Government Printing Office, October 1992.

Doyle, Sarah, with Kimberly Smith and Kemper Vest. *The Changing Shape of Peacekeeping: Conference Report.* McLean, Va.: Center for National Security Negotiations–SAIC, 1994.

Durch, William J. *The United Nations and Collective Security in the 21st Century.* Carlisle Barracks, Pa.: U.S. Army War College, Strategic Studies Institute, 1993.

Flanagan, Stephen J. "NATO and Central and Eastern Europe: From Liaison to Security Partnership." *Washington Quarterly,* vol. 15 (Spring 1992), pp. 141–52.

Fontaine, Pascal. *Jean Monnet: A Grand Design for Europe.* Luxembourg: Office for Official Publications of the European Communities, 1988.

Frye, Alton, and Werner Weidenfeld, eds. *Europe and America: between Drift and New Order.* Germany Foundation (New York: Council on Foreign Relations Press, 1993).

Freedman, Lawrence, ed. *Europe Transformed: Documents on the End of the Cold War.* New York: St. Martin's Press, 1990.

Fursdon, Edward. *The European Defense Community: A History.* New York: St. Martin's Press, 1980.

Gantz, Nanette C., and John Roper, eds. *Towards a New Partnership: U.S.-European Relations in the Post–Cold War Era.* Paris: Institute for Security Studies of the Western European Union, 1993.

Garnham, David. *The Politics of European Defense Cooperation: Germany, France, Britain, and America.* Cambridge, Mass.: Ballinger Publishing Company, 1988.

Gebhard, Paul. *The United States and European Security.* Adelphi Papers, no. 206. London: International Institute for Strategic Studies, 1994.

Ginsberg, Roy H. *Foreign Policy Actions of the European Community: The Politics of Scale.* Boulder, Colo.: Lynne Rienner, 1989.

Gnesotto, Nicole. *Lessons of Yugoslavia.* Chaillot Papers, no. 14. Paris: Western European Union Institute for Security Studies, March 1994.

Gnesotto, Nicole, and John Roper, eds. *Western Europe and the Gulf.* Paris: Western European Union Institute for Security Studies, 1992.

Goodby, James E. "Peacekeeping in the New Europe." *Washington Quarterly,* vol. 15 (Spring 1992), pp. 153–71.

Harris, Scott A., and James B. Steinberg. *European Defense and the Future of Transatlantic Cooperation.* Santa Monica, Calif.: National Defense Research Institute–Rand Corporation, 1993.

Hyde-Price, A., *European Security beyond the Cold War.* London: Sage, 1991.

Isaacson, Walter, and Evan Thomas. *The Wise Men: Six Friends and the World They Made.* New York: Simon and Schuster, 1986.

Karaganov, Sergei. *Where Is Russia Going?* PRIF Reports, no. 34. Frankfurt: Peace Research Institute Frankfurt, April 1994.

Kelleher, Catherine M. "Cooperative Security in Europe." In *Global Engagement: Cooperation and Security in the 21st Century,* edited by Janne E. Nolan. Washington, D.C.: Brookings Institution, 1994.

___. "The NATO Alliance Recast with Its Future in Doubt." *Cosmos*, vol. 4 (1994), pp. 46–50.

___. "The Future of European Security." Paper prepared for the Aspen Institute Conference on U.S. Relations with Central and Eastern Europe. Berlin, August 22–27, 1994.

___. *A New Security Order: The United States and the European Community in the 1990's*. Pittsburgh: European Community Studies Association, June 1993.

___."The Debate over the Modernization of NATO's Short-Range Nuclear Missiles." *SIPRI Yearbook, 1990: World Armaments and Disarmament*. New York: Oxford University Press and the Stockholm International Peace Research Institute, 1990.

___. "U.S. Foreign Policy and Europe, 1990–2000." *Brookings Review*, vol. 8 (Fall 1990), pp. 4–10.

Kissinger, Henry. *Years of Upheaval*. Boston: Little, Brown, 1982.

Lacy, James L., with Peter Swartz and A. I. Suma. *Beyond NATO: Institutions, Purposes, and Politics in European Security*. Washington, D.C.: Center for Naval Analysis, May 1994.

Larrabee, F. Stephen. *East European Security after the Cold War*. Santa Monica, Calif.: Rand Corporation, 1993.

Legge, Michael. "The Making of NATO's New Strategic Concept." *NATO Review*, vol. 39 (December 1991), pp. 9–13.

Lynn-Jones, Sean M., and Steven E. Miller, eds. *The Cold War and After: Prospects for Peace*. Cambridge, Mass.: MIT Press, 1993.

Mortimer, Edward. *European Security after the Cold War*. Adelphi Papers, no. 271. London: International Institute for Strategic Studies, 1992.

Murray, Douglas, and Paul R. Viottio. *The Defense Policies of Nations: A Comparative Study*. 3d ed., Baltimore, Md.: Johns Hopkins University Press, 1994.

NATO Information Service. *Basic Fact Sheets*, nos. 1–10. Brussels, 1993–94.

NATO, Peacekeeping, and the United Nations. Report 94.1. Berlin: Berlin Information Centre for Transatlantic Security, September 1994.

Nolan, Janne E., ed. *Global Engagement: Cooperative Security in the 21st Century*. Washington, D.C.: Brookings Institution, 1994.

Reinecke, Wolfgang H. *Building a New Europe: The Challenge of System Transformation and Systemic Reform*. Brookings Occasional Papers. Washington, D.C.: Brookings Institution, 1992.

Rotfeld, Adam Daniel. "Europe: Toward a New Regional Security Regime." *SIPRI Yearbook, 1994*. Oxford: Oxford University Press, 1994, pp. 208–15.

SIPRI Yearbooks. Oxford: Oxford University Press, 1991, 1992, 1993, and 1994.

Sloan, Stanley R., ed. *NATO in the 1990s*. London, Pergamon-Brassey's, 1989.

___. "Transatlantic Relations in the Wake of the Brussels Summit." *NATO Review*, vol. 42 (April 1994), pp. 27–31.

Smith, Michael, Helen Wallace, and Stephen Woolcock. "The Implications of the Treaty of European Union." *In Europe and the United States: Competition and Cooperation in the 1990s*, Hearings before the House Committee on Foreign Affairs, 102 Cong., 2 sess. Washington, D.C.: Government Printing Office, June 1992.

Stares, Paul B., ed. *The New Germany and the New Europe*. Washington, D.C.: Brookings Institution, 1992.

___. *Command Performance: The Neglected Dimension of European Security*. Washington, D.C.: Brookings Institution, 1991.

Steinberg, James B. *An Ever Closer Union*. Santa Monica, Calif.: Rand Corporation, 1993.

___. *Integration and Security in an All-European Order*. Santa Monica, Calif.: Rand Corporation, 1991.

___. *The Role of the European Institutions and Security after the Cold War*. Santa Monica, Calif.: Rand Corporation, 1992.

Treverton, Gregory. *America, Germany, and the Future of Europe*. Princeton, N.J.: Princeton University Press, 1992.

Ullman, Richard. *Securing Europe*. Princeton, N.J.: Princeton University Press, 1991.

Walker, Jenonne. *Fact and Fiction about a European Security Identity and American Interest*. Occasional Paper. Washington, D.C.: Atlantic Council of the United States, 1992.

Wells, Samuel, Jr., ed. *The Helsinki Process and the Future of Europe*. Washington, D.C.: Wilson Center Press, 1990.

Woodward, Susan. *Balkan Tragedy: Chaos and Dissolution after the Cold War*. Washington, D.C.: Brookings, 1995.

Notes

Chapter One

1.   The geographic borders of central (and eastern) Europe remain somewhat ambiguous even at the end of 1994. In this monograph, central Europe (CE) generally refers to the states of the former Warsaw Treaty Organization: Bulgaria, the Czech Republic, Hungary, Poland, Romania, and Slovakia. Central and eastern Europe is more expansive, comprising all CE states plus Albania, Bosnia-Herzegovina, Croatia, Estonia, Latvia, Lithuania, Macedonia, Slovenia, and Yugoslavia (Serbia and Montenegro). Russia, Belarus, Moldova, Ukraine, and other states in the former Soviet space are debatable but are usually explicitly mentioned when their involvement is deemed critical or inevitable.

2.   This work draws on research reported in Catherine McArdle Kelleher, "Cooperative Security in Europe," in Janne E. Nolan, ed., *Global Engagement: Cooperation and Security in the 21st Century* (Brookings, 1994), pp. 293–351. See also the related work in Catherine McArdle Kelleher, *A New Security Order: The United States and the European Community in the 1990s,* occasional paper (Pittsburgh: European Community Studies Association, June 1993). For further formulations and research on cooperative security, see the essays in Nolan, ed., *Global Engagement;* and Paul B. Stares and John D. Steinbruner, "Cooperative Security in the New Europe," in Paul B. Stares, ed., *The New Germany and the New Europe* (Brookings, 1992) pp. 218–48. The basic concept of cooperative security was first delineated in Ashton B. Carter, William J. Perry, and John D. Steinbruner, *A New Concept of Cooperative Security, Occasional Papers* (Brookings, 1992).

3.   See German foreign minister Hans-Dietrich Genscher's speech to the conference of the Tutzing Protestant Academy on January 31, 1990, reproduced in Lawrence Freedman, ed., *Europe Transformed: Documents on the End of the Cold War* (St. Martin's Press, 1990), pp. 436–45. The early leadership role of Czechoslovak president Václav Havel in promoting pan-European security is touched on in F. Stephen Larrabee, *East European Security after the Cold War* (Santa Monica, Calif.: Rand Corporation, 1993), pp. 116–17.

4.   See the latest formulation of this position by Henry Kissinger, "It's an Alliance, Not a Relic," *Washington Post,* August 16, 1994, p. A19.

5.   In reality closer to the battalion level, the Baltic Brigade represents the beginnings of new armed forces for the Baltic states. A consortium of Scandinavian countries and the United Kingdom have in effect "adopted" and begun to train and equip (though not to arm) units from the Baltic states. The United Kingdom is providing education for the fledgling officer corps, and the Scandinavian countries are including Baltic units in their own training exercises. The Danes indeed have even brought a small Lithuanian unit with them to Croatia to participate in UN peace-keeping activities.

6.   See Kelleher, "Cooperative Security in Europe," pp. 304–10.

7.   Alan Cowell, "Bush Challenges Partners in NATO over the Role of the U.S.," *New York Times,* November 8, 1991, p. A1.

8.   A leaked draft of the Bush administration's Defense Planning Guidance suggested that a clear Bush goal was to prevent an independent European security organization that would undermine NATO. Patrick Tyler, "U.S. Strategy Plan Calls for Insuring No Rivals Develop," *New York Times,* March 8, 1992, p. A1. The Bush administration's concern over an independent European defense identity was the focus of the so-called Bartholomew letter, drafted in February 1991. Sometimes called the Dobbins Démarche, the letter laid down U.S. preconditions for cooperation with the development of a European defense identity. The Bartholomew letter has not been disclosed to the public, although it has been discussed in the press and in confidential interviews. Kelleher, *New Security Order,* pp. 16–17.

9.   See President Bill Clinton's speeches to the National Assembly of France, Paris, June 7, 1994; to the Polish Sejm, Warsaw, July 7, 1994; and before the Brandenburg Gate, Berlin, July 12, 1994. The policy and attitude of the Clinton administration in 1994 were still in sharp contrast to the position of Secretary of State Warren Christopher, who, according to one press report from 1993, "seemed ready to write off Europe as an area of strategic importance to the United States in favor of Asia." Lionel Barber, "Eurothrash: Our Allies up in Arms; Why Clinton Is Giving Europe the Jitters," *Washington Post,* October 24, 1994, p. C1.

10.   For a comprehensive overview of the Combined/Joint Task Forces, see Stanley R. Sloan, *Combined Joint Task Forces (CJTF) and New Missions for NATO,* CRS Reports (Congressional Research Service, March 17, 1994). See also Les Aspin, "New Europe, New NATO," *NATO Review,* February 1994, pp. 12–14. It should also be noted that, so far, little action has been taken toward specific implementation of the CJTF concept.

11.   Catherine McArdle Kelleher and Cathleen Fisher, "The Defense Policy of Germany," in Douglas J. Murray and Paul R. Viotti, eds., *The Defense Policies of Nations: A Comparative Study,* 3d ed. (Johns Hopkins University Press, 1994), pp. 160–89.

12.   See German foreign minister Genscher's speech to the conference of the Tutzing Protestant Academy. Also of note is Genscher's speech at the CSCE follow-up meeting in Helsinki, March 24, 1992.

13.   Immediately after the fall of the Berlin Wall, Czechoslovakia was one of the strongest advocates of an all-European security organization on the model of the CSCE, but it later acknowledged the need for U.S. involvement and the role of NATO

in European security. Larrabee, *East European Security after the Cold War,* pp. 116–17. See also Jonathan C. Randel, "Czechoslovakia Offers Plan for New Security System," *Washington Post,* April 7, 1990, p. A12; and Henry Kamm, "Havel, in Rebuff to Paris, Backs U.S.-Europe Ties," *New York Times,* June 13, 1991, p. A17.

14. The German white paper released on April 5, 1994, outlines the most recent German defense policy and calls for the establishment of a rapid reaction force for international crisis management and peacekeeping missions. The legality of this policy change has subsequently been cleared by the German courts. Though representing a major shift in German policy, the paper continues to stress the need for Germany to participate in cooperative security in Europe. Giovanni de Briganti, "New German White Paper Shifts Stance on Defense," *Defense News,* March 21–27, 1994, p. 4.

15. France has played a key role throughout much of this new shared experience. Besides significant French involvement in Bosnia in 1994, France led the way in the search for humanitarian aid options during the civil war and refugee flight in Rwanda and participated alongside the United States in Somalia. John Darton, "Intervening with Elan and No Regrets," *New York Times,* June 26, 1994, p. D3. Ending a twenty-nine-year absence, France attended the September 29–30 NATO defense ministers' meeting in Seville, Spain. "France Restores Key NATO Link," *Financial Times,* September 3–4, 1994, p. 2. France has also been heavily involved in the debates surrounding the operation of the new Combined Joint Task Forces under NATO. In Haiti, the French government balked at taking part in an invasion force but agreed to participate in peacekeeping operations once democracy was restored.

16. From interviews conducted by the author at the Pentagon in May–June 1994.

17. Above all else, the keeping of irritation accounts—the retelling at points of crisis or disagreement of the record of past slights and past attacks—should be discontinued by both countries.

18. The recent French white paper called for transferring resources from nuclear to conventional arms but remained ambiguous about the future justifications of an independent French nuclear force. Issues such as whether France will build a second nuclear-powered aircraft carrier were also avoided. Giovanni de Briganti, "French Review Evades Nuclear Issues," *Defense News,* February 28–March 6, 1994, p. 4. Also the French Assembly document on nuclear tests released December 15, 1993, has further contributed to national debate over France's role in nonproliferation and technical nuclear issues.

19. See the details of the Russian-NATO agreement in Steven Greenhouse, "Russia and NATO Agree to Closer Military Links," *New York Times,* June 23, 1994, p. A3. Shortly after reaching an agreement with NATO and joining the Partnership for Peace, Russia completed an agreement to liberalize trade with the EU. See Alan Cowell, "Russia and European Union Sign Accord for Free Trade," *New York Times,* June 25, 1994, p. A3; and Andrei V. Kozyrev, "Russia and NATO: A Partnership for a United Peaceful Europe," *NATO Review,* August 1994, pp. 3–6.

20. The G-7 comprises the United States, Canada, the United Kingdom, Germany, Japan, France, and Italy.

21. Those advocating renewed assertion of Russian power and influence, both

politically and militarily, go beyond the well-publicized statements of right-wing extremist Vladimir Zhirinovsky. Former vice president Alexander Rutskoi and former parliament leader Ruslan Khasbulatov have been vocal critics of Russia's relationship with the West and of the loss of international respect and power as a result of the collapse of the Soviet Union and the end of the cold war. More ominously, the rhetoric and initiatives of President Boris Yeltsin and Foreign Minister Andrei Kozyrev have been increasingly focused on nationalist themes and couched in more aggressive tones. Celestine Bohlen, "Nationalist Vote Toughens Russian Foreign Policy," *New York Times,* January 25, 1994, p. A6. For an overview of the views of dissident Aleksander Solzhenitsyn, see Serge Schmemann, "Solzhenitsyn Is in Russia, Hoping for a 'Ray of Light,'" *New York Times,* May 28, 1994, p. A1.

22. William E. Odom, "The Ambivalent Bear: Dealing with Moscow's Two Foreign Policies," *Washington Post,* December 5, 1993, p. C1.

23. See the related work on public opinion and foreign policy formulation presented in Catherine McArdle Kelleher, "Security in the New World Order: Presidents, Polls, and the Use of Force," in Daniel Yankelovich and I. M. Destler, eds., *Beyond the Beltway: Engaging the Public in U.S. Foreign Policy* (Norton, 1994), pp. 225–52; and Catherine McArdle Kelleher, "Soldiering On," *Brookings Review,* Spring 1994, pp. 26–29.

24. The Nunn-Lugar security assistance program has been the leading congressional effort to help stabilize and eliminate the nuclear stockpiles of the former Soviet Union and assist in converting the former Soviet military industrial complex to civilian use. By the end of 1993, $111,503,000 had been obligated for the demilitarization of the former Soviet Union. Russia was to receive $103,485,000; Belarus, $4,490,000; and Kazakhstan, $111,503,000. Nothing had been obligated for Ukraine, but $177,060,000 had been proposed for Ukrainian demilitarization and conversion. These figures are taken from "Factfile: U.S. Security Assistance to the Former Soviet Union," *Arms Control Today,* January–February, 1994, pp. 32–33.

25. Some congressional arguments have questioned the desirability of paying for defense conversion in Russia when similar issues are not being adequately addressed at home.

Chapter Two

1. Baker's speech is reproduced in Lawrence Freedman, ed., *Europe Transformed* (St. Martin's Press, 1990), pp. 397–98. This speech reflected existing tensions in the European-American security relationship, but Baker's main focus was on the developing role of the European Community. His proposal for a new agreement on the formalization of U.S.-EC consultations was intended to keep the transatlantic security relationship moving at the same pace as the evolving European single market and political cooperation.

2. A sympathetic but nonideological account of the European experience is found in Derek W. Urwin, *The Community of Europe* (London: Longman, 1991).

3. One that is not is Stanley Sloan, ed., *NATO in the 1990s* (Pergamon-Brassey's International Defense Publishers, 1989).

4.   For a comprehensive account of both the history and the politics of the EDC proposal, see Edward Fursdon, *The European Defense Community: A History* (St. Martin's Press, 1980).

5.   For the views of the American architects, see Walter Isaacson and Evan Thomas, *The Wise Men: Six Friends and the World They Made* (Simon and Schuster, 1986). For the critical concepts of Jean Monnet, see Richard Mayne, *The Recovery of Europe* (Harper and Row, 1970); Jean Monnet, *Memoirs* (Paris: Librarie Artheme Fayard, 1976); and Dean Acheson, *Sketches from Life* (Harper and Row, 1959).

6.   See Alberta M. Sbragia, ed., *Europolitics* (Brookings, 1992).

7.   Article 5 states: "The Parties agree that an armed attack against one or more of them in Europe or North America shall be considered an attack against them all, and consequently they agree that, if such an armed attack occurs, each of them, in exercise of the right of individual or collective self-defense recognised by Article 51 of the Charter of the United Nations, will assist the Party or Parties so attacked by taking forthwith, individually, and in concert with the other Parties, such action as it deems necessary, including the use of armed force, to restore and maintain the security of the North Atlantic area.

"Any such armed attack and all measures taken as a result thereof shall immediately be reported to the Security Council. Such measures shall be terminated when the Security Council has taken the measures necessary to restore and maintain international peace and security."

Article 4 states: "The Parties will consult together whenever, in the opinion of any of them, the territorial integrity, political independence or security of any of the Parties is threatened." *NATO Handbook* (Brussels, 1992).

8.   Catherine McArdle Kelleher, "Arms Control in a Revolutionary Future: Europe," *Daedalus: Journal of the American Academy of Arts and Sciences,* vol. 120 (Winter 1991), pp. 111–31. See the discussion of these continuing divergences in Vojtech Mastny, *Helsinki, Human Rights, and European Security: Analysis and Documentation* (Duke University Press, 1986); and Vojtech Mastny, *The Helsinki Process and the Reintegration of Europe,* 1986–1991 (New York University Press, 1992).

9.   For more on the INF treaty, see Catherine McArdle Kelleher, "Will the Reagan Administration Accept Its Own INF Proposal?" *Arms Control Today,* vol. 17 (April 1987); and Catherine McArdle Kelleher, "Tactical Nuclear Forces and Europe," in Kari T. Takamaa, ed., *Tiede ja tutkimus rauhan palveluksessa (Science and research in the service of peace)* (Helsinki: Finnish Pugwash Committee/Helsinki University Press, 1991).

10.   For more on the CFE treaty, see Ivo H. Daalder, *The CFE Treaty: An Overview and Assessment* (Washington: Johns Hopkins Foreign Policy Institute, 1991); the articles and books of Jonathan Dean, especially Jonathan Dean and Peter Clausen, *The INF Treaty and the Future of Western Security* (Washington: Union of Concerned Scientists, 1988); and the definitive chapters by Jane M. O. Sharp in the following Stockholm International Peace Research Institute (SIPRI) *Yearbooks:* 1988: chap. 11; 1989: chap. 11; 1990: chap. 13; 1991: chap. 13; 1992: chap. 12 (Ox-

ford University Press).

11. On the evolution of the CSCE, see John Borawski, ed., *Avoiding War in the Nuclear Age—Confidence Building Measures for Crisis Stability* (Boulder, Colo.: Westview Press, 1986); and James E. Goodby, *CSCE: The Diplomacy of Europe Whole and Free,* occasional paper (Washington: Atlantic Council of the United States, July 1990). For specifics on what was actually done, see the annual compilation of activities, exercises, and inspections in *Arms Control Reporter* (Cambridge: Institute for Defense and Disarmament Studies, 1986–92), sec. 402.

12. See Victor-Yves Ghebali, *Confidence Building Measures within the CSCE Process: Paragraph-by-Paragraph Analysis of the Helsinki and Stockholm Regimes,* United Nations Institute for Disarmament Research (UNIDIR) Research Paper 3, UNIDIR/89/14 (New York: United Nations, March 1989); and John Borawski, *Security for a New Europe: The Vienna Negotiations on Confidence and Security Building Measures, 1989–1990 and Beyond* (London: Brassey's, 1992). Stockholm indeed represented a decisive blurring of the earlier arms control–CSCE division. Because all other arms control talks had broken off during the INF crisis and the coming of "the second cold War" in the 1980s, Stockholm became a primary channel for the East-West security dialogue.

13. The 1990 Military Doctrine seminar is a good example. The seminar was sponsored by the CSCE and provided for high-level military-to-military exchanges between the United States and the USSR and focused interaction on specific military topics.

14. Jane M. O. Sharp, "Conventional Arms Control in Europe," *SIPRI Yearbook,* 1993 (Oxford University Press, 1993),
pp. 591–617.

15. Karl W. Deutsch and others, *Political Community and the North Atlantic Area: International Organization in Light of Historical Experience* (Princeton University Press, 1957).

16. On American perceptions of these ties, see Catherine McArdle Kelleher, "America Looks at Europe," in Lawrence Freedman, ed., *The Troubled Alliance* (St. Martin's Press, 1983), pp. 44–66.

17. Antonia Handler Chayes and Abram Chayes, "Regime Architecture: Elements and Principles," in Janne E. Nolan, ed., *Global Engagement: Cooperative Security in the 21st Century* (Brookings, 1994), pp. 65–130.

18. Paul B. Stares, *Command Performance: The Neglected Dimension of European Security* (Brookings, 1991).

Chapter Three

1. As discussed in chapter 5, the Contact Group, composed of representatives from the United States, the United Kingdom, France, Germany, and Russia, came together in 1994 to make a third major attempt to find a political settlement for the Yugoslav crisis. It is unique in that it is the first group in the three-year history of the crisis to include Russia as a major player. The membership of the group, sometimes referred to as the quad plus one (the four key NATO states plus Russia), is seen by

some as the template for a new "Concert of Europe," paralleling the role of the post-Napoleon coalition of great European powers in the early nineteenth century.

2.   I am indebted to Desmond Dinan for this term, in *An Ever Closer Union?: An Introduction to the European Community* (Boulder, Colo.: Lynne Rienner, 1994), p. 470.

3.   During his tenure as Czechoslovak president, Vaclav Havel was an early advocate of promoting pan-European security through the CSCE. Subsequent dissatisfaction with western Europe's speed and willingness to integrate eastern Europe into the EC and other organizations has caused him to reaffirm the role of the United States in the development of greater continentwide security. Henry Kamm, "Rebuffing Mitterrand, Havel Affirms U.S. Ties," *New York Times,* June 13, 1991, p. A17. In the West, German foreign minister Hans-Dietrich Genscher's speeches, reproduced in Lawrence Freedman, ed., *Europe Transformed: Documents on the End of the Cold War* (St. Martin's Press, 1990), pp. 436–45, detail the primacy of economic assistance to the East in the development of long-term continental security.

4.   The Charter of Paris for a new Europe, signed November 21, 1990, by the CSCE heads of government, reaffirmed the values of the CSCE and, more concretely, established new structures and institutions for the CSCE process, such as regular summit meetings and meetings of the foreign ministers. Provisions were also made for establishing new negotiations on disarmament and confidence- and security-building measures. A supplementary document to the charter established a CSCE secretariat, an Office of Free Elections, and a Conflict Prevention Center. For the full text, see "The Charter of Paris for a New Europe," Stockholm International Peace Research Institute (SIPRI) *Yearbook 1991: World Armaments and Disarmament* (Oxford University Press, 1991), pp. 603–10.

5.   Sean Kay "NATO, the CSCE, and the New Russia Question," in Victor Papacosma and Maryanne Heiss, eds., *Nato after 45 Years: Does It Have a Future?* (St Martin's Press, forthcoming).

6.   The Mitterrand proposal was motivated in part by a desire to prevent a premature widening of the EC that would weaken the growing ties among the western European countries. France favored deepening the EC in the West before admitting the politically and economically troubled eastern countries. France also expressed concern over U.S. influence in post–cold war Europe and said the United Nations and Europe should "counterbalance the influence of the only superpower left." "Soviet Turmoil; France to U.S.: Don't Rule," *New York Times,* September 3, 1991, p. A8. The goals and scope of this proposed "European confederation" were never clearly formulated to the satisfaction of the eastern Europeans, and the Mitterrand proposal specifically excluded the United States. The eastern European nations saw the proposal as a diversion from their goal of rapid integration into the EC. President Vaclav Havel referred to the proposed confederation as a "political doghouse." See F. Stephen Larabee, *Eastern European Security after the Cold War* (Santa Monica, Calif.: The Rand Corporation, 1993), pp. 145-46; "Mitterrand Clarifies Scheme for Grand European Confederation," *Financial Times,* June 13, 1991; Ian Davidson, "Ambiguity Clouds of Pan-European Confederation," *Financial Times,* June 12, 1991; and Kamm, "Rebuffing Mitterrand,"

7. The proposal limits participation to forty nations: the twelve EU members, the United States, Canada, Latvia, Lithuania, Estonia, Bulgaria, the Czech Republic, Hungary, Poland, Romania, Slovakia, Albania, Russia, Ukraine, Belarus, Moldova, and the countries of the former Yugoslavia.

8. For the details of the Balladur plan, see Alan Riding, "Nine East Europe Nations Join Round Table Talks," *New York Times,* May 28, 1994, p. A–4. For further details on the history of the Mitterrand confederation proposal and the Balladur plan, see Larabee, *Eastern European Security,* pp. 145–50; and Ernst Weisenfeld, "Frankreich und Mitteleuropa—Der Plan für einen Europäischen Stabilitäts-Pakt," in Ingo Kolboom and Ernst Weisenfeld, eds., *Frankreich in Europa: Ein deutsch-französischer Rundblick* (Bonn: Europa Union Verlag, 1993), pp. 167-79. The text of the Balladur plan can be found in Kolboom and Weisenfeld, eds., *Frankreich in Europa,* pp. 180–86.

9. Lee Hockstadter, "In Moldova's East Bank, Separatists Still Cling to the Bad Old Days," *Washington Post,* March 25, 1994, p. A31. See also Report on the *Moldovan Parliamentary Elections,* February 27, 1994, prepared by the staff of the U.S. Commission on Security and Cooperation in Europe (Washington, April 1994), p. 15.

10. This help has been hampered by Russian intervention. Troops of the Commonwealth of Independent States stationed in the area are selling arms to local combatants, in part to shape the outcome of the conflict but in part just to earn a living. Neela Banerjee, "Russia Combines War And Peace to Reclaim Parts of Its Old Empire," *Wall Street Journal,* September 2, 1994, p. A1.

11. For more information, see Umit Enginsoy, "Russia Resumes Subtle Military Influence in Transcaucasia," *Defense News,* July 11–17, 1994, p. 12.

12. *Basic Reports,* vol. 4 (NATO Office of Information and Press, Brussels, October 1994), p. 5.

13. In article 25 of the 1992 Helsinki document the CSCE states "declare[d] our understanding that the CSCE is a regional arrangement in the sense of Chapter VIII of the Charter of the United Nations." They further stated their resolve to work closely with the UN in the prevention and resolution of conflicts. The 1992 Helsinki Document can be found in its entirety in *SIPRI Yearbook 1993: World Armaments and Disarmament* (Oxford University Press, 1993), pp. 190–94.

14. At the January 1992 CSCE Council of Foreign Ministers meeting the voting requirements for the decisionmaking process were altered. Unanimous consent was no longer required for a decision to enter into force. Rather, a consensus-minus-one requirement was implemented, allowing the council or the CSCE Committee of Senior Officers, in cases of gross violations of CSCE commitments, to take action in the absence of the consent of the state concerned.

15. Even then, Russia's interest stressed, primarily as a delaying tactic, the CSCE's potential utility as an umbrella institution under which principal security functions would accrue to NATO and an integrated Commonwealth of Independent States made up of post-Soviet states.

16. Because of increased belligerency in the Gulf, Britain, Italy, Belgium, France, and the Netherlands sent minesweepers to the area in 1988. Germany and

Luxembourg also contributed to the mission, providing naval forces and financing, respectively. "Information Report," European Union Assembly, Committee for Parliamentary and Public Relations, February 1993.

17. This was the so-called Franco-German proposal of October 14, 1991. See Scott A. Harris and James B. Steinberg, *European Defense and the Future of Transatlantic Cooperation* (Santa Monica, Calif.: National Defense Research Institute, Rand Corporation, 1993), pp. 13ff.

18. The smaller European states weighed in between the two positions. But most distrusted the Eurocorps initiative, fearing Franco-German hegemony in a European Union dominated by a largely Franco-German army. Thus most small states tended to lean toward the Anglo-Italian position.

19. The never public but much discussed "Bartholomew letter" is the most obvious declaration of such U.S. anxieties. As mentioned in chapter 1, the letter, also known as the Dobbins démarche, reportedly establishes preconditions for U.S. involvement in European security and defense matters. For details, see Catherine McArdle Kelleher, *A New Security Order: The United States and the European Community in the 1990s,* occasional paper (Pittsburgh: European Community Studies Association, June 1993), p. 17; and John Newhouse, "Shunning the Losers," *New Yorker,* October 26, 1992, pp. 40–52.

20. As quoted in David Buchan, *Europe: The Strange Superpower* (Brookfield: Dartmouth Publishing, 1993), p. 155.

21. An interview account suggested in late 1991 that this had been an initiative launched with only minimal consultation with the responsible military authorities, at least in Germany. Its timing was also a cause of irritation, just as the defense and military leaders of all the NATO states were meeting in Taormina to review the final strategy decision before the Rome summit. "U.S. Wary of European Corps, Seeks Assurance on NATO Role," New York Times, October 20, 1991, p. 12. See also Karen Donfried, *"The Franco-German Eurocorps: Implications for the U.S. Security Role in Europe,"* CRS Reports 5 (Congressional Research Service, October 1992) and Harris and Steinberg, *European Defense.*

22. On this point, see Dinan, *An Ever Closer Union?* and Buchan, Europe.

23. For the details of the declaration, see "Declaration on the Role of the Western European Union and Its Relations with the European Union and with the Atlantic Alliance" (appended to the Treaty on European Union, Maastricht, December 10, 1991); and the linked declaration of the nine WEU members on membership access.

24. "Report of the German and French Defense Ministers on the Creation of the European Corps," adopted May 22, 1992, by the German-French Council on Defense and Security, quoted in Harris and Steinberg, *European Defense.* For insight into the immediate heated American response to the calculated ambiguity of the German and French interpretation of their joint initiative, see Frederick Kempe, "U.S., Bonn Clash over Pact with France," *Wall Street Journal,* May 27, 1992, p. A11.

25. The policy "domains within the security dimension" on which joint actions would be taken included the CSCE process, disarmament and arms control in Europe, nuclear nonproliferation, and control of the transfer of arms and military technology to third countries. See Dinan, *An Ever Closer Union?,* p. 473, for further discussion.

26. Luisa Vierucci, "WEU—a Regional Partner of the United Nations?" *Chaillot Paper 12* (Paris: Institute for Security Studies Western European Union, December 1993), p. 23.

27. Communiqué, Extraordinary meeting of WEU Council of Ministers on the situation in Yugoslavia, Helsinki, July 10, 1992.

28. These operations have been supported by "7,000 ship days spent at sea, over 4,700 sorties by maritime patrol aircraft and over 3,100 sorties by NATO Airborne Early Warning aircraft." Participating countries are France, Germany, Greece, Italy, the Netherlands, Portugal, Spain, the United Kingdom, Belgium, Norway, the United States, Denmark, Turkey, and Canada. For more information, see *NATO/WEU Operation Sharp Guard, Fact Sheet,* (Paris: Western European Union, August 11, 1994).

29. David Huntington, "The Western European Union and the 'Architecture' of European Security," paper presented to Consensus Building Institute's Conflict Prevention Conference, Brookings, September 26–27, 1994.

30. "French Seek to Tie Arms Procurement with Germans," *Defense News,* October 18, 1993, p. 1.

31. These provisions assumed still greater significance in attempts by Russian leaders in 1993 and 1994 to suggest that these constituted a binding commitment not to expand NATO. See Yeltsin's letter to the Western allies, reproduced in *SIPRI Yearbook, 1994* (Oxford University Press, 1994), pp. 249–50, in which Yelstin refers to the Treaty on the Final Settlement with Respect to Germany as excluding, "by its meaning, the possibility of expansion to the East." The views of both the West and Russia on NATO expansion are covered in Adam Rotfeld, "Europe: Toward a New Regional Security Regime," *SIPRI Yearbook 1994,* pp. 208–15.

32. *Rome Declaration on Peace and Cooperation* (Brussels: NATO Office of Information and Press, November 8, 1991). Just what was to constitute balance among which forces was deliberately left vague. These four functions had originally been outlined at the Copenhagen summit of June 7, 1991. For a positive account of the evolution of the strategic concept, see Michael Legge, "The Making of NATO's New Strategy," *NATO Review,* December 1991, pp. 9–13.

33. At the CSCE Helsinki meeting in July 1992, members agreed that CSCE peacekeeping operations would not entail "enforcement actions." Judy Dempsey, "CSCE States to Set Up Peace-keeping Forces," *Financial Times,* July 9, 1992, p. 97. Acting in parallel, the NATO foreign ministers decided at Oslo in June 1992 to support the CSCE in certain peacekeeping missions, leaving the participation of NATO states as optional. The NATO communiqué states that "we are prepared to support, on a case-by-case basis in accordance with our own procedures, peacekeeping activities under the responsibility of the CSCE, including by making available Alliance resources and expertise." "NATO Forges Closer Ties with CSCE," *CSCE Helsinki '92,* June 1992, p. 6. The NATO decision to accept peacekeeping taskings from the United Nations as well was made public at the December 1992 meeting of the North Atlantic Council.

34. Ronald D. Asmus, Richard L. Kugler, and F. Stephen Larrabee, "Building a New NATO," *Foreign Affairs,* vol. 72 (September-October 1993), pp. 28–40.

35. "NATO's New Force Structures," NATO *Basic Fact Sheet 5* (Brussels, Sep-

tember 1993).

36. This was clearly the case, as discussed in the next section, in discussions about establishing control mechanisms for the Combined Joint Task Forces.

37. Stanley R. Sloan, *Combined/Joint Task Forces (CJTF) and New Missions for NATO, CRS Reports* (Congressional Research Service, March 17, 1994). The Combined/Joint Task Forces emerged from a U.S. proposal to the NATO allies at the January 1994 NATO summit in Brussels. The CJTF is designed to provide NATO greater military flexibility for missions and situations in area and out of area, including but not limited to UN peacekeeping missions and response to military crises around the region. The CJTF would be adaptable to U.S.-led missions but would also allow for operations conducted by the Europeans without direct U.S. military involvement. See the discussion later in this chapter.

38. Brooks Tigner, "WEU Eyes New Security Plan," *Defense News,* March 14–20, 1994, p. 34. France has consistently opposed any recognition of the continuing overall responsibilities of SACEUR and the integrated command for assets assigned to a CJTF and an operational mission command.

39. Sloan, *Combined Joint Task Forces,* p. 3.

40. These are Poland, the Czech Republic, Slovakia, Romania, Hungary, and Bulgaria.

41. Paul Gebhard credits also the shift in decisionmaking authority that followed from a French government divided between a socialist president (Mitterrand) and a conservative prime minister (Balladur). Of necessity, the task of decisionmaking moved to careful compromises at the highest levels and away from the more Gaullist, nationalist, and particularist practices of the Quai d'Orsay. Paul R. S. Gebhard, *The United States and European Security,* Adelphi Paper 206 (London: International Institute for Strategic Studies, February 1994), pp. 21–23.

42. Buchan, *Europe,* p. 155.

43. The WEU has already granted Norway, Iceland, and Turkey associate membership. Full membership hinges on entry into the EU. There is also "association," which has been granted to non-NATO states. The WEU is particularly interested in Poland, the Czech Republic, and Hungary. For a comprehensive list of membership and status in the WEU, CSCE, NACC, and EU, see Bruce Clark, "Old Enemies Make Tricky Friends," *Financial Times,* June 9, 1994, p. 15; and *The British Statement on the Defence Estimates,* white paper (U.K. Ministry of Defence, 1994).

44. According to polls conducted in August and December 1992 by the U.S. Information Agency, comfortable majorities in Germany, Britain, and Italy believe NATO is "essential to their national security," as opposed to only about half of respondents in France. The polls also show that while "there is considerable support for reducing the American military presence in Europe, majorities in all countries prefer scenarios other than the complete withdrawal of American forces from the continent." These results represent even more support for continued U.S. involvement than earlier polls indicated. Kelleher, *A New Security Order,* fn. 19, p. 73.

45. The reaction of Britain and the smaller states to the parallel French and German proposals on a more integrated European "core" demonstrate this once again.

Chapter Four

1. For a comprehensive analytic account of these extremely significant questions, see F. Stephen Larrabee, *East European Security after the Cold War* (Santa Monica, Calif.: Rand Corporation, 1994).

2. The Nunn-Lugar initiative is a series of congressionally mandated programs for U.S. assistance to Russia, focused primarily on nuclear weapons and nuclear safety issues. It provides assistance for dismantling, joint storage, accounting of fissible materials, and so on. From 1992 to 1994, $1.2 billion was authorized through Nunn-Lugar. Of that sum, $330 million has expired, and $870 million has been transferred to programs (of which $434 million has been obligated). New authorizations for fiscal year 1995 amount to $400 million. Interview with Kim Sarits, November 1, 1994.

3. Hungary was the first eastern European nation to formally accept the PFP proposal. Paul Lewis, "Hungary Officially Informs U.S. It Accepts Compromise on NATO," *New York Times,* January 9, 1994, p. A6. Support from other eastern European nations was less enthusiastic; Poland's president Lech Walesa was particularly critical of the PFP proposal (though at least some of the criticism was playing to the crowd; indeed, Poland was the first to present NATO with a full work plan). The eastern European countries soon accepted the proposal. During his trip to Ukraine President Clinton also confirmed that Ukraine would be eligible to join the PFP. Douglas Jehl, "Ukrainian Agrees to Dismantle A-Arms," *New York Times,* January 13, 1994, p. A6. Russian president Boris Yeltsin endorsed the proposal as a "good formula" during Clinton's visit to Russia on January 14, 1994. Serge Schermann, "Clinton in Europe; On Russian TV, Clinton Backs Reforms," *New York Times,* January 15, 1994, p. A1.

4. For an interesting discussion of the evolution of elite foreign policy views, see Sergei Karaganov, "Where Is Russia Going?" in *Foreign and Defence Policies in a New Era,* PRIF Report 34 (Frankfurt: Peace Research Institute Frankfurt, April 1994).

5. Often called the Falin doctrine after Valentin Falin, this was the favored position of the Central Committee's International Department. Larrabee, *East European Security after the Cold War,* pp. 154–55.

6. During his trip to Poland in August 1993, Yeltsin signaled that Russia was sympathetic to central European desires to join NATO and that these desires did not threaten Russian security. Jane Perlez, "East Europe Waits for the West's Welcome Wagon," *New York Times,* August 29, 1994, p. A6. Russia reversed this position in a letter sent by Yeltsin to President Clinton and the Western leaders several weeks later, stating that Russia emphatically opposed the expansion of NATO. Roger Cohen, "Yeltsin Opposes Expansion of NATO in Eastern Europe," *New York Times,* October 2, 1994, p. A4.

7. Edward Mortimer, *European Security after the Cold War,* Adelphi Paper 271 (London: International Institute for Strategic Studies [IISS], Summer 1992). In addition to the description of the circumstances surrounding Yeltsin's request, see the detailed description of the outreach efforts made before the summer of 1992, reported

in chapter 2.

8.   For the full text of letter see *SIPRI Yearbook 1994* (Oxford University Press, 1994), pp. 249–50.

9.   President François Mitterrand was perhaps the most extreme when in June 1991 he told the central Europeans that they were "decades and decades" away from EC membership. *Le Monde,* June 14, 1991, quoted in Larrabee, *East European Security after the Cold War,* p. 92.

10.   For two different views on France's shift in policy, see Larrabee, *East European Security after the Cold War;* and Paul Gebhard, *The United States and European Security,* Adelphi Paper 206 (London: IISS, February 1994). Larrabee emphasizes the change from socialist leadership to a less ideological conservative prime minister as the primary cause for the shift. While not ignoring the importance of the divided French government, Gebhard suggests that once the issues surrounding European union were settled, France was able to relax its policy.

11.   See Jonathan C. Randel, "Czechoslovakia Offers Plan for New Security System," *Washington Post,* April 7, 1990, p. A12; and Henry Kamm, "Havel, in Rebuff to Paris, Backs U.S.-Europe Ties," *New York Times,* June 13, 1991, p. A17.

12.   Czechoslovakia under Havel was the first to change in mid-1990; Poland in 1990 thought about adopting neutrality, and Hungary rejected a NATO role until late in 1991. Bulgaria was interested from the first because of its concerns about Turkey; Romania showed little interest until after the Soviet coup attempt. Larabee, *East European Security,* pp 54–63.

13.   Ibid., pp. 100–03.

14.   This initiative was largely the work of Italian foreign minister Gianni de Michelis and included Yugoslavia. Gianni de Michelis, "Reaching Out to the East," *Foreign Policy,* no. 79 (Summer 1990), pp. 49–52. With the addition of Poland, the organization became known as the Hexagonale. By 1992 the effort had been renamed the Central European Initiative (CEI); the former Yugoslavia was replaced by the newly recognized states of Croatia, Slovenia, and Bosnia, and eventually Macedonia; and the CEI itself became largely dormant, particularly under the weight of the conflict in the former Yugoslavia. Larabee, *East European Security,* pp. 106–08.

15.   The EC took the lead by mutual agreement with the United States. Wolfgang Reinicke, *Building a New Europe: The Challenge of Systems Transformation and Systemic Reform,* Occasional Papers (Brookings, 1992).

16.   The West in this case was the so-called G-24 countries: the EU 12 plus Austria, Finland, Iceland, Norway, Sweden, Switzerland, Australia, Canada, Japan, New Zealand, Turkey, and the United States. Catherine McArdle Kelleher, *A New Security Order: The United States and the European Community in the 1990s,* Occasional Paper (Pittsburgh: European Community Studies Association, June 1993), app. B.

17.   In 1990 this form of aid was extended to Czechoslovakia, Bulgaria, East Germany, and Yugoslavia. By late 1991 the Baltic states and eventually Romania were also included.

18.   See *Europe and the United States: Competition and Cooperation in the 1990's,* Committee Print, House Committee on Foreign Affairs, 102 Cong. 2 sess. (Government Printing Office, June 1992).

19. Perhaps the only supporters of expansion in the foreseeable future were Germany, in the interest of reassurance on its eastern borders, and Britain, still looking for ways to ensure a weaker central focus in the Community.

20. Desmond Dinan, *An Ever Closer Union?: An Introduction to the European Community* (Boulder, Colo.: Lynne Rienner, 1994), p. 478.

21. The pace of implementation of the agreements has also been graduated. Agreements with the Visegard countries entered into force on March 1, 1992 (with successive liberalization rounds beginning on January 1, 1993, and January 1, 1994), whereas the agreement with Romania did not enter into force until May 1, 1993 (with the second round beginning January 1, 1994). Bulgaria's was delayed until December 31, 1993. Trade and cooperation agreements were not finalized with the Baltic states until 1992. A similar agreement was concluded with Slovenia in November 1992. In addition to the slower pace of negotiations, compared with the association agreements, trade and cooperation agreements do not provide for the same degree of market access and do not necessarily augur eventual EU membership (perhaps the most important benefit of the association agreements).

22. This accounted for 65.14 percent of total G-24 aid as of December 31, 1993. "Scoreboard of Assistance Commitments to the CEEC, 1990–1993," European Commission, Brussels, June 1994.

23. ECU 54.2 billion (59 percent of all aid) originated in the EC and its member states, compared with ECU 15.5 billion (17 percent of all aid) from the Bush administration. European Commission, *Trade and Aid in Relations between the European Union, the Countries of Central and Eastern Europe and the Countries of the Commonwealth of Independent States* (Brussels, June 9, 1994). ECU 1 equals approximately $U.S. 1.20 for purposes of these figures.

This yawning disparity in aid levels was yet another occasion for European-American irritation. Particularly galling was Secretary James Baker's surprise announcement in December 1991 of an aid-pledging conference in Washington, a conference that essentially added only relatively small amounts of new American economic and technical aid to the far larger amounts already planned by the EC and the major European states. See the report of Baker's speech at Princeton University in Thomas L. Friedman "Soviet Disarray; Baker Presents Steps to Aid Transition by Soviets," *New York Times,* December 13, 1991, p. A1. See also the editorial on the Baker speech by Angela Stent and Daniel Yergin, "Send Help Before It's Too Late," *New York Times,* December 15, 1994, p. A15.

24. For example, of the ECU 54.2 billion in aid accounted for by the EU, fully ECU 40.1 billion (74 percent of all EU aid) is in the form of bilateral German assistance. Only ECU 3.9 billion came from the EU itself, compared with ECU 8 billion for the CEE, accounting for 31 percent of all G-24 aid from the EU and its member states. European Commission, *Trade and Aid in Relations between the European Union.* See also Karen Donfreid, *The European Bank for Reconstruction and Development: An Institution of and for the New Europe,* CRS Reports (Congressional Research Service, August 15, 1991).

25. The agreement is similar to those signed with Slovenia and the Baltic states. Although it does provide for some trade liberalization and the possibility for future

discussion of a more comprehensive free trade area, it makes no mention of any possibility for future EU membership. Telephone interview, U.S. State Department official, September 15, 1994. The agreement was signed only in June 1994 at the Corfu summit. A cooperation agreement has also been signed with Ukraine but with no other CIS state.

26. A cumulative total of $U.S. 2.4 billion to CEE versus just over $U.S. 1 billion to Russia through 1993. United Nations Economic Commission for Europe, *Economic Survey of Europe in 1993–1994* (New York: United Nations, 1994), p. 139.

27. Quoted in Larabee, *East European Security*, p. 68.

28. On the origins and evolution of the NACC, see the article by one of its initial architects, Stephen J. Flanagan, "NATO and Central and Eastern Europe: From Liaison to Security Partnership," *Washington Quarterly*, vol. 15 (Spring 1992), pp. 141–52.

29. *NATO Works with Cooperation Partners on Environmental Problems,* Basic Fact Sheet (Brussels: NATO Office of Information and Press, May 1993).

30. See the Alastair Buchan Memorial lecture given to the International Institute for Strategic Studies in March 1993 by Volker Ruehe, in *Survival,* vol. 35 (Summer 1993), pp. 129–37. Volker Ruehe repeatedly reassured the eastern Europeans that Germany was still supportive of eastern European integration into NATO. It was important, Ruehe stressed, that NATO become an inclusive rather than an exclusive alliance. Jane Perlez, "Bonn Tries to Calm East Europeans on NATO," *New York Times,* October 10, 1993, p. A6.

31. Alan Riding, "Europeans Try to Revive a Faded Dream of Unity," *New York Times,* June 20, 1993, p. A8. The EC agreements signed with the Czech republic, Slovakia, Poland, Hungary, Romania, and Bulgaria call for the integration of eastern Europe into the European Community, but by the time of the Copenhagen summit the agreements had not been ratified by all twelve European Union members.

32. See Larabee, *East European Security,* chap. 8, for a discussion of these developments and of the major strands in Russian thinking in the fall of 1993.

33. A useful description of the PFP is William T. Johnsen and Thomas-Durrell Young, *Partnership for Peace: Discerning Fact from Fiction* (Carlisle, Pa.: U.S. Army War College, August 15, 1994).

34. See, for example, Robert Zoellick, "Strobe Talbott on NATO: An Answer," *Washington Post,* January 5, 1994, p. A19.

35. Karaganov, "Where Is Russia Going?"

36. See "Partnership for Peace," Basic Fact Sheet (Brussels: NATO Information Service, June 1994); and Stanley Sloan, "Transatlantic Relations in the Wake of the Brussels Summit," *NATO Review,* vol. 42 (April 1994), pp. 27–31.

37. "Partnership for Peace," Basic Fact Sheet. There are indications that Belarus will join in the near future. Only Tajikistan has declared it will not join, and there are reports that it is now reconsidering its decision. See appendix B for the specifics of the structure of the PFP, as well as the requirements for membership.

38. William E. Odom, "The Ambivalent Bear; Dealing with Moscow's Two Foreign Policies," *Washington Post,* December 5, 1993, p. C1.

39. Karaganov, "Where Is Russia Going?" p. 7.

40. Craig Whitney, "NATO Bends to Russia to Allow It a Broader Relationship," *New York Times,* May 19, 1994, p. A3. See also William E. Schmidt, "Russian Clarifies Link with NATO," *New York Times,* May 26, 1994, p. A4.

41. See Bruce Clark's description of Yeltsin's desire to "enter three clubs, on its own terms," in "Russia Knocks on West's Doors," *Financial Times,* June 18–19, 1994, p. 2.

42. See NATO press release, "Summary of Conclusions of Discussions between the North Atlantic Council and Foreign Minister Andrei Kozyrev," NATO Office of Information and Press, Brussels, June 22, 1994. According to one press account, Kozyrev warned NATO on the pace of its expansion, saying that a large section of the Russian public needed convincing that the alliance was not intent on a "triumphant march eastward." Bruce Clark, "Russia Warns on Pace of NATO Expansion into East Europe," *Financial Times,* June 23, 1994, p. 18.

43. See the Kirchberg declaration, issued by the ministers of the Western European Union, May 9, 1994.

44. The first meeting of the WEU plus those nations with association status (Hungary, Romania, Slovakia, the Czech Republic, and the republics of Bulgaria, Estonia, Latvia, Lithuania, and Poland) took place in June 1994.

45. As of NATO Information Service data from September 27, 1994, only Poland, Romania, and Sweden had achieved full acceptance of both their Presentation Document (PD) and their individual partnership program, with Finland expected to do so shortly. PDs had also been received from Albania, Bulgaria, the Czech Republic, Estonia, Hungary, Latvia, Lithuania, Moldova, Russia, Slovakia, Slovenia, and Ukraine.

46. Initiative at the NATO summit was announced in the form of the PFP "Invitation" and an accompanying annex, "Framework Document," January 10, 1994. (See appendix B for the full texts.)

47. Because the Czech Republic is well on its way to fulfilling the obligations of the PFP program, it provides an interesting demonstration of what structural changes are required to shift from a communist system to a military dominated by democratic values and institutions. The Czech Republic will develop new systems of planning, budgeting, and programming for 1995, and by 1996 the military will be based on brigades and be reorganized into three tiers: strategic, operational, and tactical. Jaromir Novotny, "The Czech Republic—An Active Partner with NATO," *NATO Review*, vol. 41 (June 1993), pp. 12–14.

48. From an interview conducted by the author in Berlin, August 28, 1994.

49. Brooks Tigner, "Dispute Mires Partnership for Peace Efforts," *Defense News,* March 14–20, 1994, p. 3.

50. Grachev has been quoted as saying that Russia would be "pained" by any expansion of NATO. See Doug Clarke, "Grachev: Russia Will Not Join NATO," *Radio Free Europe—Radio Liberty, Daily Report,* September 9, 1994, p. 2.

51. See the speech by President Clinton to the Polich Sejm in Warsaw, July 7, 1994. Involved will be $25 million for Poland itself. With some add-on funds, there will be $30 million in fiscal year 1995 funds, and $100 million in fiscal year 1996 funds for PFP purposes.

52. "Moscow 'Cannot Join NATO,'" *Financial Times*, September 11–12, 1994, p. 2.

53. This is perhaps less true of Poland, where that country's particular and unfortunate history as a throughway for German and Russian tanks generated more enthusiasm for participation in a Western security organization. As one Polish official argued in an off-the-record seminar sponsored by the Stockholm International Peace Research Institute in Warsaw in May 1994, membership will help create security, will mark Poland as one of "us," both for the European and the transatlantic domains. Personal notes of the author, Warsaw, May 1994.

54. Even more far reaching was the vision of expansion contained in the radio speech by Vice President Albert Gore to a Berlin meeting in late August 1994,

Chapter Five

1. One of the best accounts of the international relations of the crisis is Lawrence Freedman and Efraim Karsh, *The Gulf Conflict, 1990–1991* (Princeton University Press, 1993).

2. Somalia, in essence, repeated the Gulf War pattern. The United States reached the decision to intervene in national terms and then created both a supporting coalition and the UN authority to pursue it. There were informal political consultations with key NATO allies and some movement of equipment and personnel out of NATO assignments. But only small numbers of allied forces were involved in the first phase of operations, essentially under U.S. command. All other European involvement was either financial or humanitarian aid channeled through the many private European organizations present. The transition from American command to a formal UN command in the spring of 1993 opened the way for wider European participation, albeit still at relatively low levels and within a globally recruited monitoring force.

3. Sources that deal in greater detail with the European responses to the Gulf War are Nicole Gnesotto and John Roper, eds., *Western Europe and the Gulf* (Paris: Western European Union, 1992); and "Information Report," Western European Union Assembly, Committee for Parliamentary and Public Relations, February 1993, pt. 1.

4. See the essays in Gnesotto and Roper, eds., *Western Europe and the Gulf*. In their introduction Gnesotto and Roper argue that the effect went in two directions: some concluding that European autonomy was imperative; others that the United States and NATO were indispensable in any out-of-area contingency.

5. Freedman and Karsh, *Gulf Conflict, 1990–1991*, p. 4.

6. Italy contributed only air forces to the war.

7. Arnaud Jacomet "The Role of WEU in the Gulf Crisis," in Gnesotto and Roper, eds., *Western Europe and the Gulf*, p. 163.

8. It is illustrative that several European officials gave particular emphasis to the coincidence in timing of the Bartholomew letter, or Dobbins démarche, while almost every American interviewed had forgotten it or dismissed it as being unrelated. See the discussion in chapter 3.

9. For brief critical reviews of the role of European institutions in Yugoslavia,

see James E. Goodby "Peacekeeping in the New Europe," *Washington Quarterly,* Spring 1992, pp. 153–71; and Hugh Miall, *New Conflicts in Europe: Prevention and Resolution,* Oxford Research Group Current Decisions Report 10 (July 1992).

10. This idea is suggested by Desmond Dinan, *An Ever Closer Union? An Introduction to the European Community* (Boulder, Colo.: Lynne Rienner, 1994), p. 485, and is the definite conclusion of David Buchan, *Europe: The Strange Superpower* (Brookfield, Vt.: Darthmouth Publishing, 1993), pp. 67–82.

11. See, for example, Susan Woodward's excellent analysis in *Balkan Tragedy: Chaos and Dissolution after the Cold War* (Brookings, 1995).

12. Quoted in *Financial Times,* July 1, 1991, p. 1. See also Catherine Guichard, "The Hour of Europe: Preliminary Lessons from Yugoslavia," draft paper, Center for European Community Studies, George Mason University, 1992.

13. There is as yet no exhaustive analytic study of the causes and context of this swing in German public opinion. Other factors alleged to have played a role are (1) the impact of the Croatian émigré community, largely located in Bavaria; (2) the preferences of the Christian Social Union, largely reflections of the outrage expressed by the Catholic hierarchy; (3) the role of the influential *Frankfurter Allgemeine Zeitung* and its constant drumbeat in articles and editorials; and (4) the conspiracies of German rightists supportive of Austrian "fishing" in Yugoslavia in the 1980s and the possible restoration of a German sphere of influence in the Balkans. None of these, however, seems plausible as *single* causal factors. For comments on some of these factors, see Woodward, *Balkan Tragedy.*

14. Goodby, "Peacekeeping in the New Europe," pp. 153–71.

15. This cannot be known for sure, because there may not have been any action against Kosovo and Macedonia until the Bosnia situation was "resolved" anyway.

16. Quoted in Antonia Chayes and Richard Weitz, "NATO: Conflict Prevention and Peace Operations," paper presented to the Consensus Building Institute Conference, Washington, September, 1994.

17. The monitoring mission changed in November 1992 to a sanctions enforcement mission, including stop-and-search authority.

18. NATO air assets began overflight in Bosnia under Operation Deny Flight after the UN Security Council authorization in April 1993.

19. These actions were followed by further air strikes, on August 5 and September 22, 1994.

20. Buchan, *Europe,* p. 69.

21. Yet it was in part this exclusion that atomized Yugoslavia. The attention paid to the Visegrad states to the detriment of Yugoslavia fed some of the republics' desires (notably Slovenia and Croatia because of their relatively greater wealth and proximity to the West) to dissociate from the federation and try to gain membership in Western organizations independently.

22. See, particularly, the Genscher speech at the opening of the CSCE follow-up meeting, Helsinki, March 24, 1992, which echoes themes that the foreign minister sounded in his February 1987 speech at Davos. H. D. Genscher, *Unterwegs zur Einheit, Reden und Dokumente aus Bewegter Zeit* (Berlin: Siedler Verlag, 1991), pp. 137–50. See also Genscher's address to a conference of the Tutzing Protestant

Academy on January 31, 1990, in Lawrence Freedman, ed., *Europe Transformed: Documents on the End of the Cold War* (London: Triservice Press, 1990), pp. 436–45.

Chapter Six

1.   Useful sources on the early history of NATO include Joseph M. Jones, *The Fifteen Weeks* (Harcourt, Brace, 1955); and Robert Endicott Osgood, *NATO: The Entangling Alliance* (University of Chicago Press, 1962).

2.   The basic delineation of this concept came first in a Brookings occasional paper, *A New Concept of Cooperative Security,* by Ashton B. Carter, William J. Perry, and John D. Steinbruner (Brookings, 1992).

3.   At the NATO meeting in Istanbul in June 1994, although the NATO ministers did not consent to a treaty with Russia distinct from the PFP, they did agree to a special dialogue, thereby acknowledging Russia's exceptional position in post–cold war European security. For more information, see Bruce Clark, "Old Enemies Make Tricky Friends," *Financial Times,* June 9, 1994, p. 15.

4.   For some the unacceptable extent of Germany's newfound assertiveness was reached in 1990 when Germany pressed its allies hard to recognize Slovenia and Croatia as independent states. The intervening years have seen considerable German remorse and more reticence. But Germany, with the support of the United States and others, is now expressing a clear interest in obtaining a permanent seat on the UN Security Council.

5.   The German-Russian agreements in the context of unification guaranteed that there would be no nuclear weapons or foreign troops stationed on the territory of the former German Democratic Republic in perpetuity, not just while Soviet-Russian troops remained. The question of future arrangements is clearly to be decided by the German government, which has normally kept both issues, and indeed most issues of security arrangements and defense policy, at a low public profile. A resurrection of the nuclear debates of the 1980s are clearly also not the preference of most of the opposition parties, especially the Social Democrats, who are striving for an image of being capable of governing *(Regierungsfahigkeit)* in the 1994 elections and beyond.

6.   Even the Green party now endorses the continuation of an American presence as well as a German commitment to NATO, in its present state or transformed.

7.   That is already apparent in German economic assistance policies—and aid levels—to eastern Europe and Russia, which display far more attention to the problem than is paid by American policies, and in the sponsorship, at least by Defense Minister Volker Ruehe, of near-term NATO membership for at a minimum the Visegrad states.

8.   The Open Skies treaty "commits member nations in Eurasia and North America to open their airspace, on a reciprocal basis, permitting the overflight of their territory by unarmed observation aircraft in order to strengthen confidence and transparency with respect to their military activities." Basic Fact Sheet, no. 7 (Brussels: NATO Information Service, April 1994).

9.   One relatively tepid action-forcing deadline was that for the CSCE Review Conference in Budapest in December 1994. And there is already at least one agreed

agenda, the fourteen-point programme for immediate action, established in the Helsinki document of July 1992. Two of the three general areas are specifically assigned to the Forum on Security and Cooperation: (1) harmonization of arms control, disarmament, confidence and security building; and (2) security enhancement, encompassing force planning, defense conversion, regional security, and cooperation toward nonproliferation goals.

10. For further details, see Victor-Yves Ghebali, "The CSCE Forum for Security Cooperation: The Opening Gambits," *NATO Review,* June 1993, p. 23.

11. David Gardner and Andrew Hill, "Belgium Keen to Contribute to Euro-Corps," *Financial Times,* May 24, 1993, p. 2. Spain has also indicated a willingness to contribute.

12. The Coordinating Committee for Multilateral Export Controls (COCOM) officially expired on March 31, 1994, with nothing to replace it as yet. "Cocom, Cocom, Cocom," *Baltimore Sun,* April 4, 1994, p. 8. In addition, the Clinton administration has made a number of changes in U.S. export policy, allowing the sale of previously protected equipment such as advanced supercomputers and satellite technology. Kenneth R. Timmerman, "U.S. to Rogue States: Buy American," *Wall Street Journal,* March 25, p. A8. Conventional arms are also being marketed with new alacrity. For example, in search of a resolution to the South Asian arms race, the Clinton administration proposed that Lockheed complete the delivery of U.S. F-16s to Pakistan in exchange for a verifiable ban on Pakistan's nuclear capability. The delivery had been halted in 1990 with the invocation of the Pressler amendment, which prohibits arms transfers to countries that the president cannot confirm are not engaged in a nuclear weapons program. Carroll J. Doherty, "Bid to Sell Jets to Pakistan May Provoke Fight on Hill," *Congressional Weekly Report,* April 9, 1994, p. 851. In addition, U.S. market share of arms transfers has grown substantially over the last fifteen years. According to the Arms Control and Disarmament Agency, the United States doubled its arms exports between 1981 and 1991 alone. *World Military Expenditures and Arms Transfers 1991–1992* (United States Arms Control and Disarmament Agency, March 1994); and "U.S. Doubled Arms Exports Share in 80s," *Washington Post,* April 1, 1994, p. A24.

13. Low oil prices have somewhat diminished arms sales to the Middle East, although the demand for weapons in that region grows. *Arms Exports to the Third World,* CRS Reports, (Congressional Research Service, 1994).

14. Indeed, John Ralston Saul argues that in the United States the "sums now being spent on converting defense manufacturing to civil production are so small as to be meaningless." See his article, "Arms Addiction: How the West Got Hooked on Exporting Weapons," *Washington Post,* February 6, 1994, p. C3. In Europe, overcapacities have been dealt with through the creation of large "national champions" and by increasing international (mostly intra-European) collaboration. James B. Steinberg, *The Transformation of the European Defense Industry* (Santa Monica, Calif.: Rand Corporation, 1992), pp. 65–67.

15. In general, U.S. defense firms have been far more successful in devising medium-term survival strategies than are their European counterparts. The Clinton administration has lobbied for the industry on occasion, as in the Saudi agreement to

buy $6 billion worth of U.S. commercial jets. In addition, U.S. companies, keeping internal management decisions independent of U.S. government policy, are less hesitant to lay off workers and restructure aggressively, whereas European firms tend to fall victim to government intervention. In France, for example, this has led to a delay in defense companies' difficult decisions to fire employees that have been kept on with the help of government subsidies. Keith Hodgkinson, "Coping with the Downturn," *International Defense Review*, March 1994, pp. 57–61. In the United States, the Northrop purchase of Grumman is the latest example of proactive restructuring in the industry. Calvin Sims, "Northrop Bests Martin Marietta to Buy Grumman," *New York Times*, April 5, 1994, p. A1.

16. Richard A. Bitzinger, *The Globalization of Arms Production: Defense Markets in Transition* (Washington: Defense Budget Project, 1994), p. 20.

17. Richard A. Bitzinger, "Customize Defense Industry Restructuring," *Orbis*, vol. 38 (Spring 1994), pp. 261-76.

18. This is a by-value measure and therefore subject to some distortion. But the general trend toward overwhelming U.S. dominance is clearly substantiated by the Stockholm International Peace Research Institute (SIPRI) and UN Arms Register figures.

19. The Nunn Amendment to the Fiscal Year 1993 Defense Authorization Act allocated money to weapons codevelopment with U.S. allies. Regrettably, almost all the twenty-eight collaborative weapons projects, in addition to the twenty-six memorandums of understanding, were subsequently canceled for both political and bureaucratic reasons. The U.S. military prefers to maximize control over weapons design, and to have contracting systems that cater to their perceived specific needs rather than having to consult with multiple partners. Frequently, projects funded by the Nunn amendment have been eliminated from the declining budget because of this preference and because, in some cases, collaborative ventures compete with domestically produced projects, such as when the Air Force withdrew from the NATO multiservice standoff weapon program to pursue the independently produced triservice standoff attack missile. Moreover, the United States, like other countries, prefers to support domestic employment and to limit dependence on foreign sources of arms. But unlike most countries, the United States can more readily afford to cut out foreign investment, because of the naturally large domestic market. Elizabeth Kirk, *U.S. and European Defense Industries: Changing forces for Cooperation and Competition* (Washington: American Association for the Advancement of Science, 1993), p. 12; and Bitzinger, *Globalization of Arms Production*, pp. 25–26.

20. Strong objections to the purchase of LTV by Thomson-CSF were raised on the grounds that the French company is state run, receives subsidies from the French government, and would therefore exploit LTV, imperiling the "security of secret U.S. military technologies." Additional tension between France and the United States on these issues has resulted from accusations that France engages in industrial espionage. George Graham, "French Missile Bid Stirs Row," *Financial Times*, May 22, 1992, p. 5. For a complete defense of Thomson-CSF's attempt to buy LTV and a selected listing of other transatlantic defense-industrial cooperative arrangements, see Committee on Foreign Investment in the United States, Thomson-CSF White Paper in

Support of Non-Intervention (Thomson-CSF/LTV Missiles Division Acquisition, June 11, 1992).

21. Sometime after Havel announced a ban on Czech arms imports, Prime Minister Vaclav Klaus argued that, contrary to Havel's hopes, other countries never took the bold step of discontinuing their arms trade but instead have subsumed the Czech Republic's market share, leaving Czech factories idle and Czech workers unemployed. The Czech parliament then voted to reactivate the weapons industry and to seek out new markets abroad. In the political and economic climate of the 1990s, in which defense conversion has proved prohibitively expensive and in which Western aid has not materialized to the extent it was promised, Havel's original pledge to abandon arms export was regarded as "naive and costly." Jane Perlez, "Czechs Gear Up to Resume Weapons Exports," New York Times, July 4, 1993, p. F7.

22. Thomas W. Lippman, "Ex-Soviet Arms Exports Plunge," Washington Post, June 13, 1993, p. A28. This article summarizes the testimony of William Grundmann, director of the U.S. Defense Intelligence Agency, before the Congressional Joint Economic Committee.

23. Sergey Podyapolskiy, "Glazyev Says Weapons Exports to Russia Remain at 25–30 Percent," ITAR-TASS, April 1, 1993, in Foreign Broadcast Information Service, Daily Report: Soviet Union, April 2, 1993, p. 29.

24. Lippman, "Ex-Soviet Arms Exports Plunge."

25. The term "national champion" refers to a defense firm that specializes in a particular technology or product that the government has chosen to coddle and sustain in the face of adverse market conditions in order to ensure instant access to that product or technology should a crisis occur. Even France, perhaps the most protective of its defense companies of all the western European states, is disentangling itself from long-favored firms in favor of sweeping privatization programs.

26. One measure is the number of interfirm agreements on technology transfers among members of the Organization for Economic Cooperative and Development. By 1972 there had been a total of 156 agreements; from 1985 to 1988 there were nearly 2,000 new accords. Elisabeth Skoens, "Western Europe: Internationalization of the Arms Industry," in Herbert Wulf, ed., Arms Industry Limited (Oxford University Press, 1993), p. 166.

27. The view that the United States must become more willing to engage in technology-sharing enterprises is espoused by William Walker and Philip Gummet, Nationalism, Internationalism and the European Defence Market (Alencon: Institute for Security Studies of Western European Union, 1993), p. 58; and Steinberg, Transformation of the European Defense Industry, p. 110. Kiefer and Bitzinger argue that the United States must rationalize its defense industry globalization policy by concentrating decisionmaking authority, which is currently divided among the departments of Defense, Commerce, State, and Treasury, in addition to Congress. Erik D. Kiefer and Richard A. Bitzinger, The Globalization of the Defense Industry: Roles and Responsibilities of the Federal Government (Washington: Defense Budget Project, 1994).

28. Skoens, "Western Europe," p. 169.

29. Herbert Wulf, "Arms Industry Limited: the Turning-Point in the 1990s," in

Herbert Wulf, ed., *Arms Industry Limited*, p. 26.

30. There has now been positive action on a proposal for an EC council regulation on the control of exports of certain dual-use goods and of certain nuclear products and technologies. Commission of the European Communities, COM (92) 317, Brussels, August 31, 1992.

31. The EC has also recently endorsed the assignment of responsibility for end-use declarations for arms exports to the company level. This draws on German experience with the KOBRA (Kontrolle bei der Ausfur) system, a system much discussed and revised after German firms were implicated in strategic arms exports to Iraq. The KOBRA system has many innovative computerized tracking and monitoring features. Perhaps the most unusual is that it makes a named official responsible for the assessment of any export's end use, an official who can later be held accountable for any foreseeable diversion even if that official no longer resides in Germany. For a discussion of recent Community efforts, see Wolfgang H. Reinicke, "Arms Sales Abroad," in *Brookings Review*, Summer 1992, pp. 22–25; and the narrative account given by Harold Mueller, "Prospects for the Containment of Nuclear Weapons: A European Perspective," paper prepared for the Non-Proliferation Seminar of the American Academy of Arts and Sciences Conference, Chicago, December 1992. For more proposals on European export controls, see Paul Eavis and Owen Green, "Regulating Arms Exports: A Program for the European Community," in Hans Günter Brauch and others, eds., *Controlling the Development and Spread of Military Technology* (Amsterdam: VU University Press, 1992), pp. 283–99; and Sue Willett, *Controlling the Arms Trade: Supply and Demand Dynamics*, Faraday Discussion Paper, 18 (London: Council for Arms Control, November 1991).

32. Charles Krauthammer, "The Unipolar Moment," *Foreign Affairs: America and the World*, vol. 70, no. 1 (1990–91), p. 24.

Index

Accountability, 7-8
Air traffic control, 8
Albania, 51
Arms control/reduction: détente, 36;
EU initiatives, 11; future of European
security, 146-48; information ex-
change for, 147; mutual and balanced
force reduction talks, 36-38;
prospects for, 147-48; Russia in, 148;
U.S. post–cold war policy goals, 81;
U.S.-Soviet relations, 19-20, 81
Arms industry, 152-57; U.S. NATO
policy and, 34
ARRC. *See* North Atlantic Treaty Orga-
nization (NATO), rapid reaction
forces
Aspin, Les, 95, 96

Balladur, Edouard, 50
Baltic Brigade, 7
Belarus, 81
Belgium, 62, 149
Borders: current concerns, 5; Western
European agreements, 3; Yugoslav
crisis, 114
Bosnia, 5, 7, 13, 23, 61, 107, 115, 116,
118; NATO and, 66, 72-73
Britain, 75; CEE policy, 84; in Gulf
War, 110; post–cold war support for
CSCE, 49; Western European Union
and, 56
Bulgaria, 51, 61, 88, 118

Bush administration, 11, 22, 57, 80-81;
Gulf War, 108-11; in Yugoslavia crisis, 113-14, 116, 117

CEE. *See* Central and eastern Europe
(CEE)
Central and eastern Europe (CEE): after
disestablishment of Soviet Union, 4;
arms industry, 154; challenges to European security in, 2, 23-24; Clinton
administration and, 82; in continentwide security regime, 4; current relations with West, 80; economic expectations, 86; in European security
institutions, 23, 24; evolution of security framework, 4; evolution of security policy, 86-94; evolution of
Western security outreach, 84-85,
102-03; NATO membership, 70, 94,
95, 104-05; in organizational framework of European security, 78-79;
outreach issues, 78; post–cold war
developments, 22-24; prospects, 103-
05; Russia's role in, 83; United
States and, 79, 80-82; Western European Union and, 97-99
CFE. *See* Conventional Forces in Europe (CFE) agreements
Clinton administration, 73-74, 145;
CEE outreach, 82; domestic politics
in future of European security, 19;
EU defense cooperation, 12; Partner-

ship for Peace initiative, 95; in Yugoslav crisis, 114, 118
Common foreign and security policy, 29, 57, 58, 60
Commonwealth of Independent States, 17, 139
Conference on Security and Cooperation in Europe (CSCE), 107; accomplishments, 40-41; automated continuous data exchange, 8; CEE states and, 79; conflict resolution, 120-21; current functioning, 23; evolution, 38-39; evolution of CEE security framework, 4; in future of European security, 4-5, 51-54, 77; interlocking security organizations, 75; membership, 41, 49, 53, 121; NATO and, 66; organizational structure, 52, 53; origins, 36; peacekeeping forces, 51; positive features, 52-53; post–cold war expectations for, 47-48; post–cold war experience, 48-52; Russia and, 84, 140; sanctions assistance missions, 51; Soviet Union and, 36, 38, 40, 41; transparency in, 43; United States and, 36, 38, 40; Western European Union and, 60
Confidence- and security-building measures (CSBM), 4, 6, 40
Conflict Prevention Center, 53
Continentwide security regime, 36-41; for military air traffic control, 8
Conventional Forces in Europe (CFE) agreements, 81, 146; achievements of, 38; automated continuous data exchange, 8; in evolution of CEE security framework, 4, 89; expansion of, 7, 147-48; in future of European security, 4, 5; weapons inspections and destruction, 6, 38
Council of Europe, 23, 41, 107
Croatia, 13, 51, 112, 115-16
CSCE. See Conference on Security and Cooperation in Europe
Czech Republic, 80

Czechoslovakia, 87

de Gaulle, Charles, 34
Defense: CSCE role, 52; NATO commitments, 5; NATO goals, 30-31
Delors, Jacques, 56, 87
Democratization, 4; immediate post–cold war era perceptions, 47; immediate post–cold war period, 81; NATO membership requirements, 5; Russia's role in, 83
Denmark, 88
Deutsch, Karl, 42

Economic Forum, 53
Economic issues, 55; arms industry, 152-55; CEE goals, 86; disparity among participants in cooperative security arrangement, 122-23; European Community goals, 27; European Union, 10; future challenges, 75; NACC, 93; NATO, 33; post–Soviet states, 79; Russia, 16; U.S. foreign policy, 20; U.S. outreach in CEE, 81-82; Western European initiatives in CEE, 87-89
Emergency humanitarian assistance, 5
Environmental concerns, 93
Estonia, 51
Ethnicity, 123; eastern Europe, 2; in former Yugoslavia, 115; rights of minorities, 23; significance of Yugoslavia crisis, 114
Eurocorps, 57, 58, 59; current status, 62, 73; future of, 149
European Atomic Energy Community, 42
European Bank for Reconstruction and Development, 87, 88
European Community, 41; arms production oversight, 156; basis of security, 122; CEE policy, 86-91; CFSP goals, 60; CSCE and, 52; evolution of, 27-29; Gulf War and, 109-10; NATO and, 26, 32-35; post–cold war

challenges, 54; post–cold war organizational response, 46-47; post–cold war support for CSCE, 49; prospects, 75; response to German unification, 55-56; transparency in operations of, 43; Western European Union membership, 58-59; Yugoslavia crisis, 112-13, 115-17, 119-21

European Defense Community (EDC), 25, 31, 42

European Free Trade Association, 42, 55

European Political Community, 28, 42

European security: challenges to, 1-3, 21, 23-25; chronology, 3; cold war concerns, 24-25, 32-33; conceptual basis, 121-22; current state, 1-2; disparity among participants, 121-22; European Union policy, 10; evolution of organizational structures for, 41-44; historical cooperative framework, 3-4; opportunities for, 4-8; post–cold war NATO, 64-65; role of U.S. in evolution of, 8-9, 25-35; role of U.S. in prospects for, 9-10; structural development, 25; U.S. conceptual trends, 73-74. *See also* Future of European security

European Union: arms production oversight, 156-57; CEE and, 103-04; current status, 23; economic policy, 10; European security and defense identity, 10; France and, 10, 12, 14-16; Germany and, 10, 12-13; interlocking security organizations, 75; obstacles to continued development, 11; origins of, 10; Russia and, 16, 88; United States and, 10-11

Finland, 140, 148, 152

Former Soviet Union: NATO and, 63-64; nuclear weapons in, 81; U.S. policy, 80-82; Western outreach, 80. *See also individual countries*

Forum for Cooperative Security, 148

Forum for Security Cooperation, 53

France, 75; CEE policy, 84-85; future of EU and, 11, 12, 15-16; in Gulf War, 110; NATO and, 14-15, 29, 33-34, 64, 67; Partnership for Peace and, 96, 101; response to German unification, 55; Western European Union and, 54, 55, 56. *See also* Franco-German relations

Franco-German relations, 2; Eurocorps, 52, 57, 58, 59, 61-62, 149; in evolution of European Community, 27-29, 29, 42; origins of European Union, 10

Future of European security: arms control/reduction; arms industry restructuring, 152-57; challenges, 75, 136-37, 157; challenges for NATO, 70-73; East-West relations, 103-05; France and, 10, 12, 14-16; German-United States relations, 143-46; Germany and, 3, 10, 13-14; implications of Yugoslavia crisis, 114; military policy, 4; organizational structures for, 75-77; Partnership for Peace in, 105, 151-52; peacekeeping efforts, 148-52; policy issues in CEE states, 80; political challenges, 21; political consensus-building for, 157-59; prospects, 74-77; prospects of CSCE in, 51-54; prospects of Western European Union in, 62-63; Russia and, 2, 3, 17-18, 23, 104, 137-43; United States and, 3, 136, 158; U.S. domestic politics and, 19-20, 136

Genscher, Hans-Dietrich, 13, 36, 48-49, 116

Georgia, 51

Germany: CEE policy, 85; current security, 1; in European Community, 2; European response to unification, 55-56; in evolution of European defense identity, 29, 35; foreign policy, 13; future European security and, 3; future of EU and, 11, 12-14; future of European security, 75-76; future of NATO and, 12-13; Gulf War response, 109, 110; military policy, 13, 18; NATO and, 144; NATO policy, 25; NATO role in unification, 63-64; relations with United States in future of European security, 143-46; on UN Security Council, 14; unification, 11, 12-13; United States and, 14; Western European Union and, 56; Yugoslavia crisis, 115-16, 117. *See also* Franco-German relations

Glazyev, Sergei, 154
Goodby, James, 116
Gorbachev, Mikhail, 82-83, 89
Grachev, Pavel, 97
Group of Seven: CEE and, 87; Russia and, 16, 18
Gulf War, 106; European military readiness, 110-11; political significance, 108-10, 111

Havel, Vaclev, 49, 86, 87, 154
Helsinki accords, 40-41
Hungary, 51, 61, 80, 81, 87, 118
Hussein, Sadam, 108

Independent European Program Group, 42
Information flow: for arms control/reduction, 147; CSCE accomplishments, 41, 43; military intelligence, 8
Intergovernmental Conference on Political Union, 109
Intermediate-Range Nuclear Forces treaty, 37
Iran-Iraq War, 54, 110
Iraq. *See* Gulf War

Karaganov, Sergei, 97
Kazakhstan, 81
Kohl, Helmut, 9, 13, 29, 50, 57
Korean War, 32
Kozyrev, Andrei, 95

Kuwait. *See* Gulf War

Latvia, 51
Leadership, 1; arms control/reduction, 147; challenges to future of European security, 158; of peacekeeping operations, 150; for resolution of Yugoslav crisis, 120; United States, 9, 107, 108, 136, 141
Lubbers, Ruud, 57

Maastricht Treaty, 10, 46, 55, 58, 109
Macedonia, 51, 117, 124
Marshall Plan, 8
Military agreements: arms industry restructuring, 152-57; challenges, 7; Eurocorps, 57, 58, 59, 61-62, 73; European security and defense identity, 11, 69; evolution of NATO, 5; former Soviet bloc nations, 81, 82; forms of Russian participation, 17-18; framework for future discussions, 4; French policy, 15-16; future of Russia in European security apparatus, 142-43; German policy, 13; on-site monitoring, 6; Partnership for Peace terms, 98-100; short-term concerns, 6; weapons inspections and destruction, 6, 38
Military operations: in conflict resolution, 124; continentwide air traffic control, 7; cooperative experience of European states, 7; CSCE goals, 39; German participation, 13-14; Gulf War, 110-11; information/intelligence sharing, 8; NATO rapid reaction forces, 65; Partnership for Peace exercises, 99-100; prospects for, 7; Western European Union, 61; Yugoslavia crisis, 117, 118-19
Milosevic, Slobdan, 115
Mitterand, François, 10, 11, 29, 50, 55, 57, 117
Moldova, 51
Montenegro, 51

Multilateral cooperation, conceptual basis, 44
Mutual and balanced force reduction (MBFR) talks, 36-38

NATO. *See* North Atlantic Treaty Organization
North Atlantic Cooperation Council (NACC), 7, 84, 92-94; role of, 23; Russia in, 18
North Atlantic Council, 117; France and, 70-71
North Atlantic Treaty Organization (NATO), 3, 42; achievements of, 25; action without U.S. participation, 12, 69, 74-75; basis of security, 121-22; Bosnia and, 107; CEE membership, 94, 104-05; CEE outreach efforts, 89-91; Combined/Joint Task Forces, 67-73; current status, 23, 70-73; decisionmaking process and structure, 32-34, 43, 69-72; defense goals, 30-31; economic policy, 33; Eurocorps brigade and, 59-60, 73; European Community and, 26, 32-35; European Union and, 11-12; evolution of, 30-35; evolution of CEE policy toward, 86; evolution of European defense identity and, 25-26, 43-44, 69; expanded membership, 5; France and, 14-15, 29, 33-34, 64, 67, 70-71; German military policy, 18; German unification and, 63-64; Germany and, 13-14, 18, 144; heterogeneity of membership, 5; historical evolution, 5-6; interlocking security organizations, 75; membership, 6, 32, 67; NACC and, 92-93; 1994 summit, 5, 6, 12, 74; Operation Sharp Guard, 61, 72; organizational challenges, 24; organizational structure, 64, 65, 66; origins, 30-31; out-of-area operations, 68-69, 106; Partnership for Peace and, 96, 101, 102; peacekeeping operations, 149-50; policy toward CEE states, 79; post–cold war challenges, 54, 63-66; post–cold war support for CSCE, 49; rapid reaction forces (ARRC), 65, 67; role of, 64-65; Russia and, 16, 17, 23, 83, 84, 140, 142, 143; United States goals for, 31-32; in Western European security, 3; Western European Union and, 56-57, 58-59, 67, 68, 69, 70, 71, 72; in Yugoslavia crisis, 113, 117-19. *See also* Partnership for Peace
Nuclear forces/weapons, 146; French policy, 16; Intermediate-Range Nuclear Forces treaty, 37; on-site monitoring, 6; U.S. post–cold war policy, 81, 82

Offensive forces, 3
Office for Democratic Institutions and Human Rights, 53
Open Skies agreements, 7-8, 146
Organization for Economic Cooperation and Development, 41
Organization for European Economic Cooperation, 33

Pact on Stability in Europe, 50
Partnership for Peace (PFP), 7; accomplishments of, 100-01; current status, 98-102, 103; future of, 105; NATO CJTF and, 101; obligations of participants, 98-99; obstacles to further development, 101-02, 104; origins, 67, 95; peacekeeping function, 151-52; political context, 101-02; requirements for participation, 5-6; responses to proposal for, 95-96; role of, 5, 23, 70, 82, 96; Russia and, 16, 18, 82, 84, 96-97, 137-39, 141; signatories, 67, 71, 96, 98, 99
Peacekeeping: CSCE, 51; definitional issues, 149; Eurocorps, 73; NATO, 66; NATO in former Yugoslavia, 117-19; organizational framework for, 149-50, 151-52; Partnership for

Peace in, 151-52; political context, 148-49, 150-51; prospects for cooperation in Europe for, 148-52; United States, 71, 150; Western European Union, 60-61

Pentagonale, 87

Permanent Committee, 53

Perry, William, 102

Poland, 80, 87, 101, 104

Political context: arms production industry, 153-54, 156; CEE after disestablishment of Soviet Union, 4; central issues, 45-46; challenges for Partnership for Peace, 101-02; challenges to future of European security, 21, 157-58; of conflict resolution, 124-25; for cooperative security in Europe, 3, 121-23; current organizational functioning, 107-08; European recognition of Croatia and Slovenia, 115-16; evolution of NATO in, 5; Gulf War coalition, 108-11; for multilateral action on security issues, 44; NATO CJTF, 70-71; NATO membership requirements, 6; obstacles to EU development, 11; peacekeeping operations in, 148-49, 150-51; post–cold war organizational structures, 46-47; recent development, 45-46; for resolution of Yugoslav crisis, 120-21; in Russia, 2; U.S. attitudes toward Germany, 145; U.S. domestic politics in future of European security, 19-20; U.S. outreach to CEE, 80-81; U.S. post–cold war interests, 9-10, 22, 81; Western outreach to CEE, 80

Poos, Jacques, 113

Romania, 51, 61, 83, 88

Rome Declaration, 54

Russia: after disestablishment of Soviet Union, 4; arms industry, 154; CEE NATO membership and, 95; coup attempt (1991), 91-92; CSCE and, 52; evolution of U.S. policy, 80-82; future European security and, 2, 3, 16-17, 23, 104; NATO and, 16, 17, 18, 23, 66, 83, 84, 140, 142, 143; participation in European security apparatus, 141; Partnership for Peace and, 96-97, 137-39; post–cold war relations with West, 82-84; United States and, 16, 18, 19-20, 20, 80-82, 137-43; Western outreach, 79, 80

Sanctions assistance missions, 51

Schevardnaze, Eduard, 83

Serbia, 51, 61, 118

Slovakia, 80

Slovenia, 13, 112, 115-16

Soviet Union: CSCE and, 36, 38, 40, 41, 50; in evolution of European defense identity, 26

Spain, 6, 62, 149

Sweden, 88, 140, 148, 152

Tajikistan, 51

Transparency: importance of, 6-7, 8, 43; Western European agreements, 3

Ukraine, 51, 81

United Nations, 5, 107; Gulf War role, 109; NATO and, 66; NATO and, in former Yugoslavia, 118, 119; Russia in, 140; Western European Union and, 60, 61; in Yugoslavia crisis, 113

United States: choice of partners, 9-10; cooperative arms production arrangements, 155; CSCE and, 36-37, 38, 40; current challenges, 47; domestic politics in future of European security, 19-20, 136; European Union and, 10-11; in evolution of European security, 8-9, 25-35; evolution of Western European Union and, 57-58; France and, 15; future European security and, 3, 9-10, 75; in future of German military policy, 14; future relations with Germany, 143-46; Gulf

War leadership, 108, 109; leadership
in peacekeeping operations, 150;
leadership role, 107, 108, 141, 158;
NATO CJTF and, 67, 69, 70, 71-73;
NATO goals, 31-32; NATO out-of-
area operations and, 106-07; near-
term challenges for, 9-10, 138; outreach efforts in CEE states, 80-82;
Partnership for Peace policy, 100;
post–cold war CSCE and, 49;
post–cold war interests, 8-9, 22, 81;
post–cold war NATO and, 64; responsibility toward CEE states, 79;
role in arms control/reduction, 147;
Russia and, 16, 18, 19-20, 20, 138-
43; trends in European security concepts, 73-74; weapons acquisition
system, 153-54; Western Europe and,
2; in Yugoslav crisis, 113-14, 116,
117, 118, 119, 120

Warsaw Pact, 4
Warsaw Treaty Organization, 36
Western Europe: challenges to security
in, 2; historical cooperative framework, 3; interstate rivalries, 2; organizational challenges, 24; outreach to
CEE, 84-85, 102-03

Western European Union, 10, 12, 23,
29, 41, 110, 140; CEE outreach efforts, 97-99; challenges for, 54-55;
current developments, 60-63; Eurocorps and, 73; evolution, 54-56, 62,
93-94; evolution of CEE policy toward, 86; in future of European security, 77; interlocking security organizations, 75; membership, 58-59, 94;
NATO and, 73-74; NATO CJTF and,
67, 68, 69, 70, 71; organizational
structure, 61-62; origins, 54; peacekeeping operations, 149-50
Woerner, Manfred, 117, 118

Yeltsin, Boris, 83-84, 95
Yugoslav crisis, 11, 12, 13, 21, 47;
challenges of, 112-14; chronology,
111, 126-35; CSCE response, 50-51;
European Community and, 112-13,
115-17, 119-21; European failure in
response to, 60; NATO and, 65, 72,
117-19; prospects for resolution,
119-21; significance of, 107, 111,
114, 123-24; Western European
Union response, 61

Zhironovsky, Vladimir, 84